The Wealth of Nations Rediscovered

In *The Wealth of Nations Rediscovered*, Robert E. Wright portrays the development of a modern financial sector – with a central bank, a national monetary system, and efficient capital markets – as the driving force behind America's economic transition from agricultural colony to industrial juggernaut. This new study applies the economic theory of information asymmetry to our understandings of early U.S. financial development, expanding on recent scholarship of finance-led economic growth. The book's research is original, incorporating little-used archival material and new data on early U.S. securities prices, trading volumes, and stockholder patterns. The topics covered – securities trading, market liquidity, intermediation, banking reform, emerging market success, and foreign investment – are relevant to discussions in today's business community. Drawing from and building upon Adam Smith's lesser-known insights into financial relationships, *The Wealth of Nations Rediscovered* positions itself on the cusp of emerging paradigm shifts in history and economics.

Robert E. Wright teaches Money & Banking and Financial History at the University of Virginia. He is the author of *Origins of Commercial Banking in America, 1750–1800* (2001), as well as several textbooks and numerous articles about early American financial history.

The Wealth of Nations Rediscovered

Integration and Expansion in American Financial Markets, 1780–1850

Robert E. Wright
University of Virginia

CAMBRIDGE
UNIVERSITY PRESS

PUBLISHED BY THE PRESS SYNDICATE OF THE UNIVERSITY OF CAMBRIDGE
The Pitt Building, Trumpington Street, Cambridge, United Kingdom

CAMBRIDGE UNIVERSITY PRESS
The Edinburgh Building, Cambridge CB2 2RU, UK
40 West 20th Street, New York, NY 10011-4211, USA
477 Williamstown Road, Port Melbourne, VIC 3207, Australia
Ruiz de Alarcón 13, 28014 Madrid, Spain
Dock House, The Waterfront, Cape Town 8001, South Africa

http://www.cambridge.org

First published 2002

Printed in the United Kingdom at the University Press, Cambridge

Typeface Baskerville 10/12 pt.   *System* LATEX 2$_\varepsilon$ [TB]

A catalog record for this book is available from the British Library.

Library of Congress Cataloging in Publication data

Wright, Robert E. (Robert Eric), 1969–
    The wealth of nations rediscovered: integration and expansion in
American financial markets, 1780–1850 / Robert E. Wright.
        p.   cm.
    Includes bibliographical references and index.
    ISBN 0-521-81237-2
    1. Finance – United States – History.   2. Wealth – United States –
History.   3. United States – Economic policy.   4. United States –
Economic conditions.   I. Title.
    HG181 .W75   2002
    332.63′2′0973–dc21   2001052836

ISBN 0 521 81237 2 hardback

Contents

Tables

Acknowledgments

I first thank those who gave of their wealth to support the completion of this monograph. A National Science Foundation grant provided the funds needed to acquire the securities prices that are the basis for much of the study. Harvard Business School's Alfred D. Chandler Traveling Fellowship, the American Antiquarian Society's Kate B. and Hall J. Peterson Fellowship, and the State University of New York at Buffalo's Mark Diamond Research Fellowship enabled me to make frequent visits to distant archives. The Department of Economics at the University of Virginia employed me during the two years it took to research, write, edit, and publish this monograph. Finally, UVA's Interlibrary Loan staff also deserves my thanks and appreciation for tracking down literally scores of needed microfilm reels.

I next thank those who gave of their time to help further this study. Richard Sylla was my inspiration throughout. He read the manuscript as it came out in dribs and drabs and provided constant advice and encouragement. Jack Wilson and David Cowen also provided support, encouragement, ideas, and advice. Participants in UVA's Economic History Workshop, including John James, Greg LaBlanc, Paul Mahoney, Ron Michener, Sharon Murphy, Jason Taylor, and Mark Thomas, also provided useful comments on portions of the manuscript. I am grateful to all.

I must also thank my family, wife Deborah, stepdaughter Stephanie, daughter Madison, and son Alexander, for their sacrifices. Without their loving patience, I could not have completed the book so quickly.

Finally, I must give a very hearty thanks to Frank Smith at Cambridge University Press and two anonymous readers. All three did a super job helping me to develop the manuscript. Of course, any remaining errors of fact and interpretation are mine alone.

Abbreviations

AAS	American Antiquarian Society, Worcester, Mass.
BLHU	Baker Library, Harvard University, Cambridge, Mass.
BNA	Bank of North America
BONY	The Bank of New York
BUS	Bank of the United States, 1792–1812
CCHS	Chester County Historical Society, West Chester, Pa.
CUSC	Cornell University Special Collections, Ithaca, N.Y.
DPO	direct public offering (of securities)
GDP	gross domestic product (a measure of aggregate output)
HSP	Historical Society of Pennsylvania, Philadelphia, Pa.
IPO	initial public offering (of securities)
LCP	Library Company of Philadelphia
MHS	Maryland Historical Society, Baltimore, Md.
NYHS	New York Historical Society, New York, N.Y.
NYPL	New York Public Library, New York, N.Y.
NYSL	New York State Library, Albany, N.Y.
PAH	*Papers of Alexander Hamilton*, ed. Syrett and Cooke
PRM	*Papers of Robert Morris*, ed. Ferguson et al.
PMVB	Papers of Martin Van Buren, Library of Congress
SBUS	Second Bank of the United States, 1816–1836
SEUM	Society for the Establishment of Useful Manufactures
SUNY	State University of New York
UNCSC	University of North Carolina, Special Collections, Chapel Hill, N.C.
UVA	University of Virginia, Charlottesville, Va.

A note on the footnotes: Citations to primary sources are made in full. Citations to secondary sources are made in the parenthetical social science style (last name date of publication: page number [where applicable]) in the footnotes. Only secondary sources appear in the References.

The Wealth of Nations Rediscovered

1

Introduction: The Wealth of Nations *and National Wealth*

Rulers, businesses, and scholars have long searched out the causes of wealth. Unfortunately, most of the globe's denizens remain pitifully poor, a threat to the economic and physical security of the prosperous few. One of the most influential books ever written, Adam Smith's *An Inquiry into the Nature and Causes of the Wealth of Nations*, provided a robust explanation of the causes of economic growth (increased real per capita gross domestic product or GDP), an explanation that the world would do well to study more closely. Some of the intricacies of Smith's thought regarding the financial underpinnings of wealth still elude many theorists and policy makers. Currently, a handful of scholars are explaining and expounding some of those intricacies in the hope that Smith's financial ideas will be put into practice in more places around the globe.

If you do not allow yourself to get bogged down in numbers, or regression equations, and just think about the economic history of the world for the past half millennium in general terms, a few startling observations can be made. First, an abundance of natural resources does not necessarily lead to economic wealth. The most biologically abundant and diverse areas of the globe are also the poorest. Nations with huge tracts of land, enormous numbers of people, and vast deposits of fossil fuels, precious metals, and other riches (e.g., China and the former Soviet Union) are quite poor. Some resource-rich areas (e.g., the Middle East) have found temporary wealth for a handful of people through resource exploitation, but few are under the delusion that such nations have advanced economies. On the other hand, three tiny nations, Holland, England, and Japan, each mostly barren of natural resources, thrived. None of this is to say, of course, that natural resources retard growth, or that the Falkland Islands will be the next economic superpower. It is clear, however, that the correlation between resource endowments and economic wealth is far from one to one.

Second, a broad overview of economic history reveals that nations have achieved economic superpower status only after undergoing a financial revolution. The Netherlands and Britain are the best-known

examples, but Japan and Germany underwent pre-industrial financial revolutions as well. Promising nations that never excelled in
finance, such as Argentina, continue to founder economically.[1] Financial sophistication, in other words, precedes, is highly correlated with,
and predicts economic growth. Recently, several macroeconomists
have gone a step beyond even this, asserting that financial development
outright *causes* economic growth.[2]

This book is a case study of economic growth. Its subject is the
most successful emerging market in world history, the United States
of America.[3] In just three and one-half score years (1780–1850), a
single lifetime, the United States transformed itself from a series of
loosely connected agricultural colonies into one of the world's most
powerful industrial nations. How did it do so, and so quickly? Scholars
have long debated the causes of early America's phenomenal economic success. Some point to an industrial revolution, whereas others
stress the so-called agrarian roots of American capitalism. Some, who
see a transportation, market, or price revolution as paramount, believe the creation of a free market was crucial, but others argue that a
managerial revolution led to more efficient resource allocation than
free-market mechanisms could provide. Some scholars argue for the
primacy of international trade, whereas others think that the development of domestic markets and Smithian division of labor were key. Still
others point to the existence of a flexible, progrowth legal system, or
an entire social structure geared for growth. Recently, several scholars
have noted that without adequate financial institutions, particularly
banks, and efficient capital markets, especially secondary securities
markets, early U.S. economic growth would have proceeded much
more slowly, if at all.[4]

This book elaborates on the recent work of those financial historians, and Adam Smith, to set forth a finance-focused explanation of
early American (1780–1850) economic growth. The book's thesis is
easily stated: the U.S. financial system created the conditions *necessary*
for the sustained domestic economic growth (increased real per capita
output) that scholars know occurred in the nineteenth century. In
proving that thesis, the book also shows that, despite the fulmination
of some historians,[5] the nation's early economy was capitalist to its
core.

The precise mechanism by which financial development spurs economic growth, though not accepted by all economists, has long been

[1] Sylla 1999a.   [2] King and Levine 1993; Levine and Zervos 1998.   [3] Sylla 1999a.
[4] Rostow 1960; Kulikoff 1992; Taylor 1958; Sellers 1991; Rothenberg 1992; Chandler
1977; North 1961; Lindstrom 1978; Horwitz 1977; Bruchey 1965; Sylla 1998, 1999a,
1999b; Bodenhorn 2000, 2002, Perkins 1994.
[5] Like Merrill and Wilentz 1993.

understood.[6] Most trace the idea to Joseph Schumpeter, who argued that the services that financial intermediaries, especially commercial banks, provided, such as the mobilization of savings, the evaluation of projects, risk management, and transactions facilitation, are essential for technological innovation and hence economic growth. In other words, without intermediation, the linkage of investors to entrepreneurs, visionary projects that would have created wealth wither and die. Few realize that Adam Smith also saw, though he did not stress, the importance of the financial system to growth. Smith, of course, is most remembered for his theoretical discussion of supply and demand and his metaphor of the "invisible hand," the extraordinary power of unfettered markets to produce needed goods and services. His vivid description of the division of labor in a pin-making factory also comes to mind. But his lengthy treatise contained much more, including discussions of the difficulties that arise when entrepreneurs cannot find sufficient funds to begin business, to trade in unfettered markets, to introduce additional degrees of labor specialization, or to develop scale economies. He never boldly states the finance-led thesis, but the implication of his discussion is clear – if businesses cannot raise funds, then they cannot buy the machines or make the organizational improvements necessary to increase their firms' productive efficiency. The efficiency of the overall economy therefore suffers.

Why would businesses be unable to raise the funds necessary to improve their operation? After all, improved efficiency usually means higher profits. Why could the businesses not simply borrow, for a price, from some people who have a little extra money to spare? The answer lies in the facts – the cold, hard facts of life – that the potential lenders may not know that the entrepreneur wishes to borrow, or may not be able to verify that the entrepreneur has a bona fide profitable use for the loan. Lenders do not like to part with their hard-earned wealth (or even their easily gotten wealth in most cases) unless they have decent assurances that the borrower will repay according to the terms of the contract.

If the asymmetry is too great – in other words, if one party knows much more information (usually about itself) than the other party knows – a bad outcome will likely result for the party with deficient information, usually the buyer or lender. The three major types of this "information asymmetry" are adverse selection, moral hazard, and the principal-agent problem. Adverse selection occurs before the contract. Simply stated, the worst risks (credit, insurance, inferior products) will be more anxious to contract than the best risks. Buyers or lenders who

[6]Excellent descriptions of those theories, past and present, can be found in Bodenhorn 2000, 2002.

cannot discern good risks (or products) from bad, therefore, will likely be burned. Moral hazard – and its special case, the principal-agent problem – occurs after the contract is made. If the lender (employer) does not keep adequate tabs on the borrower (employee), the borrower (employee) will have an incentive to renege on the contract by defaulting (stealing or goofing off). The problems of information asymmetry *cripple* markets, greatly reducing the number of contracts entered. Information asymmetry cannot be completely eliminated, but it can be reduced by financial institutions, such as banks, and financial markets, such as stock and bond markets.

Where levels of information asymmetry are high, relatively little private lending takes place outside of close-kin networks. Only those few with access to funds can implement new ideas or procedures, so many wealth-producing plans die due to inadequate financing. After the introduction of institutions and markets that reduce information asymmetry, some of those wealth-producing ideas, the ones most likely to succeed, find financing, are implemented, and result in productivity gains. In addition to information asymmetry, other lending or borrowing costs (e.g., the cost of searching for counterparties) can also prevent entrepreneurs from finding financing. Macroeconomic instability (e.g., large, unexpected movements in the aggregate price level, exchange rates, nominal money balances, and interest rates) also reduces the volume of lending by raising the cost or risk of lending. Financial institutions, particularly central banks, can help to increase lending levels by decreasing macroeconomic instability.

A nation undergoes a "financial revolution" when it quickly develops a banking sector; markets for the sale of government bonds, corporate debt, and equities (stock); and a central bank. Chapter 2 places the U.S. financial revolution of the 1790s, the simultaneous emergence of the new nation's commercial banking and securities sectors and central bank, in the context of the development of European financial systems and the colonial American political and legal environment. In the seventeenth century, Holland and Great Britain both underwent financial revolutions very similar to that experienced in the early national United States. In both nations, private commercial banks, a central bank, and securities markets appeared on the heels of a major political upheaval. As those institutions reduced information asymmetries, the economies of Holland and Britain blossomed. Britain also bequeathed to the early United States a tradition of stable, nonpredatory government and a legal system that reinforced the sanctity of contract. Colonial courts followed the lead of the mother country, vigorously enforcing debt contracts. Similarly, colonial governments were generally fiscally responsible. Some even managed to raise revenues through bond issuance rather than, or in addition to, traditional fiat currency (bills of credit) emissions. Finally, the early United States experienced an information revolution. Instead of traveling from one peripheral city to London and back to another peripheral city as in the colonial era, after the American Revolution (1775–83) information traveled directly between the several U.S. cities jockeying to replace London as the new nation's commercial center. The new information travel pathways significantly reduced travel times and costs. Additionally, improved roads, an expanding postal system, and, later, technological improvements also helped to reduce information costs. Although the reduced information costs did not directly reduce information asymmetry, it did enable banks and securities markets to do so more efficiently.

Chapter 3 details the major problems of information asymmetry and the methods by which early banks and securities markets sought to reduce it. Banks used specialization and economies of scale to screen applicants against adverse selection and monitor borrowers against moral hazard more efficiently than private lenders could do. Securities markets did likewise but removed the middleman, the bank, from the investment process by allowing governments and firms to sell securities directly to investors. Additionally, the joint-stock form helped to reduce the principal-agent problem. The numerous stockholders of joint-stock firms had incentives to monitor the activities of directors. The market prices of equities served as an accurate, public gauge of each company's financial outlook.

Chapter 4 addresses additional ways in which banks and securities markets improved upon colonial financial practices. Banks matched pools of investors to pools of borrowers, thereby spreading default risks. They also greatly reduced search costs; investors and borrowers need only find a bank or broker, not each other. Finally, banks provided their creditors (depositors and noteholders) with liabilities redeemable upon demand, shielding them from maturity risks. Similarly, the shareholders of banks and other joint-stock firms enjoyed access to liquid secondary securities markets that allowed them to divest cheaply and at will. Borrowers, the demand side of the equation, also enjoyed reduced search costs. Finally, the equities market allowed joint-stock companies to borrow permanent equity capital. The final section of Chapter 4 examines the important role of the U.S. central banking system, the combined efforts of the Bank of the United States (BUS) and the U.S. Treasury. The early U.S. central banking system helped to reduce lending costs and risks by increasing macroeconomic stability. After inadvertently helping to initiate the Panic of 1792, the system showed its considerable strength by stopping that financial panic in its tracks. Later that decade, the system helped to reduce inflation. All the while, the system was careful not to promote moral hazard by acting as a lender of last resort too often.

The price and ownership integration of the new capital markets is the focus of Chapter 5, which shows that the market for securities was national and even international in scope. The chapter begins with brief descriptions of the major domestic securities markets, roughly in terms of importance: New York, Philadelphia, Boston, Baltimore, Charleston, Richmond-Norfolk, and New Orleans. Trading of U.S. securities in London is also sketched. The emphasis is on the *markets*, which were intermediated by pure brokers and dealers or market makers, not on formal exchanges, which were relatively unimportant until late in the period under study. As price comparison tests show, prices of identical securities in different markets were usually close and moved in tandem. Securities prices behaved according to the Theory of Portfolio Choice, a corollary of the Theory of Asymmetric Information. Ceteris paribus, securities that were safer, more remunerative, or more liquid than otherwise comparable securities had higher prices, just as Portfolio Theory predicts. Bid-ask spreads, the price difference at which market makers promised to buy and sell securities, were reasonably small. The chapter's final section assesses the geographical dispersion of equities through a detailed study of antebellum Maine: not only was Maine's capital market capable of raising a significant volume of funds domestically but Maine corporations were also capable of attracting nonlocals, out-of-state Americans, and foreigners as owners of significant numbers of shares.

Chapter 6 describes the growth of the securities services sector, including estimates of the numbers of brokers, which grew over the period, and brokers' commissions, which were consistently low. In the initial public offering (IPO) market, early investors eagerly snapped up shares in unproven new companies if well-known businessmen backed the companies. A case study of secondary securities markets in Philadelphia shows that volumes, while low by today's standards, trended strongly upward over the period under study, as did the number of issues regularly traded. The big-city markets, however, were only the most visible parts of a much larger phenomenon; evidence shows that a large number of securities, ones not listed in major city papers, traded quietly in small, local securities markets.

Chapter 7 describes and assesses the regulatory environment. Although government sometimes enacted onerous regulations, such as New York's Revised Statutes, for the most part the market was able to circumvent or change the problems. The securities markets were lightly regulated indeed. Banks faced more strictures, including taxes. Interestingly, in many important states the existence of taxes on banks dissuaded state governments from regulating banks too severely because the bank taxes were a significant source of state revenue, too significant a source to threaten by overregulation. Early Americans enjoyed a relatively free financial sector, a fact that goes a long way toward explaining the sector's success.

Chapter 8 makes the case for finance-led economic growth by describing how finance made possible the extension of the commercial, agricultural, and manufacturing sectors. Banks provided merchants with short-term financing. Merchants also used securities, particularly government debt, to make remittances in lieu of precious metals or costly bills of exchange. Banks also sometimes lent to farmers. More important, they, and many others besides, invested in internal-improvement (road, canal, and rail) companies that expanded the market for farm produce. The secondary securities markets made the securities of such companies more liquid, and hence more valuable, also thereby indirectly helping America's huge agricultural sector. Banks accommodated manufacturers too, from small rural artisans to New England's large textile firms. The securities markets, for their part, provided joint-stock manufacturing firms, of which there were many, with sources of long-term capital. Together, early U.S. firms, be they commercial, agricultural, or industrial, had access to enough capital, long- and short-term, to allow them to take advantages of economies of scale and scope, to refine further the division of labor, and to invest in new technology – or, in other words, to improve productive efficiency.

In Chapter 9, the major themes of the study are tied to Adam Smith's *Wealth of Nations*. Scholars tend to concentrate on Smith's discussions of the division of labor and the invisible hand. Most do not realize that Smith believed in the efficacy of banks and joint-stock corporations. Fewer still realize that Smith recognized the problems of information asymmetry – adverse selection, moral hazard, and the principal-agent problem – and sought ways to reduce them. This monograph is not about the rediscovery of Smith's book per se, but it is about rediscovering Smith's ideas about how the financial system helps to produce wealth. Before the division of labor, the growth of the market, and free-market forces can do their wealth-producing work, information asymmetry must be reduced. Financial intermediaries, such as banks, and financial markets, such as secondary securities markets, are the major means of reducing information asymmetry. Ergo, economic growth fundamentally depends on the smooth functioning of the financial system.

The notion that economic growth is finance-led should prove appealing to a wide range of people around the globe. Financial service sector employees will discover that they are the heart of the mighty beast, not, as is too often asserted in some circles, bloodsucking leeches. Investors will learn to judge an emerging market's potential by analyzing the structure of its domestic financial sector. Public policy analysts will see the importance of reducing information asymmetry. Historians will be able to discuss Alexander Hamilton's financial reform program from the standpoint of economics, not just politics, and will learn to describe the financial sector before telling readers, or students, about canals, railroads, and factories. Finally, this book will help skeptical economists to see that Ross Levine and other prophets of finance-led growth just might be right. They are, after all, followers of Adam Smith, too.

2

The International and Colonial Background of America's Financial Revolution

The premise of this book is that in the 1780s and 1790s the United States experienced a financial revolution that caused the nation's nineteenth-century growth spurt. Three important new financial innovations led that financial revolution: commercial banks, the central bank (BUS and the U.S. Treasury), and securities markets. By reducing information asymmetry and other borrowing costs and risks, commercial banks and securities markets linked borrowers to savers more efficiently than had any colonial financial arrangement. The central bank, also a new addition to the economy, kept the macroeconomy on a relatively even keel, thereby reducing systemic risk. Early U.S. savers eagerly sought financial assets because, relative to other assets, like land, they were easily exchangeable and safe. Early Americans, therefore, saved more than they would have had the financial revolution not occurred. Their savings, channeled by the banks and markets into able entrepreneurial hands, financed the "internal improvements" (infrastructure), factories, and technologies that made the United States a leading industrial power by 1865.

The U.S. financial revolution of the 1790s did not, of course, occur in a vacuum. Important precedents – foreign, imperial, and domestic – laid the necessary groundwork. First Holland and then England experienced their own financial revolutions in the seventeenth century. Additionally, colonial American courts set precedents important for financial institutions and markets when they staunchly enforced debt obligations and thereby raised the expected costs of contract breaches. Colonial governments were, in the main, financially prudent, especially after about 1750. Pennsylvania and Massachusetts, for example, were even able to finance some government expenditures with bonds instead of bills of credit. Although the colonial debt markets were thin and small, they did show that at least some Americans had excess funds to invest. Also of importance was the fact that early U.S. politicians, even those opposed to the specifics of Alexander Hamilton's financial program, supported honorable debt repayment over default. Finally, the American Revolution transformed the major U.S. cities from peripheral trading posts into central trading ports. Instead of being mere spokes in London's hub, in other words, U.S. cities looked directly to each other for trade. That fundamental change in orientation, combined with decreased travel costs, helped information to flow more quickly between U.S. commercial centers. Faster and cheaper information flows made secondary securities markets more efficient and helped financial intermediaries to reduce adverse selection, moral hazard, and the principal-agent problem.

The First Financial Revolutions: Holland and Great Britain

Holland was the first nation to undergo a modern financial revolution.[1] The process appears to have begun with a rapid increase in nominal and real money balances, beginning perhaps as early as the 1540s, and an increased volume of international trade. Increases in wealth and a larger per capita money supply allowed government to collect taxes in money instead of in kind (goods and services). Indeed, over the course of the sixteenth and seventeenth centuries, Dutch governments (tentatively at first under the Hapsburgs, later with a vengeance under the republic) increased the efficiency of tax collection, eventually allowing the government to borrow from a larger segment of the population at lower interest rates. (Early on, the central government could borrow only from a handful of Antwerp bankers, at annual interest rates ranging from 12 to 22 percent.) As would later be the case in Britain in the 1690s and the United States in the 1790s, a political revolution paved the way for significant financial reforms. The Union of Utrecht, which gave tax powers to the central government of the new Republic of the United Netherlands, approximates Britain's "Glorious Revolution" and America's Constitutional Convention. The Union of Utrecht did not, as planned, create a unitary tax system for the new republic, but it did establish a workable federal system that allowed the Netherlands's most important states, especially Holland, to begin to raise taxes in a predictable, relatively efficient manner. Total and per capita revenues, and the tax burden on unskilled labor, rose and fell according to the needs of government to finance war and service debt. Overall, the level of taxation in the republic in the sixteenth through early eighteenth century was far higher than in surrounding countries, including Britain.

The solid tax base allowed government borrowing to begin in earnest. In the mid-sixteenth century, Holland, and some of the republic's other states, began to be able to borrow long-term funds at relatively favorable interest rates in a free capital market. In the

[1] Except where otherwise noted, this section is based on deVries and Woude 1997:81–158 and Neal 1990:1–14.

seventeenth century, the Dutch were able to finance their many wars by borrowing in the domestic capital market. By 1655 Dutch debt traded at yields around 4 percent. The Dutch, therefore, could afford to borrow and to spend sums much larger than their short-term ability to raise by tax. That gave them a tremendous military advantage and prevented the major disruptions to the Dutch economy that extremely high wartime taxes could have produced.

Importantly, the government's bonds were negotiable, which is to say that they could be bought and sold in "secondary" markets. The negotiable aspect of the bonds made them much more valuable because investors could "cash out" on the investment by selling it to another investor when desired. Indeed, the growing guilder volume of bonds changed ownership often. A wide variety of investors found it a relatively easy matter to purchase or sell the bonds; many a craftsman, farmer, and woman invested in them. In the 1660s a visiting statesman noted that Holland's debt, roughly 135 million guilders, was held by 65,500 different persons, or more than one-quarter of all households in the province.

In the late seventeenth century, the Netherlands fought both Britain and France simultaneously. Its capital market responded, fully meeting the government's calls, and at low interest rates. Only after several decades of heavy borrowing did the broad market demand begin to give out. After resorting to gimmicks like lottery bonds, which made huge payoffs to a lucky few, the Dutch began to rely more heavily on a few very rich families for continued funding. The rich were willing to lend when the broad middle classes were not for a number of reasons. First, the rich had more to lose should the republic lose its sovereignty. Second, richer folks can afford to take on more risk. Third, a few families could be relatively cheaply provided with very large amounts of information regarding the government's financial status. Finally, the line between the government and the rich lenders was often difficult to draw as the lenders often came from families studded with officeholders. The change from a broad base of creditors to a few drew the republic's financial revolution to a close. Thereafter, the national debt, some believe, was a great burden to the economy because it essentially redistributed wealth from the great mass of taxpayers to a wealthy few who invested almost all of it in more government debt and overseas investments.[2]

During the seventeenth century, however, the Dutch debt had been a godsend. Besides allowing the tiny country to fight, and even win, numerous wars against much larger foes, the national debt helped to spur the development of the republic's commercial financial sector,

[2] Van Winter 1977.

particularly its financial intermediaries. The government debt served to redistribute wealth from taxpayers, the bulk of the population, to the bondholders, a broad but relatively affluent part of the population. The bondholders could not always reinvest all of their interest payments in more government debt. Therefore, they demanded additional investment outlets, a demand that many business firms were happy to supply, sometimes directly through the sale of short-term commercial paper, but more often indirectly through intermediaries, including banks and insurance companies.

In 1609 the city of Amsterdam established the Bank of Amsterdam, which proved to be an almost instant success. The bank, a quasi-central bank, attracted deposits and served as a clearinghouse for transferring funds between depositors, a very conservative banking model based on Italian precedents. The Bank of Amsterdam, unlike later Anglo-American banks, did not issue demand bearer liabilities such as bank notes. In addition, it lent only to the Dutch East India Company and the city of Amsterdam. The bank indirectly regulated a system of small, private bankers that were the main source of discount loans for merchants. Lombards, which specialized in consumer loans, were also established. Insurance companies – marine, fire, and life – blossomed too. A financial press also emerged, providing the market with interest rate, exchange rate, and stock price quotations and other important financial information. Finally, a bourse or stock exchange helped to increase the liquidity of securities. Brokers and notaries also functioned as intermediaries, linking sellers of securities to buyers, and lenders to borrowers. A relatively free market encouraged financial innovation. By the 1770s, for example, Dutch financiers had created the world's first mutual funds.

"One must be blinded by dogma," a recent student of the subject has argued, "not to see the autonomous importance of financial institutions and investor behavior in giving shape to the Dutch economy." Before the Republic's financial revolution, "many people sat on vast cash hoards," a huge deadweight to the economy.[3] After the development of government debt markets and financial intermediaries reduced information asymmetry, people invested their hoards. The government could fight wars without ruinous rates of taxation, merchants could borrow to finance trading expeditions, and other firms could invest in tools or techniques that improved their efficiency. The aggregate effect of those developments was an increase in real per capita GDP.

The Dutch financial system was able to induce more savings than the republic's physical economy could handle. Dutch investors, therefore,

[3]DeVries and Woude 1997:129, 139.

became the world's capitalists. They supplied a good chunk of the credit necessary to carry on international commerce, a sizable percentage of Britain's growing national debt, and, in the 1780s and 1790s, many millions, 30 by 1803, of guilders to the emerging U.S. market.

Adam Smith well knew how the Netherlands, a loose federation of tiny nations with no special natural resource endowments, had managed to grow so rich. The answer was the same as with every other nation – free markets and free capital. Nations, and the firms within them, produce wealth by increasing the size of the market and by increasing productivity through the division of labor and through economies of scale and scope. They begin to do so, in earnest, when they can borrow funds to finance such wealth-inducing projects. They can borrow significant sums, however, only after information asymmetries have been reduced. Financial intermediaries and securities markets, Smith and the Dutch knew, were the main weapons against adverse selection and moral hazard. By the 1690s, the British government had come to the same conclusion.

The connection between the Dutch financial revolution and the British financial revolution is clear and direct.[4] The 1688 "Glorious Revolution" brought Dutch Stadhouder Willem III to the English throne. William of Orange, as the British call him, soon established, or allowed to be established, the key pillars of a modern financial system – a negotiable public debt, a secondary securities market, and a central bank. The British, who understood that their credit facilities, public and private, were deficient compared with those of the Netherlands, readily accepted, and then improved upon, the new institutions. In addition, the British soon afterward developed private financial institutions, including private banks and insurance companies, and an independent financial press that disseminated a variety of price and yield data.

Established in 1694, the Bank of England was a bank of discount, deposit, and note issue. It invested heavily in government debt and later made significant contributions to the capital stock of the big joint-stock trading companies of the early eighteenth century. The bank played a major role in establishing "publick credit." First, it helped to issue the government's bonds and notes. Second, it helped to service those debts by making prompt interest payments to the current bondholders. Third, it helped to create a secondary market for the debt instruments by maintaining the books that tracked their ownership. Finally, the bank stood ready to make loans to the government should the exchequer (treasury) have insufficient revenue to meet its obligations as they came due.

[4]Except where otherwise noted, this section is based on Dickson 1967 and Neal 1990.

In the early 1750s the British government consolidated its debt issues, which had grown to the unwieldy number of 15, 11 of which were managed by the Bank of England, the other 4 by the exchequer. The 15 debt issues were funded by 10 different revenue sources, ranging from duties on windows to the general tax fund. According to a leading historian, the consolidation "greatly strengthened and simplified the machinery of public borrowing."[5] The bank, which served as the government's main financial wing, had a monopoly on note issue. It was not, however, the only financial intermediary in the economy. A seemingly ever growing number of private banks and insurance companies also channeled funds from investors to entrepreneurs.

The financial revolution that began in the 1690s helped to launch Britain as a world economic and military power. Despite its smaller physical size and smaller population, Britain repeatedly defeated France in both war and trade. Clearly, the British financial revolution induced Britain's subsequent industrialization. The increased efficiency brought about by new technologies and new production processes were not entirely self-financed. Much finance had to be obtained externally. In other words, someone other than the entrepreneur had to supply at least part of the capital. The financial revolution provided the appropriate tools. Banks and other financial intermediaries, as was the case in the Netherlands, matched investors to entrepreneurs cheaply and efficiently. Secondary securities markets induced investment because they provided direct investors in government and corporate securities a ready market for their assets.

As early as the seventeenth century, London was home to Britain's most active securities market. Early on, when there were few securities and few holders, buyers and sellers exchanged directly and informally. As the number of securities and holders grew, brokers – who were part banker, lawyer, accountant, real-estate agent, and scrivener – appeared and began matching buyers to sellers. After the formation of the Bank of England and several large joint-stock companies in the 1690s, brokers specializing in securities appeared in London, where most of the shareholders then lived. In the early eighteenth century, trading in the new joint-stock concerns was relatively heavy, with 85 percent turnover reported for the Bank of England and the East India Company in 1704 alone. Over the course of the century, trading volumes waxed and waned from year to year, but showed a definite upward tendency. Beginning in 1697, specialized newspapers like John Castaing's *Course of the Exchange* provided the wider market with securities prices. An additional impetus to the market was the British government's enormous negotiable public debt. In the 1690s the British government

5Dickson 1967:243.

began to finance its budget deficits with transferable bonds instead of private loans from individuals. By 1700 dealers, who helped to "make a market" in securities by buying and selling them at stated prices on their own account, emerged.[6]

In 1773 a large group of London brokers and dealers constructed an edifice, "The Stock Exchange," in which to conduct securities trading. The association that constructed the building and charged the daily admission fee, however, was not a stock exchange in the formal sense but simply one of a number of renters of a convenient trading space. Not until 1801 did securities trading in London become formalized in a modern stock exchange institution, the London Stock Exchange. In addition to providing trading facilities, the exchange, which had a regular membership, made and enforced rules relating to the trading of stocks and bonds. The exchange emerged when the trading volume and complexity of the markets were high enough that brokers and dealers were willing to forgo some cash, and some autonomy, in exchange for a structured trading environment.[7]

The London experience provided the early United States with several important precedents. First, the U.S. securities markets experienced a similar progression from unintermediated transactions, to brokered markets, to markets "made" by dealers, to formal stock exchanges. Second, perhaps even better than the English securities sector, the U.S. securities sector was largely able to overcome vocal popular opposition to "speculation" and "stockjobbing."[8] Third, the U.S. financial markets quickly became efficient, again following English precedent closely. (Statistical evidence shows that securities prices in the London market exhibit "the same behavior today as they did two hundred years ago." In other words, sometime before 1800 the London securities *market* [not to be confused with the exchange, an institution] became more or less modern in form and function. Indeed, securities prices followed "essentially a random walk" even in the eighteenth century.)[9]

Colonial America and the early United States also learned much about taxation from the British. Many of the securities traded in the London market were government bonds serviced with tax revenues. By the end of the Revolutionary War, England was collecting more than £20 million sterling in taxes per year, up from just a few million pounds in the beginning of the century. In peacetime, after 1700, more than 30 percent of tax revenue went to service the debt. During and immediately after Britain's many wars, more than 60 percent of tax revenues were needed for debt service. Over the course of the century, Britain learned to carry the burden by increasing the numbers of tax

[6]Michie 1999.   [7]Michie 1999.   [8]Banner 1998.   [9]Harrison 1994:50.

collectors almost fivefold and by taking steps to make tax collection more efficient by reducing expenses per shilling of revenue raised.[10]

None of this should be taken to suggest, however, that the United States merely mimicked overseas developments. Indeed, the United States had two formal stock exchanges, in Philadelphia (1790) and New York (1792), before the London Stock Exchange formed. Additionally, the American colonies themselves provided much impetus to the financial revolution of the 1790s by extending British legal and governance precedents.

Colonial America: Courts and Experiments

In the *Wealth and Poverty of Nations*, David Landes argues that "if we learn anything from the history of economic development, it is that culture makes all the difference."[11] American society, he explains, was a "seedbed of democracy and enterprise" because of its British cultural origins and a land-to-labor ratio that led to "smallholders and relatively well-paid workers." Both ensured America's prosperity. A nation of many small proprietors created an atmosphere of Smithian business competition and an efficient, free market. The intense competition, coupled with the high cost of labor, induced U.S. firms to implement Smithian division of labor and, later, to adopt "the new technologies of the Industrial Revolution." Indeed, by the 1820s, with the aid of a slew of American inventions or adaptations, U.S. manufacturing productivity was "well ahead of Britain." The inheritance of a Lockean British governance system was also crucial. Although far from perfect, the British government, and the governments of many of its colonies, was less predatory than governments elsewhere. Furthermore, the Lockean system promoted a stable society and economy by securing personal liberty and private property rights.[12]

Indeed, if Deborah Rosen and Bruce Mann are correct, and there is little reason on this head to suspect that they are not, colonial America bequeathed to the United States a legal system that stressed the sanctity of contract. If a colonial creditor wished to push for repayment of a just debt, justices did not hesitate to sign the appropriate writs ordering sheriffs to seize the property, and even bodies, of debtors. The strong legal system per se did not eliminate defaults – the court records themselves are ample evidence of that – but it did give investors a measure of security that they would not otherwise have had. In short, the legal system raised the expected cost of defalcation or default and thereby reduced the risk of outright fraud.[13]

---

[10]Brewer 1989:88–134.   [11]Landes 1998:516.
[12]Ibid., 217–18, 297–300.   [13]Rosen 1997; Mann 1987.

If a "locked door keeps an honest man honest," then a good legal system is like a locked door. The strong legal system, in other words, lowered the threshold of private information needed before a lender was willing to part with his funds. The legal system did not reduce information asymmetry – the borrower still knew far more about himself than the lender – but both parties knew that government would help to enforce the contract if necessary. Colonial and early U.S. investors, in other words, had little worry about "political risk," the risk of government allowing a breach of contract. The biggest development in this regard in the colonial period was the elimination of jury trials in debt cases. (Judges typically rendered more impartial decisions.) Other developments included the increasingly "formalistic and unforgiving" nature of debt litigation, and more "technical" pleading, both of which made debt enforcement more predictable.[14] A recent theoretical and empirical study confirms that cross-country differences in legal systems – especially differences in creditor rights, contract enforcement, and accounting standards – explain differences in the level of financial development and hence in economic growth.[15]

Additionally, for the most part, especially late in the colonial period, colonial governments themselves were financially responsible.[16] During and after the French and Indian War, Pennsylvania was able to finance some of its operations by issuing a modest volume of negotiable bonds, the trading of which was extremely limited.[17] Under the able management of Thomas Hutchinson, Massachusetts, after its midcentury fiscal reforms, financed its deficits by borrowing in the colony's emerging capital market.[18] At times, hundreds of thousands of pounds (Massachusetts currency) of the so-called Treasurer's Notes were outstanding. The secondary market for the bonds was, however, quite limited. Apparently, no one ever thought to sell the bonds for a premium, although investors valued them highly as safe, yet remunerative, investments. Indeed, Massachusetts was able to cut the coupon interest rate on the notes from 6 to 5 percent without appreciably affecting demand.[19] Any investor lucky enough to own a Massachusetts Treasurer's Note, therefore, was loath to sell it. The turnover volume was so low that the Massachusetts government official charged with overseeing the official transfer of the bonds served as a sort of rudimentary broker, maintaining a long list of potential buyers of the essentially underpriced security. The precedent of financing an American government with debt rather than currency was an important one, but the colonial Massachusetts experience did not establish a clear

[14]Mann 1998:9.   [15]Levine et al. 2000.
[16]Perkins 1994:349.   [17]Wright 1996.   [18]Rothenberg 1992.
[19]Massachusetts Archives, "Pecuniary Volumes," 104:341, 410, microfilm; Leslie V. Brock, unpublished manuscript, 272–77, both in Leslie V. Brock Papers, UVA.

precedent for the active, efficient secondary securities markets of the early national period, where bonds and equities could sell for a premium if market forces dictated such.

The First U.S. Information Revolution:
From Periphery to Center

Problems of information asymmetry, including adverse selection, moral hazard, and the principal-agent problem, can stymie economic development, as they did in colonial America. The early national United States experienced an "information revolution" that made it easier and cheaper for the new financial intermediaries and markets to reduce information asymmetries. In short, the locus of information shifted from London to the major seaboard U.S. cities. After the Revolution, information traveled directly between, say, Boston and Philadelphia rather than traveling via London as in the colonial period. Over the period of this study, technological and transportation improvements also reduced information travel times and costs.

Tellingly, colonists merely converted colonial currencies into each other at customary rates because there were no active spot markets. In other words, Pennsylvania and New York merchants used a formula to convert their respective currencies into one another, a sure sign that there was relatively little direct trade, or information flow, between the colonies.[20] There was, on the other hand, a thriving spot market for Britain's money of account, sterling, in every colony. Those facts underscore John J. McCusker's persuasive argument that the American colonists looked primarily to home, the center, the British Isles, for commercial information. Indeed, the colonial press was small and focused largely on advertisements, politics, and international news; the commercial press was entirely based in London, the commercial, financial, and political center of the empire. Colonists, therefore, literally clamored for the London sheets, often expressing anger, or dismay, if their subscriptions did not arrive in a timely manner. There was good reason for this; even under the best circumstances, the papers delivered stale prices. Stale prices were better than extremely stale prices, though. For local prices, colonial businessmen gathered at coffeehouses, such as the aptly named London Coffee House, which was home to the Philadelphia "Merchants' Exchange." Such colonial

[20]Michener 2000. Similarly, Pennsylvania and Jamaica merchants merely converted their respective currencies into each other at a customary rate. William Pollard to Charles White, 25 September 1772; to Peter Holme, 13 October 1772, William Pollard Letter Book, HSP.

commercial gathering places often housed libraries that contained runs of back issues of the important London commercial papers and mercantile reference sources, such as Malachi Postlethwayt's *Universal Dictionary of Trade and Commerce.*[21]

After the Revolution, the situation changed drastically. The indigenous press grew in size, focused more attention on local matters, and began publishing large volumes of commercial information. North America's first "price current," *Philadelphia Price Current*, began operation in Philadelphia in June 1783. The emergence of the U.S. business press in Philadelphia, immediately after the war, McCusker persuasively argues, was no accident. By 1750 Philadelphia had emerged as the most important market in North America. With London's importance to America diminished after the Revolution, it was natural that Philadelphia would assume the preeminent position and become the first to require a local business press.

John MacPherson, publisher of the *Philadelphia Price Current*, gathered price information from a score of businessmen. He sold the paper by subscription to individuals, taverns, coffeehouses, and other public businesses and presumably allowed stationers and booksellers to retail individual issues. The paper was substantively the same as London prices current, like *Lloyd's List* and the *Course of the Exchange*. The Philadelphia paper was somewhat smaller, though, comprising a single, double-sided sheet containing some 120 price quotations.

The business press was at first quite diverse. McCusker has identified at least 11 different specific types of early business newspaper. Most broadly, there were newspapers that reported on the local economy, newspapers that reported on international trade, and newspapers that offered a combination of domestic and international news.

Publications that specialized in domestic news came in five varieties: general prices current, which published local prices of a broad range of goods; specialized prices current, which concentrated on prices of major products like cloth, grain, tobacco, and sugar; foreign-exchange papers, which published spot exchange rates (prices of bills of exchange denominated in various currencies); money publications, which listed the prices of various foreign and domestic coins in terms of the local money of account; and stock exchange papers, which tracked prices of equities and debt instruments.

International trade publications specialized in general or specialized bills of entry, which were lists of imports and exports, or marine lists, which were lists of ships entering or clearing local, regional, and foreign ports.

[21] McCusker and Gravesteijn 1991; McCusker 2000.

As the economy grew larger and more complex, and business publishing became more competitive, the commercial press began to combine domestic and foreign lists into the same paper. Combination publications always offered exchange rate information, which they combined with securities prices, marine lists, or both. As the nation grew and matured, numerous important marketplaces appeared, and the commercial press spread to cover prices and other business news. Literally scores of papers with strong commercial or business components arose and thrived between the Revolution and the Civil War.[22]

The growth of the commercial press was impressive indeed. Commercial newspaper editor Peter A. Grotjan bragged in 1815 that he enjoyed "weekly perusal of two prices Currents from Baltimore, three from New York and two from Boston."[23] In his memoirs, Grotjan claimed that "there was hardly a town in the U.S. where my report did not freely circulate according to the magnitude of the place." He also claimed to have had numerous subscribers in "England, France, Germany, Holland, Canton, Calcutta, & the West Indies."[24]

By 1800 any Philadelphian could subscribe, for just about $15 (roughly $200 in 2000 dollars), to five different local business newspapers. Those papers often carried important news and prices from other cities because commercial editors like Grotjan subscribed to many papers and freely copied from them. By 1794 commercial editors readily subscribed to commercial papers in other cities. For example, editors from Philadelphia, New York, and Boston, as well as Charleston, South Carolina, Fayetteville, North Carolina, and Wilmington, Delaware, subscribed to Philadelphia's bilingual (French and English) *American Star,* on the promise that the paper would "inform our readers of the fall or rise of public stocks, the course of exchange, the current price of

---

[22]Some of the most important, in terms of circulation, longevity, or innovation, included the following: *American Price Current* (New York), 1786; *Baltimore American and Daily Advertiser* (*Baltimore American & Commercial Daily Advertiser*), 1830–39; *Baltimore Patriot Mercantile Advertiser,* 1813–30; *Baltimore (Weekly) Price Current,* 1803–30, 1853–60; *Boston Courier,* 1837–41; *Boston Columbia Centinel,* 1811–20; *Boston Daily Advertiser,* 1830–36; *Boston Shipping List, Prices Current, &c.,* 1843–50; *Charleston Carolina Gazette,* 1823–29, 1837–40; *Charleston City Gazette,* 1815–32; *Charleston Courier,* 1803–49; *Charleston Mercury and Morning Advertiser,* 1822–33; *Comparative Price Current, and European and American Commercial Reporter* (New York), 1827; *The Diary, or Loudon's Register* (New York), 1792; *Finlay's American Naval and Commercial Register* (Philadelphia), 1795–98; *Gazette of the United States* (Philadelphia), 1798–1806; *Grotjan's Philadelphia Public Sale Report and General Price Current* (Philadelphia), 1816–30; *Hope's Philadelphia Price Current,* 1805–13; *Howard's Prices Current* (Charleston), 1832; *Lyford's Baltimore Price Current,* 1839–49; *Merchants' Daily Advertiser* (Philadelphia), 1797–98; *New Orleans Price Current & Commercial Intelligencer,* 1824–30; *New York Price Current,* 1797–1860; *Pelosi's Marine List and Price Current* (Philadelphia), 1791–93; *Pennsylvania Mercury and Philadelphia Price Current,* 1790–92; *Richmond Enquirer,* 1815–60; *Southern Patriot and Commercial Advertiser* (Charleston), 1821–43.

[23]*Grotjan's Philadelphia Prices Current,* 8 May 1815.

[24]Peter A. Grotjan's Memoirs, 1774–1850, vol. 2, HSP.

country produce, the fitting out, the arrivals and the departures of vessels for different parts of the world," and other news.[25]

For the fullest information from New York, Boston, Baltimore, or elsewhere, the Philadelphian could correspond with businessmen with similar interests in those locales. After reading his Philadelphia paper, he copied important price information into his letters and perhaps even sent his entire copy of the paper. His correspondents reciprocated, keeping the Philadelphian abreast of the nation's business news. Sometimes such information networks extended to the West Indies. Businessmen heavily engaged in international trade, however, would still want to subscribe to at least one of the London commercial papers. Those who could not afford to subscribe to many papers could read issues at various libraries, such as the Athenaeum.[26]

The volume of information exchange was impressive. In 1800, Americans sent 1.9 million copies of newspapers by post. By 1830, 16 million papers, 1.5 per capita, went through the post. A decade later, 39 million newspapers, or 2.7 per capita, were mailed. The volume of private letters sent through the mail in those years was almost identical. Just as important, the postal service, by far the largest organization in the economy, was extensive, reaching into even the most remote villages. By 1840 almost 13,500 post offices dotted the land, one for every 61.4 settled square miles and one per every 1,087 free individuals. The postal service impressed many contemporary Americans and foreign visitors.[27] The post was only one information conduit and important only for long-distance communication. Much information, especially within cities or regions, traveled by private conveyance or messenger. Just like today, the publishers' delivery persons, not postal workers, delivered most early newspapers. Unlike today, early Americans did not use the post to send a letter across town or even across county; private persons carried numerous letters for friends and family whenever they traveled for business, pleasure, or worship.[28] Clearly then, given the standards of the day, most U.S. denizens had ample access to public news and private information divulged in letters.

How quickly did those newspapers and business letters get from the major cities to those remote villages? Or to other commercial centers? Allan Pred found incremental improvements in information travel times between the major seaboard cities, and between those cities and commercial towns in the interior, over the period of this study.

[25]*Prospectus of the American Star, or, Historical, Political, Critical and Moral Journal* (Philadelphia), 1794.
[26]Peter A. Grotjan to Robert Vaux, 10 January 1816, Stauffer Collection, 16:113, HSP.
[27]John 1995:4–18, 51.
[28]Any diary or letter book from the period will provide ample evidence of the extensive use of private conveyance.

Predictably, information travel speeds were fastest where the transportation system – free roads, turnpikes, improved rivers, canals, and, later, railroads – was the most developed. Technological developments in ships also helped to decrease information travel times.[29] By the summer of 1794, for example, land travelers could hitch a ride on the mail post between Boston and New York for just four pence per mile, including a 14-pound baggage allowance. Coaches left Boston every Monday, Wednesday, and Friday.[30] By 1840 information travel times to Philadelphia, especially along the northeast corridor, were quite fast. Information could reach Philadelphia from Manhattan or Harrisburg in less than a day. Boston and Albany were only a day distant; Portland, Maine, was only two days away. To the south, Baltimore was less than a day away. Information from as far away as Petersburg, Virginia, could arrive in Philadelphia in a single day. New Orleans was eight days away, but all points east were fewer days away. Only points in Mississippi approached two weeks' time distance from Philadelphia in 1840.[31]

Faster travel information times meant more efficient markets, especially financial markets. Indeed, brokers and speculators were particularly avid information seekers, often beseeching correspondents to write more detailed letters more frequently.[32] In September 1790, for instance, George Nelson of Charleston begged Samuel Bellamy to "inform your Self as much as possible what Indents & Public Securitys are worth with you and write me by Every Opportunity with the best information concerning them."[33] During times of market volatility, brokers often sent information by "express," especially between New York and Philadelphia.[34] To facilitate trading, brokers established very wide communication networks. During the War of 1812, for example, Philadelphia's Thomas A. Biddle and J. Wharton Company corresponded with brokers, dealers, and speculators not only in Boston, Baltimore, and New York, but also in Trenton, New Jersey; Reading and Lancaster, Pennsylvania; Alexandria, Georgetown, and Richmond, Virginia; Charleston, South Carolina; and St. Bartholomew's.[35] Bankers also tapped informal information networks.[36]

---

[29]Pred 1973.

[30]Henry Wansey, *Journal of an Excursion to the United States of North America in the Summer of 1794* (1796).

[31]*Philadelphia Prices Current*, 26 December 1840.

[32]See, for example, Clement Biddle to Robert Gilchrist, 18 March 1790, Clement Biddle Letter Book, HSP.

[33]George Nelson to Samuel Bellamy, 11 September 1790, George Nelson Letter Book, UNCSC. My thanks to Jennifer Goloboy for alerting me to this source.

[34]Clement Biddle to George Lewis, 18 January 1792, Clement Biddle Letter Book, HSP.

[35]Thomas A. Biddle and J. Wharton Company Letter Book, HSP.

[36]See, for example, Minutes of the Proceedings of the Board of Directors of the Offices of Discount and Deposit at Reading, 7 November 1822, Bank of Pennsylvania Records, HSP.

This is not to say that the communication network was perfect. Far from it. For example, Nicholas Low could not sell $3,000 worth of Philip Schuyler's "Stock" in November 1798 because Schuyler's letter of attorney, dated in October 1796, was thought to be too old and hence no longer binding. The deal fell through because Schuyler could not be contacted to update the letter soon enough.[37] That is simply one of many examples of deals that could not be completed due to slow information travel times. Information was easier to obtain than during the colonial period, however, when William Pollard had to sarcastically ask his London correspondent that he "be very cautious in whom you recommend that they be men of *Real* Capital."[38] Pollard in this case had been burned because his London correspondent had provided him with stale information regarding the creditworthiness of several firms. Slow, unreliable travel also made it difficult for colonists to find endorsers; in the late colonial period, the charge was 2.5 percent for endorsing the bill of a man "not sufficiently known."[39]

What types of information circulated? Prices, of course, were of major importance. For example, when Aaron Burr, suffering from a "temporary vexation," desired to sell some of his Manhattan Company stock, he wrote William Edgar to ensure that he had been offered the going market price for the shares.[40] Credit information was also important. For example, in August 1813 Biddle and Wharton informed William Payne of Boston that the "character of the drawer" of certain bills of exchange was "well known to those in the St. Bartholomews and we believe the St. Croix Trade." "Independent of which," the brokers added, the bills were "endorsed by Daniel W. Cox, a Merchant in our City of believed large property . . . who must be well known in your City and Mr. Wilson Hunt also a man of Snug Estate, limited in his trade and whose Bills are esteemed as good as any trader, worth about 100 to 150 thousand dollars."[41] Such letters were extremely common.[42]

Securities traders also wished to know what other securities traders were up to. In July 1816, for example, Nathaniel Prime asked Thomas Biddle to give his "answer to the following questions as soon as may be:

[37] Nicholas Low to Philip Schuyler, New York, 16 November 1798, Letters to Schuyler, 1793–1804 and undated, reel 18, Schuyler Papers, SUNY Buffalo.
[38] William Pollard to William Wilson, 18 August 1772, William Pollard Letter Book, HSP.
[39] William Pollard to Peter Holmes, 13 October 1772, ibid.
[40] Aaron Burr to William Edgar, New York, 14 April 1800, William Edgar Papers, NYPL.
[41] Biddle and Wharton to William Payne, 18 August 1813, Thomas A. Biddle and J. Wharton Company Letter Book, HSP.
[42] Wright 1999a.

What amt. is there subscribed to the N[ational] Bank [?]
Who are the largest subscribers [?]
Have McEuen & Co. sb. & how many shares [?]
It is said S. & J. Nevins & Co. took 1,000 shares and but one share
    to a name for whom did they subscribe [?]
Who is most spoken of for President & Cash[ie]r. [?][43]

The revolution in information dissemination networks and information travel times, profound as it was, did not reduce information asymmetry; it merely made information acquisition faster and cheaper. It is, therefore, only the backdrop for the market and institutional changes initiated in the early national period. In other words, the theory of information asymmetry set forth here is not merely a subset of the "transportation revolution."[44] Today, entire libraries fly across the globe in just a few seconds, yet information asymmetry still disrupts markets. Indeed, the formal theory of information asymmetry arose in response to distortions in twentieth-century commodities and financial markets.[45] Conversely, information asymmetry can be reduced without great leaps in information travel times. Britain and Holland, as we have seen, experienced financial revolutions well before the "transportation revolution" of the first half of the nineteenth century or the "information revolution" of the latter half of the twentieth. Faster, and especially cheaper, information, in other words, is an aid to market participants seeking to reduce the problems of information asymmetry, not an end in itself. In the United States, banks and securities markets, as we will see in the next chapter, began to reduce information asymmetry before the "transportation revolution." In addition, those institutions and markets financed the governments and businesses that made the "transportation revolution" possible. If anything, then, the "transportation revolution" is a subset of the wider "financial revolution," not the other way around.

After all, the only ways to reduce information asymmetry, which by definition is a differential in *private* information, is to create, purchase, or steal private information about a potential counterparty. Financial intermediaries and financial markets specialize in the creation of such private information. Banks, for instance, screened loan applicants and monitored borrowers' activities. Investors attempted to discover private information about firms in order to value the firms' securities, looking for discrepancies between the going market price and the fundamental value of the security. (They also tried to obtain public information before anyone else in the market did, a practice

---

[43]Nathaniel Prime to Thomas Biddle, 3 July 1816, D, Business Correspondence, Incoming, 1815–17, Thomas A. Biddle Papers, HSP.
[44]Taylor 1958.   [45]Baskin and Miranti 1997:11–25.

that still occurs today, but one fundamentally different from creating information.) The *creation* of information is what reduced information asymmetry; improved information flows simply made it cheaper to engage in information-asymmetry-reducing activities.

The information revolution, the reorientation of information flows to the North American continent and away from London, and improvements in the post office, infrastructure, and, eventually, technology made it easier (cheaper) for banks and markets to do their job of reducing information asymmetries. Obviously, it was better for a bank if it could obtain information about a loan applicant in two days for $3 rather than in six days for $12. Nevertheless, in either case, it was the agency of the bank (or other types of lenders) that reduced the asymmetry, not the mere existence of the roads, post offices, or other infrastructure.

In the next two chapters, we will see how banks, other intermediaries, and securities markets reduced information asymmetry and other borrowing costs, and why they were better at doing so than individuals, small firms, or other colonial antecedents. The changes that the banks and markets wrought were not without European precedent, or without support from the colonial legal system or physical infrastructure, but they were fundamental, revolutionary changes nonetheless.

3

Banks, Securities Markets, and the Reduction of Asymmetric Information

Economists, historians, all thinking beings really, rely on theories to help them to make sense of a complex world. Economists tend to be very explicit about their theories, historians much less so. Historians often embed their theories in a narrative structure. Indeed, some historians deny that they use theories at all. Only the most naive epistemology would support such a view, however. Indeed, even early Americans employed theories to help them to understand reality. In 1789, for example, New Yorker George Thatcher correctly predicted, based "more upon theory than facts," that Continental securities would appreciate faster than "the securities of those States that have not certain funds for their redemption."[1] Similarly, one critic of the War of 1812 used "the theory of loans" to predict interest rate increases.[2]

The question, therefore, is not whether a scholar employs theory, but whether the theory is explicit or implicit. An important theory underlying this study, the theory of information asymmetry, is here made quite explicit. Indeed, the point of this chapter is to explain and explore that theory, which is particularly amenable to economic and business historians[3] but is straightforward enough for general historians to follow.

The theory of asymmetric information posits that differential access to relevant, private information creates market inefficiencies by interfering with the creation or fulfillment of business contracts. The theory makes one major, but highly plausible, assumption: parties to the contract with superior information will attempt to take advantage of parties with inferior information. That naturally makes potential parties to the contract wary. Of course, wary potential parties do not enter into contracts, formal or otherwise; without contracts business grinds to a halt or is channeled into less efficient pursuits. Learning how to limit information asymmetry is hence a very important economic development, one that colonial Americans did not readily

[1] George Thatcher to William Taylor, 23 April 1789, Gratz, Old Congress, HSP.
[2] *Boston Columbian Centinel*, 9 October 1811.   [3] Lee 1990.

achieve. In the early national period, by contrast, significant reductions of information asymmetry took place.

It is important to keep in mind that the theory of information asymmetry is concerned with private, and not public, information. To reduce information asymmetry, therefore, the party with inferior information must *produce*, or create, information about the counterparty. Although the dissemination of public information is not unimportant to the economy or financial markets, public information – or, in other words, "the news" – is, by definition, symmetrical. All parties have equal access to it. (Whether they use that access or not is a different story.) The theory, in other words, compares what the borrower or seller knows to what the (potential) lender or buyer knows. Both know, or could know, general information, but the borrower or seller knows more about the particular product being peddled than the lender or buyer. The lender or buyer will be burned, the theory predicts, and long experience confirms, if he or she does not create information about the product to be purchased. *Caveat emptor.*

Lending patterns in the colonial period suggest that colonists found it difficult to overcome information asymmetry. Colonial loan volumes were low and most lending occurred between members of the same family, religion, locale, or occupation. Studies by Jones and Rothenberg show that financial assets were a relatively unimportant class of assets for most colonists. No form of "precapitalist" or "communitarian" ethos or mentalité needs to be posited to explain those early lending patterns; the transactions occurred just as theory predicts, between people who had the most information about each other.[4]

Some of the most compelling evidence of colonial lending patterns comes from Remer, Thorp, and Gwyn. Remer conclusively showed that land banks in Massachusetts circa 1740 organized along denominational and occupational lines. In other words, people with close informational ties, not strangers, formed the firms. Backers of the Land Bank came primarily from New Light congregational churches and were primarily engaged in occupations focused on the internal market. The Silver Bank advocates, on the other hand, were almost entirely from Anglican and Old Light churches and were deeply engaged in international trade.

Thorp completed a detailed study of retail trade and lending in backcountry colonial North Carolina. He discovered, unsurprisingly from the standpoint of information theory, that backcountry taverns and retail stores rarely lent to persons who lived further than 10 miles from their businesses. Only in one recorded instance was a book account debt allowed to exceed £10; most accounts never exceeded £1.

[4]Jones 1980; Rothenberg 1992.

Yet, in some stores full default rates exceeded 25 percent and partial default rates approached 70 percent.

Gwyn argued that planned long-term foreign investment in the mainland colonies by non-Americans was "extremely rare." The Warren family of England constituted an exception, lending substantial sums in colonial New York. Almost all of the loans, however, went to family members or tenants of family members. Again, most loans went to people very familiar to the borrower.[5]

Colonists were not dumb or backward or believers in "moral economy." They simply lacked the institutions and human capital needed to reduce the major problems of information asymmetry – adverse selection, moral hazard, and the principal-agent problem. Furthermore, few colonial lenders had sufficient capital to spread their risks by lending to a diversified group of borrowers. The dearth of scale advantages, in other words, also served to limit the volume of colonial lending.

Early U.S. banks and securities markets greatly reduced information asymmetry. In so doing, they made borrowing cheaper and hence increased the volume of loans. Increased lending was a very good thing for the economy. Credit was, as it still is, a crucial economic activity. Without it, good ideas are left undone and humanity is left the poorer for it. When credit is ample, and correctly channeled, good ideas come to fruition and enrich us all. This chapter explains how the institutions and markets of the U.S. financial revolution reduced adverse selection, moral hazard, and the principal-agent problem.

Adverse Selection

Adverse selection is also known as the "lemons problem." Sellers of used automobiles naturally know more about their vehicles than the potential buyers know. Buyers can inspect the vehicle, take it for a test drive, and kick the tires, but are still unable to discern breakdown-prone automobiles, or so-called lemons, from dependable vehicles, or so-called peaches. They will, therefore, give no more than the average market price for vehicles of a certain make, model, mileage, and year. The owner of the "peach" finds the average offer insulting, but the owner of the "lemon" snaps it right up. The result is that buyers of used cars tend to buy lemons, so the person-to-person used car market does not function very efficiently. In extreme cases, markets can break down entirely because buyers cannot discern the good from the bad. They quickly come to believe, based on experience, that all examples of a particular good are lemons and hence refuse to offer any reasonable price. Secondhand consumer electronics, even ones not

5Remer 1990; Thorp 1991; Gwyn 1973.

technologically obsolete, for example, often sell only at steep discounts at "yard sales."

Insurance contracts offer another example of adverse selection. Ceteris paribus, those who most need insurance will be those who are most likely to purchase insurance. Shut-ins, for example, rarely buy travel insurance. Management consultants who jet all over the continent, on the other hand, almost always carry it. People who are likely to die relatively young are more likely to invest in term life insurance than people who come from a long line of octogenarians are.[6]

Adverse selection disrupted colonial financial markets. Many a merchant letter attests that the most avid insurance seekers were those engaging in the riskiest behaviors. For example, Charles Willing and Son used to forgo insurance when a seasoned captain was at the helm in known waters, but was certain to obtain insurance if the captain, or the route, was unknown.[7] Marine insurers sometimes tried to avert the adverse-selection problem by enforcing strict rules about what, and how much, the insured ship could carry. At other times, they simply raised rates. Such restrictions and price increases, of course, reduced the value of the insurance for merchants, making contracting less likely.[8] Higher rates exacerbated the adverse-selection problem because only the riskiest adventurers would offer to pay the rate. Staid businessmen like Thomas Willing simply stopped buying insurance when rates got too high. "I think the underwriters have Greatly taken the Advantage of Trade In General for 18 mos. past, & I can afford to stand my own Insurer Rather than pay such Exorbitant Premiums," Willing wrote a correspondent in June 1756.

Colonial lenders also failed to reduce the adverse-selection problem. Despite usury caps, maximum legal lending rates, in most colonies, colonists apparently tried to overcome adverse selection by raising interest rates. Market interest rates for person-to-person loans in the colonial period were generally high and usually exceeded the usury limit. The preamble of a 1750 Massachusetts law stated that, notwithstanding the usury cap, "many persons do presume to take and reserve much more for interest."[9] Benjamin Franklin also noted that market interest rates were often above the maximum allowed by law.[10]

[6] For the importance of information asymmetry to insurance firms, see D'Arcy and Doherty 1990.

[7] Charles Willing & Son to Captain Samuel Appowen, 12 November 1754; Thomas Willing to William Whitaker, Philadelphia, 7 July 1755; Thomas Willing to William Wansey, 19 August 1755, Willing Letter Book, HSP.

[8] Charles Willing & Son to John Perks, 25 October 1754, ibid.

[9] *Acts and Resolves of the Province of Massachusetts Bay* (Boston: Albert J. Wright, 1878), 3:499–500.

[10] Andrew MacFarland Davis, ed., *Colonial Currency Reprints*, 4 vols. (Boston: Prince Society, 1910–11), 3:243.

Economic historians generally agree that usury caps were often below market rates.[11] As with insurance, the price response tactic backfired. Good risks had little reason to borrow with rates so high; poor risks, however, had every reason to do so.

Early nationals also believed that colonial borrowers tended to be high-risk. Consider the following scene from a fictionalized "history" of paper money emissions in colonial Connecticut published in the *Cherry Valley Gazette*, 29 June 1819:

> *Jonathan:* Why, may it please your honors excellency the times are bad and money scarce, and some of us talk of petitioning to have paper money made, so that every body may have enough on't.
>
> *Governor:* But, friend, there is considerable money in the province now, gold, silver and copper, which you know, is of more solid value than any paper whatever. Among others, I have a small sum on hand, and if you are in want, and have any thing valuable to sell, I will be a purchaser, at a fair price, and relieve you from your embarrassments.
>
> *Jonathan:* O dear, your honor, I've nothing to sell and scarce anything to keep.
>
> *Governor:* Well, you look strong and healthy, and I presume, are willing to work for a living, I will give you employment and pay you in solid coin.
>
> *Jonathan:* Why, I work sometimes, but really I can't say I like it.
>
> *Governor:* Very well. Then supposing government should make ever so much money, and you have neither property nor labor to give in exchange for it, you would have no way of procuring it, but by borrowing or stealing.
>
> *Jonathan:* By Jingo, Mr. Governor, come to think on't, I guess you're about half right.

The governor was only "about half right" because the line between borrowing and stealing was razor thin in the colonial period. Before the Revolution, personal bonds, mortgages, and book accounts often technically defaulted. Creditors did not often sue immediately upon default; creditors to one were also debtors, and defaulters, to others. Colonial court records, therefore, are an unreliable source for determining default rates. It is clear, however, that the debt courts in colonies like Pennsylvania, New York, and Connecticut were quite active, despite their high real costs.[12]

In the early national period, financial intermediaries learned to limit adverse selection through specialization, economies of scale,

[11] Schweitzer 1987:117. [12] Horle et al. 1991; Mann 1987; Rosen 1997; Priest 1999.

and credit rationing. Commercial and savings banks and insurance companies specialized in making loans and hence got rather good at distinguishing "peach" from "lemon" applicants. Institutional financial intermediaries covered the fixed costs of information creation much more easily than the far smaller individual lenders. Finally, institutional financial intermediaries, unlike individual lenders, generally were loath to break usury laws, probably for fear of losing charter privileges. This worked to their advantage, however, because their rates were usually below the going street rate. Everyone who needed a loan therefore went first to the bank, enabling bankers to take on only the best borrowers – hence the constant complaints against banks' "political" decision-making processes.[13]

In urban areas with sufficient available bank capital, retailers reduced the percentage of their credit business, turning over the risk and trouble to banks, which, as large specialized lenders, were better equipped to create credit information. In other areas, retailers with access to bank discounts acted as quasi bankers, extending long credits to buyers but charging high implicit rates of interest in their merchandise prices, as reflected by the steep discounts that they gave for cash transactions.

Of course, personal lending did not evaporate; in fact, it exists to this day. A little appreciated fact, however, is that private lenders and retailers often took a "free ride" on bank decision making; they lent more readily to those with bank account histories than to those without. Bankers, after all, carefully screened borrowers.[14] Borrowers' application letters were important information sources where considerable dickering over terms, and lengthy explanations of credit problems, took place.[15] Printer William Patterson, for example, explained the root of his financial difficulties in great length to the board of the Bank of Columbia. "It is with painful regret that my feelings and circumstances induces [sic] me to address you once more on the subject of my accommodation paper in your Bank and I am sure if you knew all circumstance you would be disposed to relieve me," one of his long letters began.[16] Others, such as William Thornton, described their property in detail. "I have two hundred sheep, besides cattle & Horses," he explained, in addition to a contract to sell "oates & Blades at one Doll. a hundred wt."[17] George Magruder

[13]Wright 1998a.
[14]For an early textbook description, see George Rae, *The Internal Management of a Country Bank* (London: R. Groombridge & Sons, 1850), 34–40.
[15]William Slater and John McFadden to George Salmon, 15 August 1803; John Lipscomb to the Bank of Columbia, 23 April 1817, LCP.
[16]Edgar Patterson to the President and Directors of the Bank of Columbia, 18 October 1810, LCP.
[17]William Thornton to the Bank of Columbia, 17 January 1811, LCP.

noted that "the whole" of his 2,043.75 acres were "under fencing." On the land, he sowed "25 Bushels of clover seed and 5 tons plaister."[18] Stephen Lancaster told bankers that his "property near the upper Bridge in Washington . . . rents for twelve hundred Dollars a year."[19] Former treasury employee Joseph Nourse beseeched the board of the Bank of Columbia to recall his long service to the government, while informing them that his real estate was worth "in value (first cost) $35,000."[20] Similarly, entries like the following fill the directors' minutes of the Manhattan Bank: "Messrs. Few and Lewis [two of the directors] reported verbally, that they had one or more conversations with Mr. John D. Miller, one of the firm of Miller, Son, & Miller on the subject of their application for a loan, had seen their title deeds for the property proposed to be mortgaged, which property was in their opinion sufficient to secure the sum asked for." The Manhattan Bank lent the firm $35,000 for a term of six months; it was paid when due.[21]

Moral Hazard

Adverse selection is a form of information asymmetry that occurs *before* the transaction. Moral hazard is a type of information asymmetry that occurs *after* the transaction is made. Moral hazard increases when insurers or lenders find it costly to monitor the activities of their counterparties. For example, a firm applies for fire insurance; it passes the insurance company's screening procedure because its safety record hitherto is outstanding. After the policy takes effect, the number of fires increases dramatically. Now with insurance coverage, the firm has become careless. Alternatively, in a more insidious case, the firm deliberately sets fires in order to make damage claims. Indeed, many types of fraud or embezzlement are examples of moral hazard. When the pastor skips town with all of the parish's assets, that is moral hazard. So too is "welshing" on a bet or reneging on a promise. In financial matters, moral hazard results whenever a borrower does anything to jeopardize his, her, or its ability to meet an obligation. Using a loan for a purpose other than was intended, for instance, is an example of moral hazard because such practices increase the risk of default.

In the colonial era, one common type of moral hazard was to substitute higher-quality with poorer-quality goods, post sale. According to one late colonial-era Philadelphia merchant, for example, "every

[18]George Magruder to the President & c. of the Bank of Columbia, 5 January 1815, LCP.
[19]Stephen Lancaster to the Bank of Columbia, 12 September 1816, LCP.
[20]Joseph Nourse to the Bank of Columbia, 28 December 1810, LCP.
[21]Directors' Minutes, 4 February 1808, Manhattan Bank Records, Chase Manhattan Bank Archives, New York.

week" some seller watered down rum.[22] Many colonies found it necessary to establish inspectors of barrels, flour, tobacco, and other important commodities in order to reduce such fraud. Inferior dry goods
were also substituted. In 1772, for example, Philadelphia import merchant Margaret Duncan complained to her supplier: "I think you must
have sent me some of the refuse of your Warehouse." In 1774 she again
warned her British correspondent not to try to send her "unsaleable
bargains."[23]

Colonists did little to reduce moral hazard in colonial financial
markets. Borrowers often acted in ways that were not in the best interests of the lenders. Most colonial "banks," for example, were little
more than swindles.[24] That of Alexander Cummings was among the
worst. Cummings established a bank in South Carolina in the 1730s. As
a banker, Cummings both made loans to borrowers and received loans
from investors and depositors in return for his liabilities, namely his
promissory notes. When bankers are honest, we think of them as vic-
tims of moral hazard. When bankers are dishonest, they, like any other
borrower, can be the perpetrators of risky or immoral acts.[25] Cummings was of the second unfortunate variety. At first, he circulated small
quantities of bank notes, which he quickly and cheerfully redeemed
in order to gain the community's confidence. After his notes gained
some currency, he increased the volume outstanding, using them to
acquire over £10,000 sterling worth of goods, which he shipped overseas. Unfortunately for his creditors, the holders of his notes, he soon
followed his goods, leaving behind only his empty bank building.

Not all cases of moral hazard were so dramatic, but creditors were
hurt just as dearly. Backcountry colonial storekeepers, for example,
soon learned not to sell goods to distant customers on credit because
they found that they could not readily keep tabs on such customers'
businesses. Predictably, distant customers often defaulted.[26]

In the early national period, the new U.S. commercial banks learned
to limit moral hazard by monitoring borrowers after the loan was made.
The easiest way to do so was by watching the flow of cash through
customers' accounts. The old myth that checking was unimportant
until well into the nineteenth century has been repeatedly shattered;
like modern banks, early banks preferred to credit borrowers' accounts
rather than pay them directly in cash.[27] Borrowers would then draw

[22]William Pollard to William Reynolds, 10 July 1773, William Pollard Letter Book, HSP.
[23]Margaret Duncan to John Enver, 15 November 1772, 2 May 1774, Cadwalader Collection, Phineas Bond Section, HSP.
[24]Michener 1988.
[25]Sometimes, banks even take advantage of other banks. See, for example, Duke 1895:
64–90, who relates how the Schuylkill Bank of Philadelphia defrauded the Bank of
Kentucky over the latter part of the 1830s by fraudulently issuing Bank of Kentucky
shares.
[26]Thorp 1991.   [27]Adams 1978b.

on their accounts with checks. Many borrowers simply paid their cash receipts directly into the bank, sometimes running a positive balance, other times relying on discounts. Bankers, therefore, could easily discern who its borrowers were paying, and who, and how much, they were being paid.[28] They could easily spot unusual activity that might suggest a change in borrowers' creditworthiness. For example, in 1789 Seth Johnson instructed Andrew Craigie to change his financing regimen in order to "give the Bank a favorable opinion of your punctuality & ability." "It carries a much more favorable appearance to take up a note without assistance of further discounts than to seem to labor to do it by gradual decreasing," Johnson explained.[29]

Clearly, early U.S. banks monitored customers carefully. In 1804, for example, the directors of the Bank of Philadelphia "resolved, that the Cashier be directed to lay before the board at every meeting for discount the general state of the accounts of individuals in their classes as good, middling, and poor in which he shall consider principally the deposits compared with the discounts."[30] Firms willing to supply additional information secured additional privileges. For example, the Bank of Philadelphia granted the Delaware Insurance Company overdraft protection after the two companies forged a "large and beneficial connexion."[31]

Bankers sometimes called large debtors in for personal meetings with the board. Often such meetings ended with verbal restrictive covenants.[32] In other words, the banks promised to continue lending only if the debtor engaged in specific activities.[33] For instance, James Magruder pledged to use his 1815 loan to "invest towards finishing my house."[34] In 1819 the Reading branch of the Bank of Pennsylvania "agreed to continue the loan to Valentine Brobst, with his present endorsers, provided he exhibits a satisfactory statement, before the 12th

---

[28]The earliest banking textbooks describe how to monitor customers' checking accounts properly. See, for instance, George Rae, *The Internal Management of a Country Bank* (London: R. Groombridge & Sons, 1850), 26–33.

[29]Seth Johnson to Andrew Craigie, 30 August 1789, Andrew Craigie Papers, AAS.

[30]Directors' Minutes, Bank of Philadelphia, 9 July 1804, Philadelphia National Bank Records, HSP.

[31]Ibid., 12 June 1805.

[32]See, for example, William B. Magruder to Col. Deakins, 21 July 1796; John P. Van Ness to John Mason, 12 March 1804; Joseph Nourse to the Bank of Columbia, 18 December 1810; George Magruder to the President & Directors of the Bank of Columbia, 28 March 1811; J. Wiley to Mr. Daniel Kurtz, 30 June 1817, LCP. Minutes of the Proceedings of the Board of Directors of the Offices of Discount and Deposit at Reading, 25 October 1821, Bank of Pennsylvania Records, HSP. Directors' Minutes, 14 December 1802, Manhattan Bank Records, Chase Manhattan Bank Archives, New York.

[33]Directors' Minutes, 16, 26 April, 14 May 1792, Bank of North America Records, HSP; Jacob Leonard to Dr. John Ott, 17 August 1815, LCP.

[34]James A. Magruder to President and Directors of the Bank of Columbia, 3 August 1815, LCP.

of July next, of his property."[35] Restrictive covenants, of course, continue to be a major method by which modern banks reduce moral hazard.[36]

Like bankers today, early bankers often insisted on cosigners. In addition to providing the bank with extra security in the case of default, cosignatures gave the bank information about the creditworthiness of the borrower. Banks to some extent used endorsements to "free-ride" on private credit information. Consider, for example, the following letter from two Philadelphia businessmen to the Bank of Baltimore:

> Our Friend John Yates of Baltimore has suggested to us that if he could procure two or three thousand Dollars in the usual Way of Discounts it would serve him in forwarding his Business. If it suits your Convenience & meets your approbation to let him have this Accommodation in your Bank on his Notes with the Endorsements of our Friends Mess. Kent & Browne you may consider us as collateral Security for the above sum of Three Thousand Dollars till we give you Notice to the Contrary.[37]

The Reading branch of the Bank of Pennsylvania was especially fond of requesting additional endorsers.[38]

Compensatory balances were common with larger loans. Early national borrowers, in other words, sometimes received loans for tens of thousands of dollars, conditioned on the promise to draw the money over an extended period. In 1796, for example, Gustus Scott and Alexander White promised to draw down a loan of $58,000 "at the rate of about 10 or 12,000 Dollars P month."[39] That same year William Magruder promised to keep his loan in the Bank of Columbia for two full weeks before withdrawing it.[40] In 1797 Baltimoreans complained that Philadelphia banks lent only "for those who can make large deposits or, as it is termed 'KEEP GOOD ACCOUNTS.'"[41] That practice began as early as January 1796.[42] Compensatory balances are still important banking tools. In addition to raising the effective rate of

[35] Minutes of the Proceedings of the Board of Directors of the Offices of Discount and Deposit at Reading, 10 May 1819, Bank of Pennsylvania Records, HSP.
[36] Mishkin 2000.
[37] Thomas Arnat and Thomas W. Arnat to the Bank of Baltimore, 14 September 1802, LCP.
[38] Minutes of the Proceedings of the Board of Directors of the Offices of Discount and Deposit at Reading, 28 September 1819, 8 June, 26 October 1820, Bank of Pennsylvania Records, HSP.
[39] Gustus Scott and Alexander White to President and Directors of the Bank of Columbia, 21 June 1796, LCP.
[40] William B. Magruder to Benjamin Stoddert, 23 February 1796, LCP.
[41] Baltimore Weekly Museum, 15, 22, 29 January 1797.
[42] Elizabeth Meredith to David Meredith, 2 January 1796, Meredith Family Papers, HSP.

interest, the balances helped to reduce moral hazard by allowing banks to monitor borrowers' activities before the banks became fully exposed to loss.

Bankers also regularly met with other local bankers to keep tabs on borrowers and share information about general macroeconomic conditions. In 1792 the directors of the Bank of North America (BNA) unanimously resolved to form a committee to meet "once a Week, & oftener if necessary" with a committee from the BUS, "for the Purpose of communicating freely upon the Business of both, as well to prevent improper Interference with each other as to promote the accommodation of the Citizens."[43] The practice was continued and extended to new banks. In 1804 the directors of the Bank of Philadelphia "resolved that a standing Committee be appointed to confer occasionally with committees of the other banks in this City, when appointed, upon subjects of a common interest."[44] Banks in other cities, most notably New York, formed similar committees.[45]

Early U.S. bankers often rationed credit, yet another modern method for reducing moral hazard.[46] The Bank of Philadelphia, for example, capped indebtedness of any single individual or noncorporate firm at $30,000, no exceptions.[47] The Bank of Pennsylvania's branch at Reading readily mandated the rate at which loans would be paid down, on penalty of having the loans not renewed at all,[48] or the debts sued upon.[49]

Finally, early insurance companies also reduced information asymmetry by carefully screening loan and premium applicants and building restrictive covenants into policies. In addition to lending risks, of course, insurance companies faced fraudulent claims.[50] By 1830, at the latest, screening applications and insurance policies were essentially modern in form.[51]

[43]Directors' Minutes, 23 March 1792, Bank of North America Records, HSP.
[44]Directors' Minutes, Bank of Philadelphia, 7 September 1804, Philadelphia National Bank Records, HSP.
[45]Wright 1997a; *A Statement of the Correspondence Between the Banks in the City of New-York* (New York, 1805), 6, 8–11.
[46]See, for example, William B. Magruder to Benjamin Stoddert, 21 July, 1 December 1796, LCP.
[47]Directors' Minutes, Bank of Philadelphia, 22 February 1805, Philadelphia National Bank Records, HSP.
[48]See, for instance, Minutes of the Proceedings of the Board of Directors of the Offices of Discount and Deposit at Reading, 14 May 1812, 28 March, 11 April, 3 July 1816, 3 October 1822, Bank of Pennsylvania Records, HSP.
[49]Samuel Flewwelling to John P. Van Ness, 2 August 1815, box 2 folder: Correspondence with Henry Remsen Viz. Isaac Clason, Van Ness-Philip Papers, NYHS.
[50]Insurance Company of Pennsylvania Letter Books, 1794–1807, HSP.
[51]See, for example, Philadelphia Fire Company, Conditions of Insurance, 1830, Fire and Marine Insurance, Society Collection, HSP.

The Principal-Agent Problem

The principal-agent problem is a special case of moral hazard where the owner (principal) is unable to monitor the activities of his agent (employee or other person charged with the principal's property). If the agent's interests differ from those of the principal, and they usually do, the agent will take advantage of the principal through outright theft, fraud, slacking, or other means. Suppose Joe persuades his friend Maria to lend him $10,000 so that he can start a small business. If Joe is truly an agent and has no equity stake in the firm, and Maria, the owner, does not watch Joe carefully, Joe has nothing to lose. He might engage in risky behaviors, waste the money on unnecessary perquisites, or otherwise fritter away Maria's money.

The principal-agent problem is probably the most intractable form of information asymmetry. It pervades public government and corporate governance. Politicians (agents) behave as they wish until election time nears – in countries lucky enough to have elections, that is; when top managers do not have a significant equity stake in their company or are, in other words, more agents than principals, offices, trips, and other perks become more lavish; employees of fast food restaurants are often rude and slow.

Investors in colonial enterprises suffered heavily from the principal-agent problem. Indeed, one could view the American Revolution as a massive case of the principal-agent problem. The colonists (agents) did not behave as the British government (principals) desired. The government found it difficult to keep close tabs on the colonists, who responded, as any rational agent does, by getting away with as much as they could. When the principals finally began to monitor their colonial agents more closely, the agents, who were not accustomed to such close supervision, decided that an ownership change was necessary.

Because the known cases of business-related principal-agent problems in the colonial period are far too numerous to discuss, brief descriptions of a few of the more common types of cases can suffice. In 1741 Philadelphia merchant Robert Ellis was much chagrined to discover that his ship captain left £500 of gold in New York, rather than risk carrying it to Philadelphia. Ellis had to instruct the New York holder to sell the gold for "Jersey Money or Philada. if to be had," at considerable cost.[52] Three decades later, Philadelphia merchant William Pollard encountered a similar difficulty with a ship captain. "I am amazed that Capt. Lawrence Should now pretend So Much

[52] Robert Ellis to Joseph Royall, 11 June 1741, Robert Ellis Letter Book, 1736–48, HSP.

Ignorance," he told a correspondent, "as not to know a Sett of Bills of Exchange from a Bill of Loading."[53] Pollard encountered difficulties with merchants too. Although he had promised to pay promptly, Robert Hawie of Charleston failed to compensate Pollard for a "Negroe Boy" Pollard had transferred to Hawie over a year previously. Pollard suspected that Hawie was using the boy in his own house instead of selling him as instructed.[54]

Squabbles between colonial and British merchants were commonplace. Pollard attempted to mediate one such dispute between Baynton and Wharton, a Philadelphia mercantile firm, and the Hulme Brothers of Yorkshire. By contract, Baynton and Wharton was supposed to act as Hulme Brothers' agent and sell Hulme's wine for a commission. Apparently, Baynton and Wharton lied about the market for wine in Philadelphia, purchased a few pipes of the Hulmes' wine for its own account, and quickly resold the pipes for a sizable profit. It is not clear how, or if, the dispute was solved.[55]

Relations between colonial employers and employees were often contentious. For instance, Pollard felt lucky when he managed to hire "a very steady sober Fellow & very industrious" to run his paper mill. He feared, however, that his new hire "has not spirited Conduct sufficient to keep in proper Decoram a Parcell of Journeymen (should he be wanted for that Purpose)."[56] Other colonial manufacturers faced even worse situations. Philadelphia sugar baker Edward Penington, for example, lost some £1,000 because he hired "one Peter Tinges from Boston to Boil for me." Tinges, who, despite his claims to the contrary, "was by no means master of the Business," failed to use a sufficient quantity of lime water, did not know how to utilize his raw materials and secondary products efficiently, and steadfastly refused to learn from his mistakes.[57] Managers of ironworks were also notoriously poor workers. Successful ironmasters, therefore, usually employed only close family members as managers.[58]

The agent of the Warrens, an English family that lent money to New Yorkers, often failed to act in the principal's interest. The agent preferred not to sue on overdue accounts, put some of the principal's capital to his own use interest-free, and often ignored instructions.[59] Similarly, Thorp described very detailed instructions from a principal of a retail store to his agent, the storekeeper. Despite the principal's repeated insistence that the storekeeper not part with goods on credit,

[53] William Pollard to James Kinsey, 17 June 1773, William Pollard Letter Book, HSP.
[54] William Pollard to Robert Hawie, 22 June 1773, ibid.
[55] William Pollard to Doctor Joshua Hulme, 30 January 1773, ibid.
[56] William Pollard to Henry Remsen, 30 March 1773, ibid.
[57] Observations on the Making of Sugar, Penington Family Papers, 1799–1819, HSP.
[58] McCurdy 1974:94–107.   [59] Gwyn 1973.

the storekeeper quickly allowed customers to accumulate a mass of debts, many of which turned out to be uncollectable.[60]

Early national businesses were not immune to the principal-agent problem, but some of them did take steps to limit its effects. Joint-stock corporations, for example, arose partly to overcome the principal-agent problem. Directors, for example, generally were required to own corporate stock, often substantial amounts of it. That made them both principals and agents. Similarly, officers who did not have large equity stakes in the companies for which they worked had to obtain sureties before assuming their responsibilities.[61] Bank cashiers, for example, were often expressly forbade from owning stock in the bank in which they served. Unlike bank directors, who were supposed to serve the interests of their bank's owners (the stockholders), cashiers were supposed to serve the interests of the bank's customers, including noteholders, most of whom were not stockholders. Cashiers were the hands-on managers of early banks, roughly analogous to today's branch managers. Having no interest in the bank other than their salaries, cashiers could concentrate on customer service without worrying about the bottom line. Furthermore, cashiers could plunder a bank much more easily than could a director, even a president. Mere stockholding, therefore, was not a sufficient guard against fraud. Using the liquid secondary securities market, a cashier might easily sell his stock for cash and then clean out the vaults and skip town, leaving stockholders to suffer the loss. The surety bond system made it in the interest of the bond writers, in addition to that of the directors, to monitor the cashier and also provided relief to the stockholders should a defalcation occur.

Additionally, bank employees were very highly paid by the standards of the day and could look forward to higher pay if promoted up the corporate ladder. Competition for entry-level positions was keen, especially in the urban markets. Each bank employee, therefore, strove not only to keep his job but also to gain promotion, say from second bookkeeper to first bookkeeper, or third teller to second teller. Bank employees, therefore, monitored each other's activities closely, hoping to expose a cheater. Subordinates who caught a defalcating superior would gain a promotion and superiors who caught a thieving subordinate would increase their job security. For those reasons, bank frauds were rare, though widely publicized when they did occur.[62]

---

[60]Thorp 1991.
[61]Eliza Cope Harrison, ed., *Philadelphia Merchant: The Diary of Thomas P. Cope, 1800–1851* (South Bend, Ind.: Gateway Editions, 1978), 161; J. S. Gibbons, *The Banks of New-York, Their Dealers, the Clearing House, and the Panic of 1857, with a Financial Chart* (New York: D. Appleton, 1858), 23.
[62]Bodenhorn 2002.

Stockholders also monitored corporate officials. Their meetings were frequent events; most corporate charters allowed stockholders to call general stockholder meetings.[63] Stockholders steadfastly defended their right to make all nontrivial decisions.[64] In 1797, shortly after "a few of the stockholders of the Baltimore Insurance Company, had voted the president twenty-five hundred dollars per annum, for his services," one stockholder exploded with anger. "All those that were not consulted on this business," he argued, "are not bound, by either law or justice, to contribute to the payment of it." The salary was exorbitant, the stockholder argued, because "the prospects of the Insurance Company are at present dark and gloomy." Only if experience showed that "the institution requires attention from him adequate to that sum" should stockholders endorse the salary increase.[65] In 1824 stockholders of the Bank of Columbia, after replacing almost the entire board of the bank, met with the new directors to help them to lay plans to repay large debts to the Second Bank of the United States (SBUS) and the U.S. Treasury.[66] During the financial crises of the late 1830s and early 1840s, stockholders turned out to meetings en masse. In July 1840, for instance, stockholders in the Bank of Virginia held a meeting that "was very fully attended" and that took "decisive action."[67]

Early stockholders voted their shares with alacrity.[68] It should not be surprising that corporate governance was strong in the early decades of the Republic; writers drew direct comparisons between political and corporate governance principles, such as the use of term limitations to limit corruption.[69] Elaborate rules, similar to the rules enforced at political elections, sought to reduce election fraud.[70] Also like the political elections of the era, full slates of directors' candidates appeared in the newspapers.[71] Many corporate elections were hotly contested;[72] entire boards could be overturned. The stockholders of the Bank of Chester, for example, ousted the directorship when it was discovered

---

[63]For example, any 60 stockholders in the BUS who owned more than 200 shares total could call a general stockholder meeting. *Pennsylvania Gazette*, 2 March 1791.
[64]Harrison, *Philadelphia Merchant*, 124.
[65]*Federal Gazette & Baltimore Daily Advertiser*, 15 February 1797.
[66]Thomas Swann to Nicholas Biddle, 28 February, 4, 12, 20, 21, 24, 27 March 1824, LCP.
[67]*Richmond Whig*, 3 July 1840.   [68]Munsell 1850, 1:32–33.
[69]*Baltimore Weekly Museum*, 15, 22, 29 January 1797.
[70]Directors' Minutes, Bank of Philadelphia, 8, 12 February 1805, Philadelphia National Bank Records, HSP.
[71]See, for example, *Maryland Journal*, 4 March 1791; *Political and Commercial Register*, 9 February 1807.
[72]See, for example, Directors' Minutes, Bank of Philadelphia, various dates, Philadelphia National Bank Records, HSP which listed vote totals for directors' elections. Dozens of individuals received votes in the elections and the totals varied widely, suggesting that many voters did not accept "slates" but chose candidates based on their individual merits, just as in many of the political elections of the era.

that the directors had been lending primarily to a few insiders.[73] Corporate officers were sometimes compelled to explain their actions in great detail in print.[74] Similarly, stockholders were not shy about going to the media to win support for their policies or candidates. When stockholders of the Louisa Railroad of Virginia, for example, differed on whether the railroad ought to be extended to Gordonsville or Charlottesville, they slugged it out in the newspapers. Charlottesville backers eventually won, pointing to sagging stock prices as a certain sign that the market did not look upon the Gordonsville extension with favor.[75]

A few years later, a Louisa Railroad stockholder directly challenged directors in the public prints. "Isn't time we should hear something from our President and Directors concerning our Stock in this road?" he or she asked.[76] "The travel on this road, for the current year, I hear has been pretty full; the freight a good average for the year." Where then, the stockholder wondered aloud, were the profits? Surely, the revenues of the road did more than simply "pay the officers, superintendent of the road, hire of hands, &c." The stockholder then called for a statement showing how the road's revenues were "appropriated," and urged other stockholders not to give their proxies to the current board at upcoming elections.

Similarly, in 1841 "many" James River and Kanawha Company stockholders went to the papers to urge the company's directors "to stop the further progress of the Canal, until money can be borrowed at six percent interest. Also, to reduce the salaries of the officers, and dispense with those that are unnecessary."[77] Thereafter, directors found that to remain in office they had to regularly publish detailed reports of the company's current condition and future business plans.[78]

Other stockholders "voted with their feet," dumping the shares of companies they believed to be ill-managed. Discontented stockholders could run down a bad company's stock price in a hurry. The price of a company's securities, in other words, reflected the opinions and information of all of its stockholders and served as a signal to potential investors.

Finally, it should be noted that it was not merely coincidental that Holland, Great Britain, and the United States all underwent "financial revolutions" soon after experiencing a major political upheaval. Soon after confronting the principal-agent problem in politics, the

[73] *American Republican*, 24 December 1816, 4, 11 February 1817, ms. 33690, 78007, CCHS.
[74] See, for example, Shepherd Knapp, *Letter to the Stockholders of the Mechanics' Bank* (New York: H. Anstice, 1855).
[75] *Richmond Enquirer*, 10, 17 July 1838.   [76] *Richmond Whig*, 11 December 1840.
[77] *Richmond Enquirer*, 23 November 1841.
[78] See, for example, *Richmond Whig*, 3 January 1845.

revolutionaries turned to reduce the principal-agent problem in the financial realm. The sundry famous "checks and balances" built into the U.S. Constitution, for instance, can be viewed as mechanisms for making politicians accountable to the voters, the owners of the nation. In other words, the Constitution was a means of reducing the principal-agent problem.[79] The same men who successfully prevented their governments from turning tyrannical found it a relatively easy task to keep their corporations from ruining investors.

Conclusions

Banks and other financial intermediaries improved economic efficiency by reducing information asymmetries including adverse selection and moral hazard. They did so by actually creating information about parties to the contract through well-known procedures like screening, monitoring, and requiring restrictive covenants and collateral. Institutional intermediaries leveraged their specialized skills and knowledge and created economies of scale and scope that allowed them to reduce information asymmetries more cheaply than individuals or small firms could.

The corporate form helped to reduce a special form of moral hazard known as the principal-agent problem. It did so by creating incentives for employees, managers, and shareholders to monitor each other's activities closely. Early Americans were quite skilled in this aspect of corporate governance because of their experience in constitution making, which also presented them with significant agency issues. By reducing the principal-agent problem, corporations could grow much larger than firms organized as proprietorships or partnerships could. Additionally, in many sectors larger firms were more efficient than smaller ones.[80]

[79]Maier 1993.   [80]Wright 2002.

4

The Financial Sector and the Reduction
of Lending-Related Costs and Risks

As shown in Chapter 3, new institutions (particularly commercial
banks, but also insurance companies, savings banks, and brokerages)
and new markets (primary and secondary debt and equity markets)
reduced information asymmetry in the early U.S. economy. Those institutions and markets also reduced a number of other lending-related
risks. In so doing, they increased the rate of investment by inducing
more people to lend more money than they otherwise would have
done. That, in turn, made more funds available for individuals and
firms to borrow to improve their businesses through increased labor
specialization, technological improvements, and/or exploitation of
economies of scale and scope.

The new financial institutions decreased default risk, collateral risk,
and term risk and thereby expanded the loan market. They decreased
default risk by matching a *pool* of investors with a *pool* of entrepreneurs.
In case of default, all investors paid a little, instead of one investor
paying a large amount. They also decreased default risk by collecting
information on borrowers and by becoming experts at assessing that
credit information. Banks such as the Bank of Newburgh (New York),
the Utica branch of the Ontario Bank (Canandaigua, N.Y.), the
Mechanics' Bank (New York), and the BNA (Philadelphia) kept tabs on
borrowers. Directors also made personal inquiries into the back-
grounds of obscure or unknown loan applicants. Banks also collected
third-party assessments of applicants via letter or endorsement.[1] Additionally, banks obtained information by forging long-term relationships with some customers.[2]

Commercial banks actually *created* information by collecting data
on potential borrowers and assembling that data into meaningful pic-
tures of borrowers' financial status.[3] Information creation did not
come cheaply, so banks endeavored to hide their decisions in order to
prevent "free riders." (Every set of bank bylaws that I have ever seen
made the proceedings of discount meetings secret.[4] In 1819 "Friendly

[1] Wright 1999a.   [2] Bodenhorn 1999.   [3] Bodenhorn 2000; Wright 1999a.
[4] See, for example, Minutes of the Proceedings of the Board of Directors of the Offices
of Discount and Deposit at Reading, 16 July 1808, Bank of Pennsylvania Records, HSP.

Monitor" noted that, "If I ask a director, the seal of his finger is significantly impressed on his lips. There is a species of masonry in banking."[5] On the eve of the Civil War, all banks in New York City conducted their discount meetings in strict secrecy.[6]) Despite the banks' best efforts, nonbank lenders were able to discover, and use to advantage, some of the banks' lending decisions.

Securities markets also created information, in the form of securities prices. Securities holders monitored the corporations or governments in which they held an interest. Changes in their perceptions of an issuer's worth were reflected in securities prices, which were widely available to other securities holders and potential investors. Additionally, securities were liquid investments that could be used to secure bank or private loans in a process called hypothecation. After an initial contraction, the result of the rationalization of the federal debt under Hamilton, the number of new issues increased rapidly in all the major cities. In New York, the number of publicly traded issues increased from 5 in 1797 to 29 in 1817. Baltimore and Philadelphia boasted 27 issues each in 1811. In the 1830s, the number of securities issues blossomed, especially in Boston, New York, and Philadelphia.[7]

Aiding both major sectors of the financial system was a central banking system composed of a central bank, the BUS and its branches, and a central banker, the secretary of the treasury. Together, the central banker and his bank successfully checked the note issue of state banks, deflated asset bubbles, infused liquidity into the economy during panics, reduced inflation, and acted as a lender of last resort when appropriate. Colonial America lacked anything even closely resembling the early Republic's central banking system, save for the distant Bank of England, the policies of which were directed primarily toward Britain.[8]

In short, America in the final decade of the eighteenth century underwent nothing short of a financial revolution of the same magnitude and importance as had transformed Holland and Britain a century before. Banks supplied short-term credit and securities markets provided access to long-term funds for corporations while the central banking system helped to maintain macroeconomic stability. Private credit networks were also greatly loosened by the existence of banks, securities markets, and the stability that the central banking regime engendered.

[5] As cited in Krooss and Blyn 1971:19.
[6] J. S. Gibbons, *The Banks of New-York, Their Dealers, the Clearing House, and the Panic of 1857, with a Financial Chart* (New York: D. Appleton, 1858), 199.
[7] Sylla 1998:91; Rousseau and Sylla 1999; Sylla, Wilson, and Wright.
[8] Cowen 2000a, 2000b.

Commercial Banking: Intermediation and Information Creation

Americans learned to lend safely in the new economic and business environment that emerged out of the Revolution.[9] Early national financiers came to understand that they could not compensate for information asymmetry simply by raising interest rates. The adverse-selection problem is too strong; someone willing to contract to pay high interest is a desperate character, a rogue, or a major risk taker. None of those possibilities augurs well for the lender. In short, those with the riskiest projects will suffer to pay the higher rates, whereas those with safer lines of business will not. As lending rates rise, in other words, the incentives for safe businesses to borrow decreases. Soon, all the remaining applicants are risky ventures and highly likely to default. The lending rate will not save the lender; only knowing the ratio between the loan size and the borrower's net worth will.

Recall that borrowers know more about their financial situation than the lenders do, so the lenders have difficulty discerning "good" from "bad" credit risks. Lenders cannot simply raise their rates to compensate for information asymmetry; they must seek to reduce the asymmetry. In other words, lenders must subject borrowers to some sort of screening process in an effort to separate the good borrowers from the bad. Screening takes various forms according to time, place, and type of loan but generally entails probing the history of the applicant. Past problems usually eliminate applicants from consideration, but a clean slate does not allow lenders to breathe easy because lenders know that weak applicants have strong incentives to *appear* credible. One trick was to tell the directors that you wanted to borrow the money for a sensible project but then to use it to bet on horses or foreign exchange futures, both of which were options at least as early as the 1780s.

To induce borrowers to put funds to proper uses – in other words, to reduce moral hazard – lenders often build restrictive covenants into loan contracts. Those covenants attempt to limit the uses of the funds. Auto lenders, for example, want to make certain that you use the funds to buy a motor vehicle, not to buy alcohol for personal consumption. Mortgage lenders likewise strongly prefer that borrowers use their loans to purchase real estate, not lottery tickets. Therefore, even after making loans, lenders must continue to monitor and restrict borrowers' activities. Early bankers often required oral restrictive covenants that they monitored after making the loan. If the borrower broke the covenant, he or she was not welcome to apply for future loans at

[9]For a narrative analysis of the origins of commercial banking in the United States, see Wright 2001.

the bank.[10] For example, in 1811 the Pleasant Valley Manufacturing Company applied for a loan from the Bank of Newburgh on the promise that "the avails will be taken in small notes & paid to the workmen they employ, in small sums."[11]

Overcoming information asymmetries like adverse selection and moral hazard is usually cost-prohibitive on a small scale. So too is finding a counterparty whose needs are the precise opposites of one's own. Colonists overcame those problems by lending to those about whom they possessed ample information – relations, neighbors, and colleagues. Sometimes, parties unknown to each other but introduced through a third person would contract. Nevertheless, contracts between complete strangers were rare and, when made, highly overcollateralized.[12] Credit, of course, is a very good thing. Were they not beneficial to both lender and borrower, loans would not be made. Unfortunately for the colonists, a nasty catch-22 limited their ability to enter mutually beneficial loan contracts. As the amount of information lenders had about potential borrowers increased, the number of potential borrowers rapidly decreased. In other words, colonial lenders could lend with absolute certainty to, say, siblings, but the odds that their siblings desired to borrow the amount and for the term the lenders desired were slim. As a particular lender widened his market, he had increasingly less information about potential borrowers. When he finally found a borrower who wanted exactly £100 for exactly five years, he was chagrined to find him a stranger living in the next county. If enough information could be procured cheaply enough, a contract might ensue, if the borrower posted collateral, usually to twice or thrice the value of the loan.

Colonial retail credit was also limited. Established local property owners, long-term tenants, and businesses obtained book credit with the local grocer, tobacconist, or cobbler. The retailers kept the balances due from any given customer low, however, in order to spread default risk. They also charged higher prices for goods purchased on credit rather than for "ready money."[13] Apprentices, itinerate workers, and short-term renters received no credit except through their masters or employers. Of course, the bosses were not extending credit to their employees, most of whom were without property or local ties. The bosses merely debited the purchases from their workers' accrued pay.

---

[10]Bodenhorn 2000.

[11]Robert Abbot Jr. to John Humm, 19 December 1811, Bank of Newburgh Papers, NYHS.

[12]See, for example, the historical commentary of "Common Sense" in the *Pennsylvania Gazette*, 21 June 1786.

[13]*PRM*, 5:166.

The net effect of the small colonial credit market was to limit the productivity of the economy. Businesses with productive uses for funds could not cheaply find people willing to lend. Even those who did find loans often could not borrow as much as they needed because the market value of their main source of collateral, land, was volatile and difficult to measure, leading to rampant overcollateralization.

By 1800 the credit scene, though far from perfect, had dramatically improved. First, financial intermediaries called commercial banks had arisen and become quite good at matching investors with entrepreneurs, producing information about loan applicants, and taking advantage of economies of scale to reduce transaction costs associated with the creation and monitoring of restrictive covenants. Though per capita bank capital was still quite low, each bank loan created a ripple or multiplier effect. The ready availability of short-term commercial credit allowed wholesalers to extend more credit to their customers, the retailers, and for retailers to extend more credit to their customers, consumers.

To the extent that they could not keep their dealings secret, banks made private lending easier. Businesspeople who paid their bills due with checks, for example, clearly had bank accounts and, hence, probably bank loans. That information made it easier for them to borrow funds privately; the private lenders gladly took a "free ride" on the banks' decision making.

The First U.S. Commercial Bank: The Bank of North America

Based in Philadelphia, the BNA was the nation's first full-fledged commercial bank, and its operations (though not its first charter, which was quickly revoked) indirectly served as a prototype for hundreds, nay thousands, of the nation's first banks. The BNA helped other early banks, such as The Bank of New York (BONY) and the Bank of Massachusetts, to begin operations. Those early banks in turn influenced many other institutions, if only through the repeated defection of directors and employees to new banks.[14]

The BNA used its initial capital as a sort of cushion or buffer to meet unexpected contingencies that arose in the course of its business. That business consisted primarily of discounting the bills receivable of businesses, at first mostly merchants, but later retailers, artisans, and even women. (Yes, women engaged in business as *feme sole* traders received bank discounts.) The discount process worked as follows. On discount day, businesspeople took bills or notes due in the near future to the bank. In a secret meeting, the directors decided which applications to

[14]Wright 1997a; Bodenhorn 2000.

grant and which to reject. Successful applicants received the present discounted value, with interest at 6 percent, of the receivable. In Robert Morris's words that meant for the borrower "receiving ninety nine and paying an hundred at the End of two Months."[15] Another way of thinking about discounts is that the bank took the interest at the beginning of the loan rather than at the end.

In any event, the bank credited the discount to the successful applicant's account. He or she could then write a check against it, withdraw it in bank notes, or withdraw it in specie. The BNA had to stand ready at all times to pay specie to its nonequity liability holders; the convertibility of its notes and deposits was the basis of its credit. Interestingly, one did not have to live in Philadelphia or even be a direct customer of the bank in order to benefit from its discount operations. As Morris explained to John Wendell of New Hampshire in May 1782, anyone could draw a bill on a "Merchant of Reputation payable at sixty day's Sight" in favor of a Philadelphia supplier. If the merchant accepted the bill, the supplier could get it discounted at the BNA for immediate cash. That would allow him to ship an order of goods to the drawer. Two credit extensions had occurred: the bank lent to the supplier and the merchant lent to the drawer, but the latter took place only because of the bank.[16] This is not to imply that only Philadelphians could get direct discounts; Morris intimated that well-known citizens in New Hampshire could get discounts, even accommodation loans.[17] Indeed, in 1782 a little over one-quarter of the dollar value of the BNA's nongovernment loans went to non-Philadelphians.[18]

The BNA also helped American businesses to obtain credit overseas. All touted how the bank introduced "a punctuality and method in business not practiced previous to it's [sic] establishment." Of course, potential creditors, especially those overseas, looked upon punctuality with favor.[19]

The BNA, like other early U.S. banks, also accepted lodged deposits, or "real" deposits not arising from a bank's lending.[20] The key to business was for the bank to match up calls for its nonequity liabilities (lodged and created deposits and its own notes) with the availability of its assets (its specie reserves, loans, and secondary reserves). When its creditors, noteholders and depositors, called for their money faster than its debtors, discount recipients, repaid, trouble ensued for the bank. In such circumstances, it responded as all early national banks responded, by restricting new loans and by not renewing existing loans when they fell due. Such was the case in spring 1782, when

[15] PRM, 5:96.   [16] Ibid.   [17] PRM, 4:454.   [18] Rappaport 1996.
[19] PRM, 7:754, 9:517.   [20] PRM, 4:616.

the bank's biggest debtor, the national government, could not reduce its indebtedness to the bank. The British blockade had stymied trade and hence greatly reduced demand for the bills of exchange on France that Morris used to raise money for the nation's account.[21] The fact that the notes of the bank did not at first find an extensive circulation exacerbated the situation.[22] In 1782 the notes remained current only near Philadelphia, making it all-too-convenient to exchange them for silver dollars for remittance to New York, an illegal but nevertheless thriving entrepôt.[23]

Morris clearly saw the BNA's role as an intermediary between investors and entrepreneurs. In July 1781 he informed John Jay that "placing the collected Mass of private Credit between the Lenders and Borrowers [would] supply at once the Want of Ability in the one and of Credit in the other."[24] Morris also realized that the bank's corporate structure reduced the principal-agent problem, a specific type of moral hazard that occurs when owners (principals) do not properly monitor the activities of their workers (agents), thereby allowing them to find ways not to behave in the best interest of the principals. For instance, when queried about the bank's "Manner of doing Business" by some "Subscribers at a Distance from Philadelphia," Morris noted that the directors or agents were also stockholders or principals, elected by other stockholders or principals, and hence were the best judges of the bank's daily operations.[25]

Although the BNA got off to a rather rocky start politically, many Americans immediately saw the extensive benefits of commercial banking. James McHenry, for instance, tried to establish a bank in Maryland in January 1782. His plan actually passed the Maryland Senate before meeting defeat in the House of Delegates.[26] In May 1782 there was also some talk, though apparently much less serious, of "a Bank in New Hampshire."[27] The BNA, though at first opposed to other banks in Philadelphia,[28] welcomed and even aided commercial banks that formed in New York and Boston in 1784.[29] As the nation emerged from the economic disruptions of the war, and rampant currency depreciation, the BNA increased its capital base and extended its discounts to a wider circle.[30]

Early national banks also overcame information asymmetries by eagerly accepting securities as collateral for loans. The BNA was a little slow to implement the practice[31] but by 1792 admitted that it had sometimes secured loans with "Publick Securities."[32] Collateralizing loans with securities soon became an important practice.

---

[21] *PRM*, 5:145, 243, 268, 377, 390.   [22] *PRM*, 5:459–60, 559.   [23] *PRM*, 5:436.
[24] *PRM*, 1:287.   [25] *PRM*, 1:357–58.   [26] *PRM*, 4:260–61.   [27] *PRM*, 5:95.
[28] Schwartz 1947.   [29] *PRM*, 9:644.   [30] Buel 1998.   [31] *PRM*, 4:58, 69.
[32] Directors' Minutes, February 1792, Bank of North America Records, HSP.

Initially, many charters prevented banks from owning securities outright as assets on bank balance sheets. Some early banks, however, such as the Bank of Philadelphia, held significant amounts of U.S. bonds.[33] By the mid-1790s the BNA kept between $20,000 and $40,000 worth of U.S. bonds on its books.[34] By the War of 1812, many banks, with the aid of legal changes,[35] regularly owned securities as "secondary reserves" – a highly liquid but income-generating asset that could be cheaply converted to cash to meet deposit outflows.[36] In 1814, for example, the Bank of America (New York) "sold nearly if not upwards of 500,000 dollars stock to command specie."[37] In 1816 the Bank of Somerset purchased shares in the SBUS through the brokerage firm of Biddle and Wharton of Philadelphia.[38] In 1823 the Bank of Philadelphia owned $3,050 worth of turnpike stock, $1,465 worth of Harrisburg Bank stock, and $250,000 worth of Pennsylvania Five Percent coupon bonds.[39] By 1826 political economists noted "that several of our most solid banks, keep stock in preference to specie, to a certain amount, relying upon its convertibility into cash, and retaining it because it yields an interest and diminishes their dead capital in the precious metals."[40] One of those banks was the BNA, which in 1826 owned over $60,000 of government bonds and shares of two dozen corporations.[41] Earlier, the BNA had held even larger portfolios of securities, amounting, for example, to almost $150,000 in 1791 and $140,000 in 1817, though in some years it held no securities whatsoever.[42] Similarly, the BONY owned over $1 million worth of U.S. bonds for three consecutive years in the late 1790s[43] and the Manhattan Bank owned hundreds of thousands of dollars worth of U.S. bonds at times in the 1810s.[44]

[33]Thomas McKean to Philadelphia Bank, 12 April 1804, Directors' Minutes, Bank of Philadelphia, Philadelphia National Bank Records, HSP.
[34]General Ledgers, Bank of North America Records, HSP.
[35]See, for example, "An Act for the payment of certain Officers of Government, and for other purposes" chapter 239, 19 June 1812, *Laws of the State of New York*, 35th session (1812).
[36]A Citizen, *An Appeal to the Public on the Conduct of the Banks in the City of New-York* (New York: Courier Office, 1815), 4–8. English banks began purchasing securities as secondary reserves in the eighteenth century (Michie, 1999:27).
[37]Biddle and Wharton to Joseph & George Marx, 1 February 1814, Thomas A. Biddle and J. Wharton Company Letter Book, HSP.
[38]Contract, 11 July 1816, ibid.
[39]Directors' Minutes, Bank of Philadelphia, 6 March 1823, Philadelphia National Bank Records, HSP.
[40]Thomas Law, *Considerations Tending to Render the Policy Questionable of Plans for Liquidating, Within the Next Four Years, the Six Per Cent Stocks of the United States* (Washington, D.C.: S. A. Elliot, 1826), 9.
[41]General Ledgers, Bank of North America Records, HSP.
[42]"Condition of the Bank," ibid.
[43]Records of The Bank of New York, The Bank of New York Archives, New York.
[44]General Ledgers, "Statements of Condition," Manhattan Bank Records, Chase Manhattan Bank Archives, New York.

The Emergence of Secondary Securities Markets

Until very recently, scholars have largely ignored the role of secondary securities markets in the early U.S. economy. Perkins's recent treatment of the financial services sector, for example, discusses securities markets only briefly (in conjunction with lotteries). Recent scholarship has argued that the secondary securities markets were an important part of the financial sector and hence an important, perhaps crucial, element in U.S. economic growth.[45] Like any new good or service, the emergence and proliferation of markets for financial instruments can be explained in terms of demand-side and supply-side factors. In other words, why did investors wish to purchase securities? Why did issuers wish to create and sell them? Investors purchased securities because they were cheaply bought and sold, provided good returns, and could be used to secure loans. Firms issued securities when they needed access to long-term capital, or when they could borrow more cheaply directly from investors rather than indirectly from banks.

Demand for Investment Securities

In short, investors desired financial instruments like equities and corporate or government debt instruments because, holding yields constant, those securities were safer and more liquid than the available alternatives. Consider, for example, the analysis of "An Old Banker" in his rebuttal of anti-BNA writers who claimed that banks limited private lending:

> Destroy the Bank, and these foreign [investors in the Bank will] remit their money to some more stable institution, spreading, wherever they go, the history of our folly and disgrace. Let us suppose the bank destroyed. Do you imagine the Bank Proprietors of Pennsylvania will instantly place their money out at interest? – He that believes this, has more credulity than I would willingly hope, for the honor of Pennsylvania, possesses the mind of the most ignorant man in the state.[46]

"An Old Banker" clearly understood that bank stock was more desirable than personal loans because it was easier to acquire, monitor, and sell. A description of the investment options facing colonists shows the tremendous advantages of the new financial instruments that arose during the financial revolution of the 1790s.

Colonists had not found investing easy. Benjamin Franklin's Poor Richard made a virtue of investing; but, without any commercial or

45 Perkins 1994; Sylla 1998, 1999a; Sylla, Wilson, and Wright 1997.
46 *Pennsylvania Gazette*, 30 March 1785.

savings banks anywhere in the colonies, how were colonists to save? There were few formal financial intermediaries to help savers to make investment decisions or to spread risks. Savers and borrowers generally dealt with each other directly. Although both sides saved the modest cost of intermediation, they had to spend inordinate amounts of time ascertaining the reliability of the other party or suffer pecuniary losses.

A major way that colonial investors saved was to purchase cheap land in unsettled areas and then wait for the land to appreciate. If all went well, in a few years, or more likely decades, the market value of the land rose and the saver sold it for a profit. Such investments had disadvantages, however, the biggest being that it was difficult to time the market. The investor might die 10 years before prices rose, leaving his widowed spouse and children to fend for themselves in the interim. Investors also had to contend with squatters, taxes, poorly executed surveys, changing land conditions, and a host of other problems. Perhaps most troubling was the extreme illiquidity of frontier investment lands. Until the frontier line passed, they were difficult to sell. Without improvements, they were next to impossible to mortgage. Frontier land investments were, in a word, more "speculations" (to wit gambles) than investments with solid, predictable rates of return and due dates.

The same was true of local investments in improved lands including farms, mills, and forges. With that savings tactic, a head of household, usually a father, bought a local tract and leased it to tenants until his eldest son got married or turned 21. That tactic was a good one in the sense that the child was almost certain of receiving something. Unfortunately, however, the market value of what the son inherited was often less, and sometimes substantially less, than what the father had paid for the land. Sometimes tenants "wasted" the property and moved on. Other times, tenants made significant improvements to the property but demanded, and usually received, monetary compensation for making fences, clearings, and buildings. In addition, real estate, as an asset class, did not always appreciate. Colonial land prices often decreased, sometimes in Florida-like busts, but also in long, gentle undulations probably reflecting long-term population shifts and changes in regional economic activity.[47]

Early national investors came to understand that investment in land was like buying any type of tangible property in that the value could go up or down because of market conditions or because of the physical condition of the property itself. Such persons gave up the age-old prejudice against intangible forms of property because paper property reduced what might be termed "physical risk." For instance, the

[47]Michener 2000.

ownership of an equity instrument burned up in a fire could be determined and a new stock certificate issued. A burned uninsured barn, on the other hand, lost its value irrevocably.

Colonial investors could also save by making or buying several different types of intangible property in the form of commercial instruments, especially book balances, promissory notes, bonds, and mortgages. Book balances are most often associated with book accounts arising in the course of trade. It was possible, however, for savers to create a book credit by physically lodging a deposit with a merchant, lawyer, or other person of means in the same way savers of later generations would deposit money in their local bank. Merchants accepted the deposits and made use of the money until the saver called for it in person or by check or draft. As it was not customary to pay interest on such credits, there was little incentive for savers to use this vehicle except for convenience and safety's sake.

Promissory notes, bonds, and mortgages are all contracts for the payment of money at a specified point or points in the future, usually, especially in the case of the last two, with interest. The instruments vary mostly in the type of security offered. Promissory notes are most like today's "signature loans" or "IOUs." If a promissory note remained unpaid after its due date, or became too large due to accrued interest or additional debts, creditors often insisted that debtors convert the notes to bonds. Bonds were more formal instruments that specified a default penalty. Interestingly, most colonial investors did not sue if the principal of a bond was not paid on time but only if interest payments were not kept up, and even then not always. Because savers had few reliable investment opportunities, many did not want to be inconvenienced by having their principals returned. When a borrower defaulted on bond interest payments, or the sums involved were very large, savers often insisted on taking a mortgage on the borrower's real property as extra security. The biggest problems with personal notes, bonds, and mortgages were the risks associated with information asymmetry.

The personal, illiquid nature of colonial credit markets made it very difficult for colonial businesses to grow. Partners had to supply all of their own capital, perhaps with some borrowing from family members or very close business associates. Total liability combined with moral hazard to keep the number of principals very small; colonial partnerships rarely exceeded 3 principals and almost never exceeded 10 principals. The result was a very small average firm size and little possibility of exploiting economies of scale or scope. Only with improved access to external funding, therefore, could average firm size grow.

In order to increase efficiency, after all, businesses often need to borrow large sums for long periods. Lenders are usually reluctant to part with a portion of their wealth for so long because of two major risks: default risk, the risk that the borrower cannot repay the principal and stipulated interest; and term risk, the risk that the lender will need the money back before the end of the loan term. Information deficiencies form the core of both risks. The lender must collect information in order to judge whether the borrower will repay the principal and interest in a timely fashion. The lender must also carefully collect information to consider his or her own future need for the principal. Despite their best efforts, lenders encounter information deficiencies. Borrowers seek to withhold information that might dissuade lenders from lending; acquisition of reliable information has at least an opportunity cost and often an out of pocket cost.

Lenders sometimes compensated for informational deficiencies and asymmetries by seeking a higher rate of return. The longer the contract, the less information available, the higher the price. (Longer loan terms usually have higher yields. Look in your bank, for example, at the higher yields on 5-year versus 1-year certificates of deposit, or the yields of 30- versus 15-year mortgages, on any given day.) Similarly, greater geographical, or social, distances led to higher rates. The lender must know something of the borrower before making the loan and must monitor the borrower to ensure that he or she is putting the money to productive use.

As interest rates increase, the number of businesses that can profitably borrow decreases rapidly. The additional interest itself raises the risk of default and leads to a still higher rate, and so on, and so forth, until the rate becomes so ridiculously high that neither the borrower nor the lender desires to contract. Compounding this issue were early America's usury laws. Although the details varied by colony or state, almost each one set a maximum legal interest rate that was lower than the usual market rate for private loans. Under such conditions, supply and demand had less influence on interest rates. Lenders first had to decide whether to lend at a usurious rate. If they broke the law, they had to charge even more interest to cover default risk because the illegal contract was not enforceable in court. If they abided by the law, they had to decide whether to lend at the maximum legal rate. Loans, some legal, others not, were made, but the number of loans was much lower than what it would have been had the usury laws not existed.[48] Also, as we have seen, the "lemons" or adverse-selection problem cannot be compensated for by raising the cost of borrowing and, hence, limits the number and size of loans.

---

[48]Usury laws added either to the cost of lending or to the cost of borrowing, depending on which party bore the brunt of the potential punishment. In either case, the increased cost would necessarily reduce the number of transactions.

Here, then, are two major causes of early Americans' incessant cries for "credit."[49]

One way that colonial lenders tried to decrease the amount of information they needed about borrowers was to secure loans with some type of collateral, usually real estate but sometimes ships or personal property. Unfortunately, lenders were most likely forced to seize the security when the economy was doing poorly – when the collateral was usually at its lowest market price. Additionally, colonial courts were not always keen on real-estate foreclosures during economic downturns. Furthermore, real-estate values could decrease because of changes in local conditions, like unfavorable relative access to new roads, and incompetent farming practices and other forms of wastage. Finally, land was extremely illiquid; it could take years to get clear title. A relatively eloquent expression of the illiquid nature of land comes from the following poem, taken from *Vade-Mecum, or the Dealer's Pocket Companion:*

> FIRST, see the Land which thou intend'st to buy
> Within the Seller's Title clear doth lie:
> And that no Woman to it doth lay Claim,
> By Dow'ry, Jointure, or some other Name,
> That may it cumber. Know if bound or free
> The Tenure stand, and that from each Feoffee
> It be releas'd; That the Seller be so old
> That he may lawful sell, thou lawful hold:
> Have special Care that it not mortgag'd be,
> Nor be entailed on Posterity.
> Then if it stand in Statute, bound or no,
> Be well advis'd what Quit-Rent out must go,
> What Custom Serve hath been done of old,
> By those who formerly the same did hold:
> And if a wedded Woman put to Sale,
> Deal not with her unless she bring her Male:
> For she doth under Covert Baron go,
> Altho' sometimes some traffic so (we know.)
> The Bargain being made, and all this done,
> Have special Care to let thy Charter run,
> To thee, thy Heirs, Executors, Assigns,
> For that beyond thy Life securely binds.
> These Things foreknown and done you may prevent
> Those Things rash Buyers many Times repent!
> And yet when you have done all that you can,
> If you'll be sure, deal with an honest Man.[50]

[49]This discussion owes much to McCusker and Menard 1985:335–36.
[50]*Vade-Mecum, or the Dealer's Pocket Companion* (Boston: T. & J. Fleet, 1772).

Land titles, in other words, often floated in a netherworld of doubt. It almost never seemed clear who owned what land, how much that land was worth, and whether prospective borrowers had mortgaged those lots elsewhere. This was a problem because the holder of the first mortgage held the first lien on the property in case of default. Mortgages and liens were only sometimes advertised, and checking back issues of newspapers or public record books was a difficult and unsure way to determine a lot or tract's eligibility.[51] There were no specialized "title searchers" (as we now call them) in colonial or early national America. As late as 1832, the Farmers' Loan and Trust Company hired full-priced lawyers like Abraham Van Vechten of Albany to conduct title searches: "This company are about to loan on Mortgage to Peter Gansevoort Esq. of $30,000 on [certain city lots... please to] investigate the title [and send us a bill of your charge and expenses]."[52]

Lenders tried to counter those problems, which we could term security or collateral risk, by seeking security twice and thrice the current value of the mortgaged property.[53] Mortgage lending, especially person-to-person mortgage lending, was notoriously difficult. The U.S. mortgage market, even with the increased level of intermediation of the nineteenth century, has begun to function well only in the past few decades, with the invention and proliferation of securitization.[54] Early national borrowers found it difficult to obtain loans secured with mortgages at times. In early 1811, for example, Luther Martin of Maryland offered "landed property to the amount, in value of forty thousand dollars at least" to secure a $12,000 yearlong loan in 1811.[55] Also in early 1811 an unnamed borrower in Boston offered to secure a loan of "3 or 4,000 dollars" with "real estate given as security to double the amount, which is greatly increasing in value yearly."[56] By the autumn of 1812 Boston borrowers had to post "security to three times the amount" for a loan of "two or three thousand Dollars."[57]

Bills of exchange, with bills of lading listing loan collateral in detail, to some extent reduced information asymmetry. But although bills of exchange were among the most ubiquitous financial instruments of the eighteenth century, usually only merchants, a small fraction of the population, could readily invest in them. Often drawn on distant payers

[51]For an example of a mortgage announcement by Roeloff Duryee, see *New York Independent Journal*, 10 March 1784.
[52]Elisha Tibbits to Abraham Van Vechten, 28 November 1832, 41, Farmers' Loan and Trust Company Letter Book, CUSC.
[53]The public loan offices in Pennsylvania, for example, sought double security for unimproved land and treble for improved land. Bonds all required double indemnity, almost as a matter of course. Since most mortgages were simply bonds collateralized into mortgages, there is little doubt that mortgages were overcollateralized (Schweitzer 1987:123–29, 144, 150–51).
[54]Snowden 1987; Mishkin 2000.   [55]*Baltimore Whig*, 20 March 1811.
[56]*Boston Columbia Centinel*, 19 January 1811.   [57]Ibid., 23 September 1812.

(bankers), bills of exchange were not free from defalcation or default. The so-called real bills doctrine, a guide to the use of bills of exchange in mercantile trade, therefore, called for the overcollateralization of loans secured by bills of exchange, often to thrice the value of the loan.

Such overcollateralization had the effect of limiting loan volume because it decreased the potential size of loans on any given property and effectively raised the cost of borrowing by forcing the borrower to pledge more property for repayment. As noted, real estate was not an ideal form of collateral because property values fluctuated violently and were difficult to ascertain.[58] Seemingly minor differences in similar properties, such as location, can have large price consequences. Furthermore, market participants know with certainty the market value of a particular property only at the time of actual sale. Worse yet, real property can be quickly "run down." To protect themselves from miscalculations, price swings, or wastage, therefore, colonial lenders insisted on mortgages to twice or thrice the value of the loan – which, of course, limited the amount borrowed. Stocks and bonds of the same type, on the other hand, were complete equivalents incapable of wastage. Additionally, the secondary markets provided constant valuations of the collateral. The market for stocks and bonds greatly increased private lending because borrowers who were able to post financial securities as collateral found willing private lenders.

Financial institutions also decreased collateral risk by providing lenders and borrowers with a wider choice of assets to collateralize. Early national borrowers, for example, hypothecated stocks and bonds to secure loans. In other words, they deposited financial assets with borrowers in order to obtain, enlarge, or continue loans. In 1790 the concept of hypothecation was unknown to such a learned judge as Robert R. Livingston of New York. One of Livingston's arguments against Hamilton's funding system was that "stock will be sold below par to raise . . . money."[59] One of the virtues of financial securities was that they did not have to be sold to raise money; they could be used instead to secure a loan. In 1790 even some businessmen were only dimly aware of hypothecation. Moore Furman, for example, complained to William Edgar that he needed cash because he was "about to settle my old Concerns with my partners." "I have a few thousand pounds in United State Securities," he explained, "but our funds not being fixed they remain much under Value." Furman also owned real estate, "but

[58]An Anglo-American, *American Securities: Practical Hints on the Tests of Stability and Profit, For the Guidance and Warning of British Investors* (London: W. P. Metchim, 1860).
[59]Robert R. Livingston, *Considerations on the Nature of a Funded Debt, Tending to Shew that it can never be considered as a Circulating Medium and that the Interest of the United States Renders it Essentially necessary to fund it agreeably to Terms of the Original Contract at this Time, and not to adopt the Debts of the Respective States* (New York, 1790).

Lands are very low and unsalable." Furman then noted that New York merchant William Constable "mentioned that he could get securities funded, or money advanced on them" but Furman had yet to "enquire of the plan."[60]

One can excuse Furman for his ignorance of hypothecation. Early on, even Robert Morris did not appreciate the importance of hypothecation, refusing to allow the BNA to accept securities as loan collateral. Within a few weeks of the bank's opening in early January 1782, one of the directors, Thomas Fitzsimons, consulted Morris about whether the bank "should discount to Individuals on Public Securities." Morris "told him those Securities would be Ultimately Good but they would soon absorp [*sic*] their whole Capital and therefore [were] too dangerous to the Institution." He later wrote Thomas Procter that the bank had too little capital "to go through with so extensive a Scene as such Discounts would open to them, consequently they are compelled by necessity to decline the Undertaking." The bank changed its policy, but only after Hamilton, and the market, proved the effectiveness of hypothecation.[61]

By the late 1780s sophisticated securities dealers like Andrew Craigie of Boston readily used hypothecation to secure loans.[62] Similarly, in the 1780s the BONY, as yet unincorporated, lent on the hypothecation of securities.[63] In the 1790s Hamilton taught the less informed portions of the market about the power of hypothecation. Article Ten of the BONY's 1791 act of incorporation, which Hamilton wrote, forbade the bank from "buying or selling any stock, created under any Act of the Congress of the United States, or of any particular State, *unless in selling the same*, when truly pledged to it by way of security, for debts due to the said corporation."[64] Hamilton used that hypothecation clause to help quell the Panic of 1792. By the end of March 1792, the BONY, under Hamilton's instructions, began to "extend their loans upon deposits being made of Six Pcents @ 20/ Three Pcents @ 10 & deferred @ 12/." The action afforded borrowers "a great Accom[m]odation" and raised "the Price of Stocks."[65] Hamilton also directly instructed his successor as secretary of treasury, Oliver Wolcott, about hypothecation.[66]

[60]Moore Furman to William Edgar, 22 May 1790, William Edgar Papers, NYPL.
[61]*PRM*, 4:58, 69.
[62]Seth Johnson to Andrew Craigie, 23 December 1789, AAS.
[63]William Duer to William Constable, 11 January 1785, box 1, folder 1: Wm. Constable Letters, 1774–1784, Constable-Pierpont Papers, NYPL.
[64]Herman Krooss, ed., *Documentary History of Banking and Currency in the United States* (New York: McGraw-Hill, 1969), 1:332–37.
[65]Daniel McCormick to William Constable, New York, 29 March 1792, box 2, Constable-Pierpont Papers, NYPL.
[66]Alexander Hamilton to Oliver Wolcott Jr., New York, 5 August 1796, *PAH*, 20:290.

Market participants learned well. Securities dealers continued to secure loans "on the Stocks."[67] By the late 1790s large-scale speculators like John Nicholson regularly hypothecated equities to obtain loans.[68] The Manhattan Bank, established in 1799, accepted securities as collateral for loans, especially large ones.[69] After the War of 1812, borrowers asked for discounts on the security of equities or U.S. bonds without apology.[70] By the 1820s stock hypothecation was ubiquitous.[71] In 1826, for example, voting stockholders of the Dry Dock Bank had to affirm the following declaration: "The shares on which I now offer to vote, do not belong and are not hypothecated to the New York Dry Dock Company, and that they are not hypothecated or pledged to any other corporation or person whatever"[72] By the 1830s stock hypothecation was the basis of the emerging "call market."[73] "Our terms for loaning money on notes secured by the hypothecation of Stock, are the charge of legal interest accompanied with the right to call in the amt. loaned, or demand additional security whenever in our opinion the safety of the debt requires it," Henry Seymour informed John Delafield in December 1836.[74] By 1840 loans made on security of hypothecated stock were very prominent in the portfolios of some banks.[75]

Lenders typically preferred hypothecation because the market value of financial instruments held up much better than real-estate prices, even during the Panics of 1792 and 1819[76] and the War of 1812, and

[67] Alexander Macomb to William Constable, 1 August 1792, box 2, Constable-Pierpont Papers, NYPL.
[68] John Nicholson to William Young, 8 February 1798, Dreer collection, HSP.
[69] See the General Ledger of the Manhattan Company, Chase Manhattan Bank Archives, New York.
[70] S. Pleasonton to William Whann, 5 March 1816, LCP.
[71] *Span of a Century, 1811–1911: Mechanics and Farmers Bank Albany, New York* (Albany: Quayle St., 1911); Charles Glidden Haines, *Arguments Against the Justice and Policy of Taxing the Capital Stock of Banks and Insurance Companies, in the State of New York* (New York: G. F. Hopkins, 1824), 10; *Origin, Provisions and Effect of the Safety Fund Law* (Albany: Packard and Van Benthuysen, 1834), 4.
[72] Ezra Weeks to Simon N. Dexter, 24 December 1827, Simon Newton Dexter Papers, CUSC.
[73] Myers 1931.
[74] Farmers' Loan and Trust Company Letter Book, 315, CUSC.
[75] Allan Nevins, ed., *The Diary of Philip Hone, 1828–1851* (New York: Dodd, Mead, 1927), 467.
[76] Newly available price information shows that the Early National period experienced no stock market "crashes." The prices of individual securities sometimes slumped, and occasionally trading halted for short periods, but no prolonged, across-the-board drops were experienced until the late 1830s. Simple arbitrage and open market operations quickly squelched the Panic of 1792. Trading stopped for a few weeks in some markets during the Panic of 1819, but when trading reopened most securities remained at their prepanic levels. For the Panic of 1792, see Cowen 2000a, 2000b. For the securities price movements, see Sylla, Wilson, and Wright 2002.

because the value of a given instrument was uniform and not subject to degradation, local caprice, or the political atmosphere.[77] (A share in a given bank was like any other share in that bank and always would be; a plot of land in a given town was of variable quality and could be "run down" after being posted as security.) In July 1812, for example, the nation's "political affairs may be considered as an unpropitious period for the Sale of Lands." Benjamin Chew, for example, discovered that "the Price admitted for the Sale of the lands now sold is short of the Estimate that we affixed to them" shortly before.[78] The shock of war did not seriously affect the securities markets until the sacking of Washington; government bond prices dropped slightly (interest rates increased) for a few months, but bank share prices increased. The only part of the securities market that suffered early on was marine insurance stocks, but even they had bounced back by late October 1812.

The legal nature of negotiable public securities was crucial to their success. The importance of negotiability was long understood. Robert Morris, for example, argued that allowing for "the Transfer of debts due by the United States to Individuals so as to enable the Sale of such debts by one Man to another" would greatly aid public credit by reducing the "Great Inconveniences" that arose from a want of transferability. Accordingly, he instructed Joseph Nourse, the register of the treasury, to allow for the transfer of public debt by a three-step process. First, the seller assigned the certificate to the buyer by endorsement. A government official then noted the change in ownership in the official registry and issued a new certificate to the new owner.[79] Morris rejected proposals to further increase the liquidity of the debt by creating bearer instruments. He understood that bearer obligations circulated too much like money and were subject to theft, loss by fire, and other calamities making them "less valuable from that Circumstance."[80]

Financial institutions decreased term risk by establishing markets that allowed investors to sell their investments, virtually at will, usually for much less than 1 percent of the sale price, plus the cost of postage if they lived outside of Boston, Charleston, or one of the other securities market centers. Freed from finding information about each potential borrower, lenders or investors still needed to decide in which institutions to invest. The task was a relatively simple one because there were far fewer potential institutional investments than individual borrowers.

---

[77]For the volatility of land prices, see *Pennsylvania Gazette*, 3 February 1790; Bogue and Bogue 1957; Lebergott 1985; Michener 2000.

[78]Benjamin Chew to Abraham Morrison, 20 July 1812, box 277, Chew Family Papers, HSP.

[79]*PRM*, 4:156–57, 161, 164–65.   [80]*PRM*, 8:360.

In addition, information regarding the profitability of institutions, in the form of dividends and the market price of their shares, was widely available. The custom of distributing profits to stockholders as dividends persists to this day, despite the fact that the practice is economically unnecessary, except as a signaling mechanism to investors.[81]

Dividend notices were an important shorthand means of informing potential investors about company performance; investors used dividend information to decide in which companies to invest. In the first decade of the nineteenth century, for example, Ebenezer Hazard of Pennsylvania and Jedediah Morse of Massachusetts often exchanged information regarding local investment opportunities – canals, turnpikes, bridges, and insurance companies. The two pieces of information they most eagerly sought were the dividend payment and the current price of shares. From those two figures they calculated their expected return on investment. Whenever that return approached or exceeded 6 percent, they made purchases because they could not make as much profit by lending to individuals.[82] Clearly, other market participants made similar calculations.[83] When the BUS announced an unexpectedly large dividend in 1794, for instance, the price of BUS shares rose.[84]

The dividend rate, in other words, helped to establish the market price of the company's equities, or ownership shares. Secondary securities markets in the nation's major seaboard cities allowed investors to sell their investments in government debt instruments or equities. Because of those markets, investors readily purchased the debt instruments, which were redeemable decades later, and the corporate equities, which in most cases were never redeemable. Investors realized the importance of secondary securities markets immediately. As Samson Fleming informed William Edgar in early 1784, "it is an amazing Advantage to have Stock in Bank... [because investors] can take out & put in as reason directs."[85]

"Take out & put in as reason directs" is exactly what early investors did. The stock transfer books of early corporations show a steady turnover of ownership. Brokers' records show a large volume of transactions. In the 1790s share turnover rates of some Pennsylvania and

---

[81]For the unnecessary nature of dividends, see Baskin and Miranti 1997. The gist of the idea is that a stockholder is an equity holder and hence owns his or her share of the company's profit whether the profit is distributed or retained.
[82]Ebenezer Hazard to Jedediah Morse, 14 November, 24 December 1799; 25 January 1800; 2 February 1804; 17 January, 9 April 1805; 13 February, 6 December 1808, Ebenezer Hazard Papers, HSP.
[83]See, for example, David Grim and Philip Grim to Watson & Paul, 4 February 1799, LCP.
[84]George Nelson to Mr. Bell, 19 March 1794, George Nelson Letter Book, UNCSC.
[85]Samson Fleming to William Edgar, 9 February 1784, William Edgar Papers, NYPL.

New York banks often exceeded 20 percent per year. By the 1810s, single brokerage firms in Philadelphia annually bought or sold tens of thousands of shares, and hundreds of thousands of dollars of bonds. By the 1830s, hundreds of thousands of shares, and millions of dollars of bonds, changed hands in the Philadelphia market. (See Chapter 6 for details.) Volume figures for Boston were similar, while somewhat lower, but still substantial, numbers of securities changed hands in Baltimore; various cities in Virginia; Charleston, South Carolina; and New Orleans. New York outpaced them all.[86]

The Informational Virtues of Hamilton's Funding System

The elegant simplicity of Alexander Hamilton's funding system was largely responsible for the high volume of securities transactions. Before the funding system, the public debt was highly variegated and hence difficult to track. Further compounding matters, colonial Americans did not have much experience trading public debt. The debt markets, therefore, were generally in shambles. Hamilton's system rationalized the market by bringing information needs within existing market and technological constraints.

American investors informally traded a small volume of provincial and British securities in the late colonial period but very few individuals were involved in this activity.[87] The financial pressures of the Revolution and early Confederation period led the various American governments to create a wide variety of debt instruments, including, but not limited to, loan office certificates, indents, final settlements, soldiers' certificates, depreciation certificates, state agents' certificates, and the notes of Morris, Hillegas, Nourse, Pickering, Pierce, and Barber.[88] The Continental Congress backed some of the instruments, while state governments pledged to service others. Some good came out of this diversity, mainly the formation of intercity information and exchange links between brokers. Immediately after the war, a half dozen or so men entered the brokerage business in each of the major seaports.[89] Flows of securities appear, however, to have been rather random, based more on guesses than fundamentals, like interest rates. One dealer

---

[86]For the Boston stock market, see Martin and Barron 1975. For New York, see Werner and Smith 1991.

[87]Matson 1985:249.

[88]Jonathan Elliott, *The Funding System of the United States and of Great Britain* (Washington, D.C.: Blair and Rives, 1845); Rafael Bayley, *The National Loans of the United States, from July 4, 1776 to June 30, 1880* (Washington, D.C.: Government Printing Office, 1882).

[89]Early brokers included: New York: John Delafield, Hayman Levy, Daniel Phoenix, Samuel Hay, John Keating, Viner Van Zandt, Philip Lott, and the partnerships of Daniel Parker, Elisha Hopkins, and Daniel McLane and of Elihu Marshall and James Bingham. Philadelphia: James Dunlap, Matthew McConnell, Haym Solomon. Boston: Andrew Craigie.

suggested as late as 1789 that securities trading was little more than "a lottery."[90]

Evidence suggests that competition kept transaction costs down. "Quakenbos had a quantity of Pickerings [a type of security] but Platt [another broker] worked cheaper than I offered to do," one early broker informed a correspondent. The securities dealers facilitated intermarket and intramarket sales and even tried to sell some of the debt instruments in London. However, structural limitations appear to have impeded market integration.[91]

The sheer complexity of the revolutionary debt constituted a major problem. How were investors to make rational calculations about returns when repayment terms were unpredictable and uneven? Superintendent of Finance Robert Morris, for instance, regularly instructed Continental Treasurer Michael Hillegas, Cashier of the Superintendent John Swanwick, and Paymaster General John Pierce to use various combinations of their quasi-personal notes to "pay" – or, to be more precise, to "put off" – the obligations of the other three until specie could be acquired. As an entry in Morris's diary shows, the Confederation government deliberately complicated repayment, making it difficult for liability holders to assess the government's creditworthiness:

> I sent for Mr. Swanwick and directed him to Collect the several Debts above mentioned and to provide Mr. Pierce with Money to pay his Notes as fast as demanded if possible, I then drew a Warrant on the Treasurer of the United States in favor of the Pay Master Genl. for the whole amount of his notes, Mr. Swanwick will pay Mr. Pierce the Money for it and finally pay the Warrant to Mr. Hilligas the Treasurer instead of so much Money on account of the Bills and I directed Solomon the Broker to Sell more Bills to provide for the Balance as well as for other purposes.

Additionally, state governments often passed legislation that severely hindered investors' ability to liquidate holdings quickly. A Pennsylvania statute requiring certification that the original holders of certain securities were Pennsylvania citizens, for example, prevented Ebenezer Hazard from making a timely sale of debt instruments that he had held for three years without gain.[92]

Plagued by uncertain redemption, counterfeits, and uneven coupon payments, securities' prices fluctuated widely over time and space.[93]

[90]Seth Johnson to Andrew Craigie, 2, 19, 26, 29 July 1788, 13 December 1789, Andrew Craigie Papers, AAS.

[91]John Delafield to John Delafield, 6 September 1784, John Delafield to James Farlie, 24 March 1785, John Delafield Letter Book, NYPL.

[92]*PRM*, 6:118; Ebenezer Hazard to unknown, New York, 16 August 1786, Ebenezer Hazard Papers, Gratz – American Miscellaneous, HSP.

[93]Those not conversant with these matters can consult Perkins 1994 or Ferguson 1961.

In 1784 New York broker John Delafield reported selling securities between 3 shillings and 14 shillings in the pound (15 percent to 70 percent of their face value). Although he optimistically reassured potential investors that the sundry securities were good risks, he admitted that "local circumstances have tended to raise or fall their value." Although a major broker for over a year, Delafield did not know the amount of a major security that had been issued or remained outstanding, crucial factors in determining a target price. Other brokers also had difficulty finding basic information about securities.[94]

Delafield tried, usually unsuccessfully, to convince investors that piecemeal, state funding was a good thing.[95] Investors must have realized then what seems so obvious now – the technology of the day could not meet the information needs of investors. There were too many types of debt issued by too many types of governments under too volatile political situations for much market integration to occur. For example, in Philadelphia in 1786 the following securities were listed for sale:

> Militia certificates, of Pennsylvania, Depreciation funded on the excise, Ditto unfunded, but purchase land, Stelle's and Story's certificates, Loan-Office ditto of Pennsylvania, Nicholson's, or new loan, Dollar money [Pennsylvania bills of credit denominated in dollars], Shilling money, Indents or Facilities, Continental securities, Land-office papers, of Pennsylvania, Jersey finals that draw interest, Thompson's, Virginia depreciation, finals, treasury land warrants, Maryland finals, Depreciation, Delaware finals, depreciation, Continental money, New York finals that purchase land, Nourse's certificates of Pennsylvania, Nourse's, not adopted by any state.

To make rational trading decisions, investors would have needed good sources of information in each state and the national government.[96]

The information situation was so bad that Philadelphia broker Mathew McConnell tried to profit from the situation by publishing in 1787 *An Essay on the Domestic Debts*.[97] "Ever since public securities have been in circulation," he explained in the preface, "their variety were found so great, that a knowledge of them was considered by those who did not attend to their rise and progress, as a profession." Nevertheless,

94Seth Johnson to Andrew Craigie, 4 September 1784, Andrew Craigie Papers, AAS.
95*Pennsylvania Gazette*, 15 March 1786.
96John Delafield to John Delafield, 6 September 1784, John Delafield to Udney Hay, 23 October 1785, John Delafield Letter Book, NYPL. The best survey of pretelegraphic information dissemination is Pred 1973. For later periods, see Garbade and Silber 1978; Garg 2000.
97Mathew McConnell, *An Essay on the Domestic Debts of the United States of America* (Philadelphia: Robert Adiken, 1787).

even McConnell, who had been "a dealer therein for some time," was, by his own admission, "inadequate to the task." He apologized to readers, noting that "he was not so fully aware that the field into which he was entering had been so extensive, or that the subject would have required so much attention." The tiny pamphlet, a mere reprinting of Pennsylvania's securities laws, bears out McConnell's harsh self-appraisal.

Alexander Hamilton's funding system changed that cacophony of uncertainty to the euphony of just three major bonds, each entirely under federal control.[98] Under Hamilton's system, investors in revolutionary debt needed only to stay apprised of the outlook of the national government's ability to service its debts. State securities quickly disappeared as holders used them to subscribe to the national bonds. By the end of 1791, in other words, the amount of information that investors needed to make rational decisions decreased significantly and finally came within the existing technological bounds. The multitude of state payment schedules and transfer regulations gave way to dependable, predictable payments and a uniform transfer system. "Sixes" paid 6 percent interest, while "Threes" paid, as one might guess, 3 percent. Both paid interest quarterly. Hamilton's third bond, usually called "Deferreds," paid no interest until 1802 when they effectively became "Sixes." Investors correctly valued the Deferreds as zero-coupon or discount bonds and correctly noted that they made excellent investments for minors.[99]

Hamilton's financial program, the funding of the debt and the passage of the first BUS, brought the young republic roughly on par with Great Britain, at least on paper.[100] America, like Britain, now had a national bank and a nationally funded debt. Would the bank and the markets perform as in Britain? Yes, because Hamilton made sure of it. Hamilton's role, in other words, extended beyond merely initiating and engineering the passage of important financial legislation. Many regard him as a genius because he made the legislation work in the real world. On one level, Hamilton was a skilled administrator who helped to establish important procedures and precedents regarding the way that the U.S. Treasury interacted with the national bank,

[98] Some of Hamilton's contemporaries also noted the necessity for reducing the complexity of the debt. See, for instance, *Pennsylvania Gazette*, 9 September 1789.

[99] Historical treatments of these events include McDonald 1958, 1979; Perkins 1994; Ferguson 1961. E. F. Thomas Fortune, *An Epitome of the Stocks and Publick Funds . . . Together with an Appendix, containing the only Account ever yet published of the Bank Stock and Funds of the United States of America, Second Edition with Additions* (London: T. Boosey, 1796), 67–68.

[100] The United States was certainly at least the equal of Britain by the end of the period under study. "We think it will be taken as evidence that the credit system of the United States at large is better than that of England at large." H. C. Carey, *The Credit System in France, Great Britain, and the United States* (Philadelphia, 1838), 30.

state banks, and the securities markets.[101] More dramatically, he also helped to steer the financial sector through its first test, the Panic of 1792. In the early months of 1792, all of the nation's banks, including the BUS, felt overextended and hence began to curtail credit. That action caused the failure of several securities speculators, including the notorious William Duer. Prices of securities, including U.S. debt instruments, briefly plummeted. At critical junctures, Hamilton used treasury funds to purchase U.S. securities on the open market, thereby bolstering their prices. Simultaneously, he added liquidity to the system by selling guilder bills, bills of exchange drawn on the proceeds of a U.S. loan in Amsterdam, on credit. Because of Hamilton's interventions, and simple arbitrage, securities prices quickly rebounded and the financial sector continued to grow apace.[102]

Of course, Hamilton did not function in a vacuum. When Hamilton arrived in late colonial America, he found a thriving commercial community thoroughly conversant with small-scale personal financial instruments, like bills of exchange and promissory notes, and possessed of active markets in foreign exchange and maritime insurance. Historians have long known that restrictions on the colonial economy were heavy, so heavy, in fact, that some believe the main causes of the American Revolution were economic.[103] Commercial banks were nonexistent, loan offices were too small to meet demand, brokers were rare, and the overall scope of operations was relatively small. The largest colonial maritime insurance firm, for example, was Thomas Willing's partnership, Thomas Willing and Company. The firm underwrote only £80,000 (approximately $215,000) worth of risks at a time; the Insurance Company of North America, one of several Philadelphia maritime insurance corporations formed in the 1790s, underwrote well over $1 million worth of risks. Despite Willing's tremendous business acumen, the insurance concern was unprofitable, a victim of information asymmetry and Willing's myriad other commitments. The Insurance Company of North America, on the other hand, proved extremely profitable. It overcame information asymmetry through specialization and economies of scale.[104]

Colonial merchants were, by necessity, experts in foreign exchange. However, from a developmental standpoint the exchange markets were relatively unimportant. Most of the time, America was on a specie standard, restricting exchange rates to a narrow band between specie shipment points, outside of which specie and securities became the preferred media of remittance.[105] Additionally, after 1784 banks helped the exchange markets to function more efficiently by

---

[101]Flaumenhaft 1992.   [102]Cowen 2000a, 2000b.   [103]Egnal and Ernst 1972.
[104]Wright 1996.   [105]Officer 1996.

lending on the security of bills of exchange, the major foreign exchange instrument.[106]

Hamilton also benefited from a large degree of agreement on financial issues. Historians have tended to exaggerate the ideological distance between early U.S. political parties.[107] In fact, there was considerable political consensus that local banks were necessary for economic growth, that the national debt needed to be funded, that incorporated insurance companies were necessary, and that capital markets should be allowed to develop relatively unimpeded.[108] Indeed, Jefferson may have owed his first election to the presidency to probank urban artisans.[109]

Strong rhetorical stances against certain aspects of the financial system, like the national debt, did not constrain government borrowing. Indeed, over the period of this study, the U.S. government completed several other bond issues in order to consolidate its foreign debt (5.5 percent, in 1795), fight the French in a naval Quasi-War (6 percent, in 1799), build an army (8 percent, in 1799), buy Louisiana (6 percent, in 1803), fight its second war for Independence (6 percent, in 1812, 1813, 1814, 1815), redeem Treasury notes (6 percent, in 1815), and subscribe to the SBUS (5 percent, in 1816), among other purposes. Andrew Jackson paid off the national debt in the 1830s, but Jacksonians later borrowed to fund the Mexican War.

Although later bond issues somewhat complicated matters for investors, rapid redemption of some of the issues meant that investors could choose from rarely more than a half-dozen or so types of bonds at any one time. Because the payment and transferal terms of the bonds were similar, the federal government remained the sole issuer, information speeds increased over the period, and investors became more adept, the increased number of bonds did not cause serious information problems.[110]

Women and Widespread Securities Ownership

Perhaps the best evidence of that is the fact that a wide spectrum of Americans owned corporate stock and government debt in the early national and antebellum periods. Merchants, women, orphans, artisans, retailers, and farmers owned "stock."[111] Despite a picture of powerless and wealthless early American women drawn by some historians,

---

[106]Doerflinger 1986.   [107]For a recent example, see Larson 2001.
[108]Perkins 1994.   [109]Wright 1998a.
[110]Jonathan Elliott, *The Funding System of the United States and of Great Britain* (Washington, D.C.: Blair and Rives, 1845); Rafael Bayley, *The National Loans of the United States, from July 4, 1776 to June 30, 1880* (Washington, D.C.: Government Printing Office, 1882).
[111]Wright 1999a; Majewski 2000.

considerable numbers of women owned equity stakes in banks, insurance companies, and other joint-stock corporations. Of the 89 persons and companies who held stock in the Insurance Company of North America from 1792 until 1799, for example, 11 were women.[112] Similarly, some 53 of the Manhattan Company's first 388 subscribers (about 14 percent) were women. A considerable number of women owned stock in the Bank of Pennsylvania in the mid-1790s.[113] Of the first 69 subscribers to the Commercial and Farmers Bank of Baltimore, 10 (14.5 percent) were women. Women accounted for 12.5 percent of the total capital subscription to that bank in its 1810 initial public offering (IPO).[114] In 1812 some 45 females, mostly unmarried women and widows, owned stock in the Bank of Utica.[115] Nine percent of the 89 investors in the IPO of the Central Bank of Worcester, Massachusetts, were women, though they purchased only 24 of the 1,000 shares offered. When that bank offered an additional 517 shares in 1848, 12 percent of the purchasers were women, but again they took on average fewer shares than the average subscriber took. During the Central Bank's 1850 offering of 1,000 shares, 14.6 percent of the investors were women, but this time their portion of the shares purchased, 9.8 percent, was much closer to the average subscription.[116] Twelve percent of the initial subscribers to the Bank of Chester County (1814) were women, who accounted for only 4.8 percent of the total number of shares taken.[117] If anything, women increased their stake in that institution over the next several decades.[118] Indeed, women were probably more extensively engaged in the secondary markets than in IPOs. For example, women were transactors in 21.6 percent of the 111 transfers of Worcester Bank stock between 1812 and 1846 for which records still exist.[119] Women owned 7.8 percent of the dollar value of Ohio bank stock in 1841.[120]

Women were less active investors in transportation companies. Of the first 427 investors in the Permanent Bridge, near Philadelphia, only 22 (5.15 percent) were women. Women accounted for only 553 (3.69 percent) of the 15,000 shares initially subscribed between April

---

[112]Ruwell 1993.
[113]Nancy Patterson Bright Collection, Bank of Pennsylvania Manuscripts, 1790–1831, HSP.
[114]Commercial and Farmers Bank of Baltimore Director's Minutes, 1810, ms. no. 2189, MHS.
[115]Carey, *The Credit System in France, Great Britain, and the United States*, 82.
[116]Central Bank of Worcester Business Records, Stock Record Book, 1830–64, AAS.
[117]Bank of Chester County, Stock Ledger & Dividend Ledger, 1814–22, ms. 78004, CCHS.
[118]Bank of Chester County, Record of Stock Transfers, 1814–72, ms. 78010, CCHS.
[119]Worcester Bank Records, folders 7, 8, Stock Certificates and Transfers, 1812–29, 1844–46, AAS.
[120]*Philadelphia Prices Current*, 27 February 1841.

1798 and April 1800.[121] When 241 additional investors joined the company in 1803, 21 (8.7 percent) were women who accounted for just 3.5 percent of the 5,477 new shares. Between January 1800 and May 1815, 32,153 shares of the company's stock changed hands in 716 transactions (44.9 shares per trade average). During that span, 30 women sold 540 shares and 53 purchased 1,064 shares, for a net increase of women's holdings of 524 shares.

Other types of nonbank corporations attracted female investors but not always in droves. The spotty records that remain of the Chester County Silk Company make clear that women owned shares of its stock but allow for little else to be said with certainty.[122] In Pennsylvania in the early 1840s, 7 of the 49 subscribers to the tiny ($1,000 par capitalization) Agricultural and Mechanics Association of Pennsylvania and New Jersey were women.[123] In Maine in 1844, women were just 7.5 percent of all nonbank stockholders and accounted for only 4 percent of the nonbank capital of the state's 19 nonbank corporations.[124]

The most comprehensive data on women's bank stockholding now extant also comes from Maine and dates from 1839 and 1841. In 1839, 15.33 percent (472 of 3,079) of the stockholders of the state's 50 banks were women. Women accounted for 8.93 percent of the par value of stock in that year. The figures for 1841 were similar (17.33 percent of stockholders; 9.55 percent of stock value).[125] By 1853 women composed 24.7 percent of Maine bank stockholders and owned a full 16 percent of the par value of Maine bank stock.[126] Women's investment in Maine's banks may have paled compared with women's investment in Massachusetts. According to nineteenth-century political economist Henry C. Carey, by the late 1830s women owned some 38.5 percent of Massachusetts's total banking capital. Carey applauded limited-liability corporations because small tradesmen, servants, and women could buy stock without fear. Under such a principle, he noted, an association of even the "poorest persons" could fund its activities.[127] Indeed, women's benevolent associations, such as "The Association

[121] Schuylkill Permanent Bridge Co. Stock Books, HSP.

[122] Chester County Silk Company, ms. 7237, CCHS.

[123] Agricultural and Mechanics Association of Pennsylvania and New Jersey, Constitution and Stock Transfer Book, 1840–46, HSP.

[124] [Secretary of State of Maine], *An Abstract of the Returns of Corporations, Made to the Office of the Secretary of State, in January, 1845, for the Year 1844* (Augusta, Maine: William T. Johnson, 1845).

[125] Asaph R. Nichols, *List of Stockholders, With Amount of Stock Held by Each, in the Banks of Maine* (Augusta, Maine: Smith & Robinson, 1839); Samuel P. Benson, *List of Stockholders, (With Amount of Stock Held by Each,) in the Banks of Maine* (Augusta, Maine: Severance & Dorr, 1841).

[126] John G. Sawyer, *List of Stockholders, (With Amount of Stock Held by Each Jan. 1 1853,) in the Banks of Maine* (Augusta, Maine: William T. Johnson, 1853).

[127] Carey, *The Credit System in France, Great Britain, and the United States*, 82–83.

for the relief of respectable aged indigent females," often invested in equities. That organization gave its wards cash, wood, and tea. The organization paid for the handouts from current donations, of course, but also received a "dividend on Stock in Mechanics Bank $40.50."[128]

The considerable extent of female shareholding shows that early financial markets were impersonal and inclusive. Markets existed simply to raise capital for firms and governments, not to allow one class or gender to gain power or to exert control over another group. At least in the free states, *all* investors were welcomed, and many did join the market. The shares of the first corporations, mostly banks, were priced too high for most investors, but par values for subsequent corporations quickly dropped to the $35 to $100 range, well within the purchasing power of the top half of wealth owners.[129] Early federal securities were available in a range of values, from a few dollars to thousands of dollars. Later government and corporate debt issues were usually available in $100 increments. Holding securities became widespread enough that school arithmetic books taught students how to price bonds, equities, loans, and discounts.[130]

The equities of banks, insurance companies, and internal-improvement companies were extremely important investment instruments. Extant stockholder lists for the BNA, for example, show that between 1785 and 1830, 11,947 BNA shares traded hands in 3,618 transactions, an average of about 3.3 shares per trade. That the median trade size in those years never exceeded 2 shares, and the mode and lower quartile never exceeded 1 share, strongly suggest that the Bank's 1,800 to 2,500 shares were widely held. (Because the market value of BNA shares was usually well over their par value of $400, or roughly $4,000 in today's dollars, the trading volume of BNA shares, measured as share units, was somewhat less than the volumes of Pennsylvania's other early banks, which traded even more actively due to their lower per share value.) Bank shares were extremely good investments; they usually paid excellent dividends, could be hypothecated to secure loans, and were easily sold.[131]

After 1816 even the very poor could also invest in "stock," albeit indirectly through savings banks. Those banks received deposits, often as low as $1, in exchange for regular dividends a point or two below prevailing bond yields. Although their deposits were more like modern certificates of deposit than modern savings accounts, and hence

---

[128] *New York Weekly Visitor, and Ladies' Museum* 1 (1817–18): 94–95. The organization owned around $600 worth of bank stock.
[129] Sturm 1969.
[130] Alice Arnold, "Al[i]ce Arnold Her Ciphering Book, 1795"; Sarah B. Pollock, "Practical Arithmetic Comprising all the rules for transacting business executed at Mrs. Rowan's Academy, 1810," both in AAS.
[131] Wright 1999a.

relatively illiquid, savings banks still managed to accumulate millions of dollars, which they reinvested in the secondary securities markets. In addition, like insurance companies, savings banks lent significant sums on bond or mortgage.[132] Depositors in the Bank for Savings in New York in 1820 included boot cleaners, coachmen, cartmen, chamber maids, nurses, students, laborers, waiters, and a huge number (143 of 1,527 total depositors) of domestics. New York newspaper editor Mordecai M. Noah noted that the poor denizens of Manhattan often accumulated surprisingly large sums. "Domestics" with "several hundred dollars" invested in the Bank for Savings were not uncommon as early as 1819.[133] Growth in the number and deposits of savings banks were strong.[134] As in other places, such as Central Europe after 1820,[135] savings banks aided economic growth by mobilizing the savings of many small investors.

The ability to sell securities at will was so critical to early national investors that they created secondary markets for more traditional investment instruments, including ground rents. A recent study of ground rents shows that the rights to receive the rents traded regularly in Pennsylvania, especially after the Revolution. The "rents," really contracts for the conveyance of land in *fee simple* in return for a perpetual annual payment, were supported by common, statutory, and case law. They gave the grantor (seller or ground rent landlord) a secure income stream while allowing the grantee (buyer or ground tenant) to acquire full ownership for little initial investment. Ground rent landlords who later wished to have a lump-sum payment instead of many smaller payments simply sold the income stream to a third party. A similar market existed in Baltimore.[136]

Southerners also sought liquid investments. There were small stock markets in Alexandria, Richmond, Norfolk, Charleston, and New Orleans. Those cities, and smaller commercial centers (e.g., Savannah, Georgia; Mobile, Alabama; and Natchez, Mississippi) also supported thriving commercial paper and secondary mortgage markets. Increasingly, investors treated slaves as a type of financial security. Like stocks and bonds, they were highly liquid, almost always commanded specie, served as collateral for debts to banks and other large-scale lenders, and could be leased to create income streams rather than worked directly.[137] The dearth of large urban centers and the large volume of funds invested in slaves, however, hindered southern financial and economic development.[138]

---

[132] See, for example, the balance sheets of the Worcester County Institution for Savings, 1828–82, box 6, folder 1, Worcester Collection, AAS.

[133] *New York National Advocate*, 7 July 1819.

[134] Keyes 1876; Manning 1917; Horne 1947; Olmstead 1976.   [135] Pammer 2000.

[136] Wright 1998b, 1999b; Mayer 1883.   [137] Kilbourne 1995.   [138] Majewski 2000.

Supply of Investment Securities

Entrepreneurs needed two types of loans, long-term and short-term. They needed long-term loans, of a year or longer, to make capital improvements, such as erecting buildings, purchasing machines, clearing land, and digging wells. They used shorter loans, from a few days to a few months, to smooth out cash flows. Goods often could not be sold before the expenses required to create or purchase them needed to be paid. Short-term loans bridged the gap.

Before advanced financial intermediation, information deficiencies also plagued borrowers. They had to discover for themselves who had money to invest, how much those potential investors had, how long they were willing and able to part with their money, the collateral security they required, and the interest rate they sought or the likelihood that they would lend at the lawful limit. Borrowers made inquiries orally, by letter, and by advertisement, and then waited for responses. Lenders were not always found, or found in a timely fashion. Thus the constant cry for money in the colonial period, especially from those with the fewest contacts and least collateral. In economic jargon, search costs were prohibitively high.[139]

Advanced financial intermediaries made it easier for entrepreneurs to secure both long- and short-term loans. Early commercial banks, for example, generally specialized in making short-term loans from a few days to a few months in duration. In exchange for the discount, "an allowance made for the payment of any sum of money before it becomes due, ... [which is to say] the difference between that sum, due sometime hence, and its present worth,"[140] banks advanced their notes, non-interest-bearing, nonlegal tender promissory bearer instruments convertible into specie or credit on their books, to businesspersons with accounts receivable or other visible means of repayment.

Short-term credit was essential to business success in many regions and sectors. Printers in early national Virginia, for example, found it difficult to compete with Philadelphia printers well lubricated with discounts.[141] Artisans in New York and Philadelphia who received bank discounts in the early 1790s got angry enough when they lost those accommodations in the last years of the 1790s to abandon the Federalists for the commercial wing of the Republican Party. Those artisans who obtained discounts tended to do much better than their competitors. Access to short-term credit was important enough that,

---

[139]Kohn 1999.
[140]Arnold, "Al[i]ce Arnold Her Ciphering Book, 1795"; Pollock, "Practical Arithmetic Comprising."
[141]Rawson 1998:256, 284, 302, 317–18; Remer 1996.

north of the Rappahannock, the electorate supported the controlled growth of banks and banking.[142]

At least two bank lending models were used in the early national and antebellum United States. One was the "insider lending" model by which banks overcame information asymmetry by essentially owning the firms to which they lent. There was nothing at all sinister about that method; it may very well have fueled supply-side economic growth.[143] Indeed, in many advanced economies today, including Germany and Japan, insider lending is the norm. Insider lending sounds evil or inefficient to most Americans today because the current U.S. banking system is based on the "outsider lending" model that prevailed in most places in the early United States outside of the industrializing regions of New England that Lamoreaux studied. In the outsider model, banks overcame information asymmetry by collecting information on applicants, not by owning the applicants.[144] They did so cost-effectively by specializing in information collection, taking advantage of economies of scale, and keeping loan maturities short.

Most early U.S. banks rarely lent sums for long terms. Even when they did, the money was subject to call every few months. Banks did not lend much for long terms because they did not have to; other institutions developed to intermediate long-term lending. The least studied of those institutions was the government loan office. Although, unlike their colonial predecessors, they did not issue their own notes, government loan offices in New York, Pennsylvania, and elsewhere lent large sums, for long terms, at low interest, to yeomen and artisans. When properly managed, loan offices took applications, verified applicants' property claims, and apportioned mortgages accordingly. Like colonial and confederation loan offices, they undoubtedly contributed to capital deepening in the areas where they operated.[145] Unfortunately, at the legislated maximum interest rate there were usually more applicants than could be accommodated. Commissioners therefore used a nonprice mechanism to determine who received loans and who did not. Conscientious commissioners lent to the safest risks. Less scrupulous commissioners, however, made loan decisions based on political or other favors, a clear case of the principal-agent problem. Such loans were not as economically beneficial as loans made on sound business principles, and many contemporaries knew it.[146]

[142]Wright 1997a, 1997b, 1998a; Crothers 1997; Karmel 1999.
[143]Lamoreaux 1994. [144]Wright 1999a; Lockard 2000.
[145]Schweitzer 1987; Kaminski 1972:76, 159.
[146]Albany Balance, 9 March 1810; Van Vechten to Fowler, 10 August 1786, Van Vechten Correspondence, 1780–1835, James T. Mitchell Collection, HSP; Laws of the State of New York (1808), chapter 24; Farmers' Loan and Trust Company Papers, CUSC.

The pinnacle of long-term business financing was the capital market – the market for equities and long-term debt instruments. Entrepreneurs sold standardized shares of their businesses to investors. Unlike colonial entrepreneurs, early national entrepreneurs could offer limited liability to investors. If a corporation failed, in other words, each investor was responsible only to the extent of his or her investment, not all of the firm's debts, as in noncorporate business firms.[147] The payments for those shares constituted the concern's working capital, a loan that the corporation had to repay only when it ceased to exist. As we have seen, investors were willing to enter such arrangements because they realized that they could sell their shares at fair prices to other investors virtually at will.

Governments – federal, state, and local – found that they could defer taxes by selling interest-bearing debt certificates to investors. After Alexander Hamilton's financial reforms restored the public's confidence in government debt, which was badly shaken during and after the Revolution, national, state, and city governments issued long-term debt in order to finance wars, territory purchases, and infrastructure projects like waterworks and canals. By the 1830s, corporations, especially transportation companies like railroads, noticed the idea and began to raise funds by issuing corporate bonds in addition to the usual sales of equities. The amount of money raised through sales of equity and debt was enormous by the standards of the day. By 1840 hundreds of corporations, and even some unincorporated companies, including banks, insurance companies, transportation concerns, factories, mining companies, hotels, and theaters, had borrowed hundreds of millions of dollars, for indefinite periods, to finance their operations.[148]

Those companies made the economy more efficient (increased output per unit of input). The processes by which they did so are well understood. Sometimes they developed or implemented new technologies or organizational schemes. At other times, the companies simply grew larger and broader, using economies of scale and scope to become more efficient.[149] In all cases, financial institutions and markets provided entrepreneurs with the funds that they needed to implement their ideas. Some specific examples may serve to clarify this point. After the Revolutionary War in northern Virginia and many other places in the country, a sort of "projecting spirit" for economic development suffused the thoughts and actions of many businesspeople.[150] Because those businesspeople were generally long on ideas but short on cash, that spirit of enterprise may have been lost to inertia. The

[147]Perkins 1994.
[148]Sylla, Wilson, and Wright 2002; Fenstermaker 1965; Evans 1948.
[149]Chandler 1990.   [150]Crothers 1997, 1999.

emerging, dynamic financial system, however, gave those businesspeople means of raising money to implement projects like canals and turnpikes, which scholars have long considered important elements of economic growth.[151] Similarly, entrepreneurs like Philadelphia tin manufacturer Thomas Passmore used the financial system to improve their businesses; however, not until the 1790s, when Passmore gained access to bank discounts, was he able to implement a plan to extend his customer base into new markets, including several southern states.[152] Finally, even merchants primarily engaged in the foreign carrying trade made extensive use of the financial sector for short-term financing, to hypothecate securities to obtain longer trade loans, and to make safe investments during business cycle downturns or trade stagnations caused by war or government regulations. In short, by 1800 the financial sector aided almost the entire market-oriented part of the economy, from farmers using corporate turnpikes or canals to get goods to market, to artisans and nascent manufacturers who obtained bank loans or ground rents, to merchants who used the new financial securities to facilitate domestic, foreign, and carrying trade commerce.

The National Bank and the Panic of 1792

The most salient aspects of the financial revolution were the first Bank of the United States and the Panic of 1792. The BUS, part of Hamilton's financial reform package, was a large, but not all-powerful, force in the early U.S. economy. Under the leadership of Hamilton, and the stewardship of President Thomas Willing, the BUS was the primary agent of federal monetary policy. The BUS and the U.S. Treasury, acting in concert, created essentially a central bank. Together, they exerted considerable influence over other banks and the securities markets. In fact, the BUS-treasury team first initiated, then stopped, the Panic of 1792, the first test of the young nation's new financial system. Later, the central banking system stopped inflation and prudently acted as a lender of last resort.

The Economic Role of the First Bank of the United States

The BUS helped to regulate the nation's money supply, which by 1800 was mostly composed of bank notes and demand deposits.[153] Bank notes were the bearer promissory notes (liabilities) of banks,

[151] Taylor 1958.
[152] Smith 1776: book 1, chapter 1. Passmore's business can be traced in great detail by consulting the Thomas Passmore Record Books. His bank accounts can be found in the Bank of North America Records, Individual Ledgers. Both sources are in the H.S.P.
[153] This section is based on Cowen 2000a, 2000b.

designed to circulate from hand to hand without endorsement, like cash. They were not a legal tender, like coins (specie), but enjoyed extensive circulation. By emitting notes of higher value than the coins in their vaults (fractional reserve banking), early banks increased the nation's money supply. In retrospect, the system of bank notes fared far better than many early experiments with fiat government paper money like bills of credit, the value of which depended on legislators' desire to tax their constituents. Just as the theory of information asymmetry predicts, the market could better judge the credit of a bank, a private institution beholden to its stockholders, than the composition and disposition of future legislatures.

Of course, some degree of information asymmetry between the general public and early banks still existed; many feared that banks would emit too many promises and be unable to redeem their notes with specie in a timely fashion. In other words, the public did not know what a particular bank's reserve ratio was, or if that ratio was adequate. The BUS, however, helped to reduce that asymmetry.

The BUS was by far the largest and most ubiquitous of the early banks, most of which were single "units" bereft of branches. Its capital, $10 million, was enormous for the day. Additionally, it had fully functional branches in Boston, New York, Baltimore, and Charleston, South Carolina, and later in New Orleans, Washington, D.C., and elsewhere. Government deposits further swelled the size of the national bank. "The large amount of public deposits," Treasury Secretary Albert Gallatin noted, "necessarily gives a more than usual preponderance to the Bank of the United States over other Banks." Indeed, by 1800 the BUS boasted of assets in excess of $28.5 million.[154]

Whenever the BUS in the course of its business, collecting loan repayments or accepting deposits, came into ownership of the notes of another bank, it returned the notes to the issuing bank for redemption in specie rather than suffer the note to remain outstanding. By insisting on rapid redemption, the BUS prevented the state-chartered banks from emitting too many notes. "The old Bank never overtraded," Thomas Willing told a correspondent in 1815, "neither was it possible for any other institution to do so and preserve its credit for a day." The BUS, in other words, freed the market from monitoring every bank in the rapidly growing system. As long as the BUS was functioning properly, chances were that the notes of any U.S. bank were literally as good as gold. Bank notes, in other words, enjoyed a wider geographical circulation thanks to the BUS's redemption policy.

The BUS also directly aided regional money movements; its notes and postnotes enjoyed a national circulation. Additionally, it sold drafts

[154]Wettereau 1985.

on its branches. The easy movement of funds from city to city greatly aided the securities markets. An investor in Boston desirous of buying securities in Baltimore, for instance, could remit the notes of state banks, BUS notes, or a draft on the BUS-Baltimore purchased at the BUS-Boston.

The government used the BUS likewise. Revenue sources and disbursement sites were rarely the same. The BUS and its branch system helped the government shift funds from major revenue centers like Philadelphia and New York to places like the western frontier, where purchases had to be made.

The BUS helped the economy in other ways as well. For example, the BUS safeguarded government funds. A stockholder-owned institution with scores of directors and dozens of officers, the BUS was full of checks and balances that prevented fraudulent use of government monies. That was a major improvement over the colonial period, which was rife with financial scandals perpetrated by colonial and county treasurers. The corporate structure of the BUS, in other words, reduced moral hazard, ensuring that the new national government would suffer no pecuniary losses due to embezzlement.[155]

Governments, like firms, sometimes need to anticipate future revenues. Moreover, like firms, governments can do so by borrowing on bond in the capital market or by obtaining a bank loan. The BUS provided the government with the latter, especially in the early years of the Republic, before sufficient tax revenue systems were in place. At one point in 1795 the U.S. government owed the BUS $5.5 million, or over half its capital.

A Central Banking Regime Emerges

In today's Federal Reserve System, a series of Reserve banks throughout the country act as agents of the central banker, the chairman of the board of governors, currently Alan Greenspan. The early nation's system was quite similar. The BUS and its branches served as a *central bank*; the secretary of the treasury was the de facto *central banker*, charged with maintaining macroeconomic stability. As a private institution, the BUS was staunchly independent, an important trait for central banks.[156] Its private ownership, however, did not prevent the BUS from foregoing profits in order to implement the treasury's policies. Of course, the BUS was not unusually magnanimous; it did the treasury's bidding in order to retain government deposits.

[155] The best discussion of how bank governance procedures reduced moral hazard that I have seen is Bodenhorn 2002.
[156] Mishkin 2000.

Throughout its existence, the BUS helped the treasury to contain state banks, although many believed that the practice limited the national bank's profitability. One BUS-Boston president put it this way: "We are charged with doing injury to other Banks by draining them of their specie and retaining it by the limitation of our discounts. Now is there any man of sense who does not see that there is a sacrifice of our profit to the public safety?" The BUS sacrificed profits to the general good in other ways too. For example, it opened branches in suboptimal places, such as newly acquired New Orleans, in order to aid federal revenue collection. Also, rather than export specie out of the country, it sometimes bought bills of exchange for prices above the specie ship point, in other words at a price so high that it would have been cheaper for the bank to denude the nation of its supplies of precious metal.

Most important, the BUS acted as a lender of last resort. It lent to the BONY during the Panic of 1792, for example, and saved the Columbia Bank of Washington, D.C., from bankruptcy in 1801. It did not aid all failing financial institutions because the Treasury Department understood the moral-hazard problem involved in acting as a lender of last resort too often. "Government cannot be supposed," Gallatin persuasively argued, "to become on that account pledged for the folly, knavery or imprudence of every small Bank."

The Treasury's concerns were similar to the Federal Reserve's concerns today. Early secretaries of the treasury, like the modern chairman of the board of governors, sought to keep close tabs on the aggregate price level. In 1795, for example, the BUS curtailed loans in response to the treasury's inflation fears. Specie exports, high corporate dividends, and "inordinate Prices" (the wholesale price index jumped from 102 in 1793 to 131 in 1795) induced the treasury to pressure the BUS to put the brakes on the economy by reducing its lending. The tactic worked.

The treasury also concerned itself with easing potential liquidity crises. In 1805, for instance, Gallatin informed Willing that:

> I have within these two days, received information from several quarters, intimating that the actual scarcity of specie in New York, combined with the conduct of the directors of the Manhattan Bank, might be attended with some danger, as it has already with great inconvenience, to the commercial interest of that city generally. . . . You must be sensible that a very sudden & great diminution of discounts by any of the considerable Banks might cause distress and ruin to many.

Gallatin moved quickly to ease the New York money market, ordering the BUS to shift $200,000 to the Manhattan Bank from banks in Philadelphia and Rhode Island. Gallatin also ordered Willing to "support also the Manhattan and New York Banks." Again, the central banker, with the help of the BUS, succeeded.

The Panic of 1792

The central bankers and bank were not always quite so successful. The first major episode of the secretary of the treasury acting as a central banker, in fact, triggered the infamous Panic of 1792. William Duer and other speculators, who usually take the blame for the panic, were proximate causes of the downturn. Its root cause was a credit restriction initiated by Hamilton in his role as central banker. Hamilton ordered the BUS to restrict credit in February 1792 because "the superstructure of Credit," as he put it, "is now too vast for the foundation. It must be gradually brought within more reasonable dimensions or it will tumble." Hamilton, like Greenspan today, sought to engineer a soft landing for an economy that had grown overheated. When the BUS curbed its loans, other banks had to follow suit for fear of falling too deeply indebted to the central bank. According to Philadelphia broker Clement Biddle, "not only the National Bank but the Bank of NY & the Bank of N.A. all restrained their Discounts within very narrow limits about the same time wch. Occasioned the greatest Demand for Money."

The balance sheets of the BUS tell the same tale; the bills discounted dropped from $2,675,441 on 31 January to $2,051,564 on 9 March. The BNA also restricted lending, by some 7 percent, at the end of February and the beginning of March.[157]

The banks, apparently at Hamilton's prompting, refused to continue loans to speculators. Speculator Alexander Macomb, for example, told a correspondent that "the National Bank have taken the conduct of things in such a light, that they refuse the paper of all those persons [speculators]. The New York Bank does the same in a great degree." The result was to force speculators to sell securities at ruinously low prices in order to raise cash to repay their bank obligations. BONY director Daniel McCormick noted that the BUS "checked without mercy on Application for renewal and [have] been the means of bringing a quantity of paper [securities] into the market suddenly and of course lowered the prices." Indeed, prices of U.S. Sixes dropped from a high of about 120 in January 1792 to just over par (100) in March. U.S. Threes similarly plummeted, from 70 in January to 60 in March. After the failure of speculator William Duer in mid-March, the markets began to break down and panic ensued. Stephen Higginson noted that the banks were "short," that credit was "low among speculators," and that there were "no steady prices to anything." Everyone wished

[157]Balance Sheets, Bank of North America Records, HSP.

to sell and no one wished to buy, until, that is, the central banker and his central bank stepped in.

BUS cashier John Kean and other BUS officials knew that someone had to add liquidity to the system. "In these stormy times it requires great attention and prudent cautious measures tempered at the same time with as liberal an extension of credit as the funds of the institution & other circumstances will admit of," he argued. "Credit which was a short time ago pampered and overfed," he continued, "is now sick very sick indeed & requires tender nursing and renovating cordials to keep her from totally expiring." When Hamilton approached the BUS for aid, therefore, the central bank stood ready.

Hamilton's main goal was to restore faith in government securities and allow the market to correct itself through arbitrage after the restoration of liquidity to the money market. He did so brilliantly, purchasing U.S. securities in the open market while simultaneously persuading state banks to lend more freely. He accomplished the latter feat by promising state banks increased government deposits and by encouraging them to accept U.S. securities at par as collateral for loans. Hamilton further bolstered the securities market by allowing purchasers of the government's guilder bills (bills of exchange drawn on Holland, the proceeds of a loan) to buy them on credit upon the hypothecation of U.S. securities. Finally, Hamilton helped to draft the Buttonwood Agreement, the contract that created the forerunner of the New York Stock Exchange, in a successful attempt to persuade securities brokers and dealers to regulate their own industry. All of those actions decreased uncertainty and the risks of information asymmetry, leading to an influx of arbitrage funds that stopped the skid in securities prices. Confidence was restored quickly, and the economy steamed forward.

Nevertheless, many supporters of the young nation's new financial regime feared that their political opponents would use the panic to excite "public indignation" sufficient to "demolish all the money systems of our country."[158] Although the regulatory response to the panic was inconsequential, most policy makers understood that the panic proved the tremendous power of the nation's new financial system, not its weakness. Market forces like arbitrage, coupled with sound central banking theories, and a powerful central banking system, allowed the central banker, Hamilton, to easily correct the Panic. Most policy makers also understood that speculation was a good sign, not a problem. As Hamilton explained to William Short, U.S. loan agent in Europe, speculation arose from speculators' belief in the government's ability to pay off the national debt with ease. "The moderate size of the

[158]George Cabot to Israel Thorndike, 19 March 1792, mss. 781 – 1792 U58, BLHU.

domestic debt of the United States," he wrote, "appears to have created the most intemperate ideas of speculation in the minds of a very few persons, whose natural ardor has been encreased by great success in some of the early stages of the melioration of the market value of the Stock." Speculation and fluctuating prices, in other words, spoke well for the nation's excellent credit, which was unsullied by the panic.

The panic also showed that early U.S. financial markets were already quite transparent, despite the lack of a Securities and Exchange Commission–like regulatory body. Although some unscrupulous brokers did make false or "sham" sales in order to influence prices, newspaper editors made note of the fact, and few market participants suffered losses as a result. False price information was occasionally reported throughout the rest of the century, but competitors, editors, and stock boards kept the fraudulent practice at a minimum.[159]

The U.S. government itself also deserves praise for keeping the market informed of its revenues, expenditures, and debts. Most of the information it produced was reliable and widely disseminated. There is little wonder in this. The new nation's politicians, after all, were steeped in the theory of information asymmetry, though they did not call it such. Most of the debates in the constitutional conventions revolved around the best way to reduce the principal-agent problem in government. In the Lockean tradition, citizens considered themselves the principals (owners) of the nation and considered politicians mere agents entrusted to manage the nation in the interest of its owners. Americans rightly believed that the federal nature of the governance system and the sundry checks and balances of the federal and state constitutions would keep government from turning predatory. Investors, therefore, used the government's data to make business projections with full confidence.

[159]John Hickling, *Men and Idioms of Wall Street: Explaining the Daily Operations in Stocks, Bonds and Gold* (New York: John Hickling, 1875), 19.

5

Evidence of Capital Market Integration, 1800–1850

Price and securities ownership data show that securities markets rapidly integrated; prices for identical or comparable securities fluctuated in unison and moved closer together over time, and ownership of securities was local, regional, national, and even international. Price integration occurred quickly in the 1790s but suffered minor setbacks in some later periods. In all periods studied, however, the markets behaved rationally, in accordance with the Theory of Portfolio Choice. The markets were also transactionally efficient, as measured by bid-ask spreads; though higher than spreads today, the bid-ask spreads of early U.S. market makers were surprisingly small. Also, as an analysis of stock ownership patterns in antebellum Maine will show, ownership of capital market instruments was geographically integrated. Other scholars have come to similar conclusions using different data and different analyses.[1]

It has taken scholars so long to recognize the integration and efficiency of early national and antebellum capital markets because postbellum capital markets were not very good. Because scholars often assumed that development was linear, it was easy, a priori, to dismiss antebellum capital markets as inefficient. Development, however, was not linear, at least not when it came to financial markets. The death of a few million men, the destruction or emancipation of millions of dollars worth of property, the implementation of new banking and currency systems, and the near destruction of the Constitution were the causes of postbellum capital market inefficiencies, not endemic financial backwardness.

Brief Descriptions of the Major Securities Markets

All of the major U.S. securities markets followed much the same development path as the London securities market but did so much more quickly. At first, buyers and sellers searched for each other directly, perhaps in person, then through newspaper advertisements.

[1] Most notably Bodenhorn 2000 and Majewski 2000.

Soon after, brokers appeared. They reduced search costs for both buyers and sellers, taking a small commission in return. Soon after that, brokers began to act, at least at times, as dealers (market makers), buying and selling securities on their own account. In the larger, more active northern markets, the broker-dealers created formal stock exchanges, self-regulatory membership-based organizations. Indeed, Philadelphia and New York developed stock exchanges before London. It took many decades, however, for the exchanges to monopolize the secondary securities market. Significant amounts of trading occurred "out of doors," "at the curb," "in the alley," or "under the tree" throughout the period of this study. That is why the emphasis here is on the securities *markets*, not the exchanges.

New York

New York is the early nation's most studied securities market.[2] By 1825 it was the largest capital market in the United States. Even in the early 1790s, however, when Boston and especially Philadelphia still posed credible threats, New York possessed the nation's most important market. The other markets usually looked to New York for price signals. Philadelphians and Bostonians both recognized that fact early on. In June 1791, for example, Stephen Higginson of Boston noted that the price of securities in Boston "will depend chiefly on the course of the York market."[3] As early as January 1790, Philadelphia broker Clement Biddle admitted that securities prices "are and will be for some time governed by New York."[4] In late April of that year, Biddle still believed that the New York market "entirely governed" the Philadelphia market, albeit with a lag of "two Days."[5] New York's lead apparently never was reversed, at least for long.

New York was also the most sophisticated market of the young republic. In early January 1790 Biddle admitted that "Dealings" in Philadelphia were "more limited than" in New York. He also noted, as he had twice in 1789,[6] that it was "out of all question making any Contract here for Certificates at a future Day or even buying on a Credit by best houses." Philadelphia, he later explained, possessed "few monied men ... who speculate out of the Beaten Tract."[7] That was in sharp

[2] Werner and Smith 1991.
[3] Stephen Higginson to LeRoy & Bayard, 21 June 1791, Gratz, Old Congress, HSP.
[4] Clement Biddle to Robert Gilchrist, 24 January 1790, Clement Biddle Letter Book, HSP.
[5] Clement Biddle to John Dougherty, 29 April 1790, William Rogers, 29 April 1790, ibid.
[6] Clement Biddle to John Groves, 12 June 1789, to George Joy, 9 September 1789, ibid.
[7] Clement Biddle to Robert Gilchrist, 14 March 1790, ibid.

contrast to New York, where time contracts were already widespread.[8]
The following securities sales list, from *The Diary, or Loudon's Register*
of 6 March 1792, is an excellent example of the sophistication of the
New York market at that time:

sales of stock at auction yesterday at noon	
6s for cash	24/3
d now p 10th March	24/4 – 24/5.75
d now p 9th inst.	24/5.5
d now p 30 days	25/9.25
d now p 13 March	24/4.25
d now p 13 April	26/2
p&d 10 June	26/2.5
p&d 25 June	26/3
3s for cash	13/9 – 13/10.75
d tomorrow p 20 March	14/4
p&d on Wednesday	13/9.75
d now p 15 April	14/8
deferred for cash	14/7.75 – 14/10.5
d now p 15 March	15/
d now p 15 April	15/7.25
B.U.S. 1/2s for cash	200.5 – 195.5
p&d on Friday	198 – 198.5
p&d 15 March	201.25 – 192
d now p in 30 days	208.25 – 197.25
p&d 10 April	207.75 – 297
15 April	210.5 – 197.25
21 May	215
23 May	214.5 – 216.25
2 June	217.75 – 211.5
10 June	219 – 219.25
25 June	219.25 – 220
3/4 shares 15 June	186
manufacturing scripts for cash	$55

P stood for "payable," d for "deliverable," / for "shilling," and other
abbreviations for various types of U.S. bonds, BUS stock, or Society
for the Establishment of Useful Manufactures (SEUM) stock. The list
shows that New Yorkers bought securities on credit (d now, p in the
future at a price fixed now), by forward contract (p&d in the future at
a price fixed now), and by straight cash sale.

---

[8]Clement Biddle to Robert Gilchrist, 6 January 1790, ibid.; *Pennsylvania Gazette*, 2 March
1791.

The published lists of securities traded in New York were extensive. By 1825, for example, the *New York Prices Current* regularly listed more than 100 securities, some issued by upstate and out of state corporations. The New York market also soon came to dominate trading volumes.

Philadelphia

Philadelphia enjoyed one of the first, largest, and most active of the nation's securities markets. Listed securities, which numbered just 8 in 1795, grew to almost 50 by 1825, and about 120 by 1835. Trading volumes and the number of nonlisted securities traded were second only to New York.

The securities market in Philadelphia suffered from periodic liquidity problems during yellow fever epidemics and long, cold winters that froze the Delaware River and thereby reduced Philadelphia's share of international trade.[9] In addition, Philadelphia investors tended to be much more conservative than their New York counterparts. When Philadelphia brokers finally began quoting securities prices in decimal percentages of par (base 10), rather than in pound and shilling percentages of par (base 20 in shillings or base 240 in pence), they felt obliged to publish copious conversion tables so as "to prevent any inconvenience which may arise to those who have been habituated to the *old method.*"[10] The tables were wholly unnecessary on computational grounds; an old quotation of 10 shillings in the pound was simply rendered as 50 percent (10/20 = 50 in shilling terms or 120/240 = 50 in pence terms).

Whatever their faults, Philadelphia investors made heavy investments in federal debt instruments and both national banks. For example, on 1 January 1820 Philadelphians owned $43.5 million of the $90.4 million U.S. national debt – more than investors in New York, Boston, or any other U.S. city or foreign country held. About the same time, Philadelphians owned 37,269 shares in the SBUS, about 3,000 shares fewer than New Yorkers owned, and 1,000 shares fewer than Baltimoreans, but over 10,000 more than held in Massachusetts, and far more than owned elsewhere.[11]

Boston

The Boston capital market had a big head start on other cities. British regulations forced late colonial Massachusetts to borrow money

[9] Thomas Forrest, P. Baynton, Benjamin R. Morgan, James Ash, to President & Directors of the Bank of the United States, 20 September 1798, Etting Collection, HSP.
[10] *Poulson's American Daily Advertiser,* 4 November 1800.
[11] Carey Manuscripts, LCP.

rather than to emit tax anticipation script (bills of credit), as other colonies could. Although other colonies, most notably Pennsylvania,[12] issued small amounts of bonds, colonial Massachusetts, led by Thomas Hutchinson, had by far the biggest, and most successful, public debt issues. According to contemporary accounts, the bonds were liquid and virtually riskless:

> The Provincial Notes of the Massachusetts Bay, are in such high Esteem and Repute that they are all in the Hands of Gentlemen of Fortune, who really make Interest to secure them to themselves, and give Cash in the Room of them; That Government has been so very punctual in paying the Interest Annually, and the Credit of the Province being pledged in Security, every Gentleman chooses to get his Monies into that Bank if he can, as he knows that at any Time that he Wants to turn his Notes into Cash he may do it.[13]

Despite its head start, the Boston market appears to have lagged behind those of New York and Philadelphia. In 1795 Boston papers listed 6 securities. In 1810 the number stood at 9, in 1820 at 15, and in 1830 at 19. Not until the 1840s did the Boston market fully blossom. In 1844 the *Boston Shipping List* quoted prices for over 120 securities, including 31 varieties of national, state, municipal, and corporate bonds, and the equities of 24 banks, 19 insurance companies, 19 railroads, 26 manufacturers, and some 17 miscellaneous securities. Thanks to stockbroker Joseph Martin, scholars know much about the late antebellum Boston securities market.[14]

Volume figures for Boston, however, remain elusive. Lists of sales by individual brokers published in the *Boston Courier* between 1837 and 1843 suggest that trading in equities was sometimes heavy. In just those six years, the broker sold almost 70,000 shares in some 200 different varieties of bank, insurance, railroad, steamboat, manufacturing, and trading company stocks – many of them, of course, not listed in the commercial papers.

Baltimore

Baltimore was home to the South's largest and most active securities market. Scattered evidence indicates that securities trading in Baltimore began at least by 1789[15] and was well established by 1798,[16]

---

[12] Wright 1996.   [13] *New Hampshire Gazette*, 12 November 1773.
[14] Martin and Barron 1975.
[15] *Maryland Journal*, 28 September, 14 December 1789, 30 August 1791; *Maryland Gazette*, 24 February, 3 March 1791.
[16] *Federal Gazette & Baltimore Daily Advertiser*, 6, 17 January, 14 February, 7 April 1798.

after commercial control had been wrested from rival Annapolis, where limited securities trading also took place.[17] Regular newspaper quotations, which began in 1803, continued at least until the Civil War. In 1803 the papers listed 4 varieties of federal bonds, 4 bank stocks, and the equities of 3 insurance companies. By 1830 Baltimore papers listed 6 debt instruments, and the equities of 11 banks, 7 insurance companies, and 9 transportation companies. The following is a list of the miscellaneous and road securities from the 17 October 1829 *Baltimore Price Current*:

Miscellaneous:
    City Corporation 6s
    City Corporation 5s
    State 5s
    Annuities
    Water Company Stock
    Union Manufacturing Co.
    Gas Light Co.
    Temascaltepec Co.
    Tlalcotal Mining
    Cerralvo Mining
    N.C. Gold Mining
    Masonic Hall 6s
    Screw Dock Co. Stock
    Maryland and Virginia Steam Navigation
    Pennsylvania, Delaware and Maryland Steam Navigation
    Baltimore & Potomac Steam Line
    Alexandria, Washington & Georgetown Line
    Baltimore Flint Glass Co.
    Baltimore Shot Tower Co.
    Phoenix Shot Tower
Road Stocks:
    Reistertown
    Frederick
    York
    Washington and Baltimore
    Baltimore and Harford
    Baltimore and Ohio Railroad
    Baltimore and Susquehanna Rail Road

Over the entire period 1803 to 1850, Baltimore papers listed 20 different varieties of debt instruments, and the equities of 31 banks, 20 insurance companies, 25 transportation companies, 2 utilities, and a

[17]Papenfuse 1975.

dozen miscellaneous stocks, including shares of theaters, shot towers, a flint glass company, other manufacturing concerns, mines, and trading companies.

Again, trading volumes have been elusive. Indications of trading activity from the *Baltimore Telegraph and Mercantile Advertiser*, however, suggest that trading was *active*, if not heavy. Between 1 March and 28 June 1815, the paper listed prices of 544 securities (32 different securities for 17 weeks). The newspaper listed only 159 securities, slightly less than 30 percent, as not having traded in the previous week.

Charleston, South Carolina

Regular price quotations for securities traded in Charleston begin in April 1803, although a few sporadic quotations from the eighteenth century have also been found, and literary sources make clear that there were several active dealers by the early 1790s.[18] In 1803 U.S. Eight Percent bonds, U.S. Sixes, Navy Sixes, and U.S. Threes were listed, in addition to South Carolina Six and Three Percent bonds, South Carolina discount bonds, and shares of the BUS, the South Carolina Bank, and the State Bank of South Carolina. The breadth of the market was largely stagnant for several decades; the depth of the market is unknown. At various times, however, newspapers noted that "Stocks of all kinds, and Bank Shares, are still much in demand" in the Charleston market.[19]

Beginning in the 1830s the numbers of listed securities slowly grew. In 1835 the newspapers listed 7 bank stocks; a decade later, they listed 10. The number of listed insurance companies, however, remained at only 2 over that period. The heyday of the antebellum South Carolina insurance industry was the early 1820s, when 3 were listed. The Charleston transportation market was also thin. Only 3 transportation companies – a bridge company, a railroad company, and the Santee Canal Company – enjoyed listed securities. Not until 1849 did the newspapers list the first utility company, a gas firm. In early 1810 the papers also listed a theater company for a short time.

Richmond, Norfolk, and Other Virginia Cities

Securities markets existed in cities in northern Virginia, including Alexandria, Washington, D.C., and Georgetown. Newspaper quotations, however, were sporadic at best, though the prices of shares in the Alexandria Bank and Potomac Bank in Alexandria have been discovered for the period 1806–14.

[18] See the George Nelson Letter Book, UNCSC.
[19] *Grotjan's Philadelphia Prices Current*, 25 September 1815.

Richmond and Norfolk were much fuller markets, at least in terms of newspaper coverage. Indeed, the earliest Richmond quotations date from 1786.[20] Between at least 1804 and 1819, Norfolk's securities market was important enough for newspaper editors to take notice. Papers at first listed three securities: the equities of the Bank of Virginia, the BUS, and the Norfolk Marine Insurance Company. After the War of 1812, listed securities included the old shares of the bank of Virginia, that bank's new issue, Farmers' Bank shares, SBUS shares, and shares in the Marine Insurance Company and the Union Insurance Company.

Quotations for Richmond begin in earnest in 1815. Richmond and Norfolk seem to have battled for predominance until 1839, when the number of equities listed in Richmond papers jumped from 4 to 7. Thereafter, Richmond's dominance was clear. By 1855 Richmond papers listed the prices of Virginia state bonds, the bonds of the cities of Richmond, Petersburg, Lynchburg, and Norfolk, the bonds of 10 railroads, and the equities of 4 banks, 3 insurance companies, 1 gas company, and 6 transportation companies, including 5 railroads. Even at times in Richmond in the late antebellum period, however, newspapers were more likely to quote securities prices in Baltimore, Philadelphia, or New York than prices of Virginia securities in Virginia markets.

New Orleans

New Orleans also had a securities market, but the city papers were not always keen on publishing prices, especially between 1838 and 1845. During the 1820s the listed securities were the equities of the Louisiana State Bank, the Orleans Bank, the SBUS, the Bank of Louisiana, the Louisiana State Insurance Company, the Louisiana Insurance Company, the Orleans Insurance Company, the Orleans Navigation Company, the Mississippi Marine and Fire Insurance Company, and the Consolidated Association. The business of the last is unknown, as is the depth of the Louisiana market. By 1835 the securities lists had grown to about 30 issues, a dozen of which were bank equities. Other issuers included 10 insurance companies, 3 transportation companies, and 2 cotton press firms.

Overall, the southern securities markets were smaller than their northern counterparts, in absolute terms, per capita, and per dollar of sectional aggregate output. Given the stylized fact that southern investors put all of their savings into land and slaves, however, it is extremely interesting that the South had any securities markets at all. More detailed studies of the southern markets are certainly in

---

[20] *Virginia Independent Chronicle* (Richmond), 13, 20 September 1786.

order and may yield insights into the causes of the region's divergent economic path.[21]

Other Domestic Markets

Securities, even national ones, traded, at least occasionally, in other urban U.S. areas too, including Albany, New York;[22] Providence, Rhode Island;[23] Wilmington, Delaware;[24] and Hartford, Connecticut.[25] For national securities, however, investors often turned to the larger, thicker U.S. markets. As discussed in Chapter 6, local securities also traded in many towns but only occasionally left traces in the newspapers.

London

U.S. securities traded in Europe in the late 1780s[26] and were ubiquitous in London as early as 1792.[27] Passage of the Jay Treaty gave added impetus to the trade.[28] In May 1795 a Londoner wrote that the "nature" of U.S. securities was "fully known to many brokers in this city."[29] The brokers, with the help of pamphlets like Thomas Fortune's *Epitome of the Stocks* series,[30] stayed abreast of details concerning U.S. securities. More than 50 price quotations of U.S. securities in London have been found in U.S. newspapers. By the 1810s several London prices current regularly published the prices of U.S. securities in London. U.S. securities also occasionally traded in Britain's provincial exchanges,[31] and direct sales of securities from U.S. brokers to non-Londoners, including English investors in the West Indies, were not unheard of.[32] Shares of large state chartered banks also traded in London.[33]

---

[21] Majewski 2000 makes a good start in this direction.

[22] Farmers' Loan and Trust to G. B. Throop, 10 May 1837, Farmers' Loan and Trust Company Letter Book, CUSC.

[23] *Providence Gazette and Country Journal,* 18 January 1794.

[24] *Delaware and Eastern Shore Advertiser,* 21 February 1795.

[25] *Connecticut Courant,* 23 February, 26 October 1795, 19 June 1797.

[26] See the Clement Biddle Letter Book, HSP, for conclusive proof.

[27] "If you will inform me the prices of American Stock in London I shall be obliged to you." George Nelson to Mr. Lambert, 2 June 1792, George Nelson Letter Book, UNCSC.

[28] *Pennsylvania Gazette,* 4 February 1795.

[29] *Philadelphia Gazette of the United States,* 22 May 1795.

[30] Thomas Fortune, *An Epitome of the Stocks* (London, 1796, 1802, 1810, 1824, 1833, 1838).

[31] Michie 1981.

[32] Edmond Britten to Thomas Biddle, 26 March 1810, Thomas Wright Jr. to Thomas Biddle, 15 October 1814, Business Correspondence, Incoming, 1800–14; Thomas Wright to Thomas Biddle, 22 February 1815, Business Correspondence, Incoming, 1815–17, Thomas A. Biddle Papers, HSP.

[33] *Report and Observations on the Banks, and Other Incorporated Institutions in the State of New York* (New York: William Mercein, 1828).

Price Comparisons between Markets

Early U.S. securities markets were price-integrated. Prices in each market, in other words, moved up and down together, and price differences between markets were usually small. If a local economy heated up, funds quickly and easily flowed in from elsewhere to help meet the increased demand. Liquid investment instruments flowed freely from state to state, region to region, and even nation to nation. Consider what occurred when business activity increased in a particular area, say, Philadelphia. At first, because entrepreneurs sought more money than was available, interest rates increased. Increased rates decreased the prices of debt instruments in the Philadelphia market. (The price of bonds and interest rates are inversely proportional. As interest rates increase, the market prices of coupon bonds sink to keep yields in line with market interest rates. The yield of a bond purchased at its face value that pays 6 percent interest once a year is 6 percent. That same instrument, purchased at half of its face value, essentially gives to the purchaser twice the instrument's coupon rate, in this case, 12 percent. This is because the purchaser paid only $50 for an instrument that pays $6 per year interest.) Arbitrageurs in other markets, say, New York and Baltimore, saw the price decrease as a buying opportunity. They bought the securities low in Philadelphia for resale at a higher price in their home markets. Because of those purchases, several things happened. First, the increased demand for securities in Philadelphia tended to raise their price. Second, the increased supply of securities in Baltimore and New York tended to decrease securities prices in those places. Finally, money (in the form of specie, bank notes, or, in most cases, simply credits) flowed from Baltimore and New York to Philadelphia. That money, of course, lowered commercial interest rates in Philadelphia by increasing the money supply there. Philadelphia entrepreneurs could then acquire the loans they needed in order to make their businesses more efficient. For example, in the second week of February 1803, Six Percent U.S. bonds cost $95.75 per $100 par value in Philadelphia. At the same time, those same bonds cost $98.00 in Baltimore and $100 in Boston. Interest rates, in other words, were higher in Philadelphia than in those other two cities. Funds quickly flowed to Philadelphia to buy bonds. By the last week in February, U.S. Six Percents cost $96.00 in Baltimore and $97.50 in both Philadelphia and Boston.[34] Arbitrage, in other words, greatly reduced interest rate differentials. Philadelphians owned more cash, and investors in Baltimore and Boston owned more bonds. The net effect of such transfers was to get money, in a timely fashion, to where it would do the most good, for the lowest cost then possible.

[34] Sylla, Wilson, and Wright 2002.

Similar scenarios played themselves out many times in early America and involved the securities markets of Europe, especially London, as well as those in the United States.[35]

There appear not to have been any specialized arbitrageurs, although many dealers were constantly on the prowl for opportunities.[36] Sellers naturally seeking the highest price for their property did much of the work. In late July 1814, for example, John Jacob Astor instructed William Payne of New York to "transfer $25M Dollars of my Stock to Thomas Biddle and Wharton to be plac'd in the Books at Phila where stocks are better sale than with you. . . . If your market has improved so as that you can dispose of the Stock at 83 then sell it."[37] Clearly, then, for market integration to occur, liquidity must have been adequate, a point that some contemporaries well understood.[38] Bank stocks appear to have gained sufficient liquidity by the early 1790s. In August 1791 Seth Johnson informed Andrew Craigie that the directors of the BUS would likely "be guided in their discounts not by the quantity of Stock standing on the name of any individual but by established credit." "Formerly Stockholders in the Bank of New York had a preference in discounts," he explained, "but since the Stock has become so negotiable in the market this preference has ceased to exist." "The Stock of the National Bank being also negotiable & transferable at the pleasure of the holder," he continued, "the possession of it can give no security to the Bank nor influence the directors in discounts."[39] U.S. public securities were probably at least as liquid as bank stock.

We can begin to look for price integration, therefore, in the 1790s. The method used was to compare average prices of U.S. Six Percent bonds in Boston and Philadelphia, beginning in 1796. Only price quotations dated within two or fewer days of each other were used; 63 such quotations were available. Using the absolute value of the difference between the price in Boston and the price in Philadelphia, the average price difference between the two markets was $1.25, the median $.96. The largest price difference was $3.96, the smallest $.00 Interestingly, the bonds sold at a premium in Boston all but 7 of the observations. Except for the periods from 18 April to 16 May and from 3 November to 5 December, the price differential never exceeded $2.00 for more than a few days. In Boston, prices of Sixes that year ranged from a low of $84.375 to a high of $91.50. In Philadelphia, Sixes ranged between $82.50 and $90.42.[40]

---

[35] Thomas Fortune, *An Epitome of the Stocks* (London, 1796), 56–71.
[36] George Nelson to Samuel Bellamy, 14 July 1791; to Josiah Adams, 25 January 1792, George Nelson Letter Book, UNCSC.
[37] John Jacob Astor to William Payne, 23 July 1814, John Jacob Astor Papers, BLHU.
[38] *Pennsylvania Gazette*, 30 December 1789.
[39] Seth Johnson to Andrew Craigie, 20 August 1791, Andrew Craigie Papers, AAS.
[40] Price quotations are in terms of dollars per $100 face or par value.

In 1800 the same security in the same markets under the same procedure showed somewhat less price integration. Prices diverged by an average of $1.26 and a median of $1.18 over 38 observations. The highest divergence was $4.00, and the prices never got closer than $.08. The bonds again sold at a premium in Boston in all but 4 of the observations. Only from 15 September until 13 October did the price differential exceed $2.00 for more than a few days. In 1800 prices of Sixes ranged from $82.00 to $92.50 in Boston and from $81.67 to $92.75 in Philadelphia.

In 1805 the same test of the same securities and markets showed a further decrease in integration. Prices diverged by an average of $1.89 and a median of $1.75 over 44 observations. The highest divergence was $5.00, the lowest $.00. Bostonians paid a premium for the bonds over Philadelphia in all but one of the observations. Prices diverged by more than $2.00 from the beginning of January until early July; thereafter, the markets were closely matched until late December. Over the course of the year, Sixes ranged from $91.00 to $96.50 in Boston and from $89.00 to $95.50 in Philadelphia.

The year 1810 brought improved price integration. In 32 observations, the prices of Sixes in Boston and Philadelphia differed by an average of $1.30 and a median of $1.125. The highest price divergence was $3.00, and divergences of greater than $2.00 persisted only between 24 September and the end of the available Boston price quotations in early November. Boston again paid a premium most of the time; prices of Sixes were higher in Philadelphia for only 2 observations. The Sixes traded within tight ranges in both cities, from $102.00 to $103.75 in Boston and from $100.50 to $103.00 in Philadelphia.

The War of 1812 – and, more specifically, the fact that Boston banks maintained specie payments while banks in New York and points south and west did not – makes nominal price comparisons of securities, any assets for that matter, impossible between the autumn of 1814 and the end of the depression the Panic of 1819 caused. Tests using adjusted prices, however, have shown a fair degree of price integration.[41] Our analysis of market integration, therefore, resumes with a comparison of prices of shares of the SBUS in Baltimore and Philadelphia between May 1821 and August 1823, inclusive. Over that period, 116 SBUS quotations within a few days of each other were found. The mean absolute difference in SBUS prices between the two markets was just $.56, the median exactly $.50. The price differential exceeded $2.00 only twice; there was no price differential at all 11 percent of the time. SBUS prices over that period ranged between $102.00 and $119.75 in Baltimore and $101.00 and $119.00 in Philadelphia. Investors in the

[41] Sylla, Wilson, and Wright 1997.

latter city paid a premium for SBUS stock 58 times, exactly 50 percent of the sample.

The same test run over the period from May 1825 until December 1826, inclusive, produced similar results, though with fewer (86) observations. The average price difference for SBUS shares was only $.365, the median exactly $.25. The highest price differential was $2.00, and that level was reached only twice, widely separated in time. Over 15 percent of the time, no price differential existed. Over the period of the test, SBUS shares reached as high as $121.00 in Baltimore and $121.50 in Philadelphia and went as low as $112.25 in Baltimore and $112.50 in Philadelphia. Baltimoreans paid a premium 56 percent of the time.

A comparison of prices of U.S. Three Percent bonds in Baltimore and Philadelphia between January 1830 and December 1832 also shows a considerable degree of market integration. In that span, 140 price quotations for Threes in both markets within a few days of each other are available. The absolute value of the differences between the prices in the two markets, the same methodology used in all the preceding tests, was $.525. The median difference was only $.375. Prices in the two markets never differed by more than $2.75 and jumps over $2.00 were rare and short-lived. On 14 occasions, or exactly 10 percent of the time, there was no price difference between the two markets. Prices for Threes were higher in Philadelphia exactly 75 percent of the time.

Given the technological limits of the era, early U.S. securities markets were remarkably price-integrated. Markets in close physical proximity of each other, such as Philadelphia and Baltimore, of course displayed the most price integration, meaning that prices in those two markets for identical securities were usually very close. Price divergences between more distant markets, such as Philadelphia and Boston, were larger but still quite small in dollar and percentage terms. When it came to the national securities – federal bonds and SBUS shares – the early republic's major securities markets were clearly part of a larger national capital market.

Price Movements and the Theory of Portfolio Choice

The Theory of Portfolio Choice predicts that all else being equal, demand for an asset will increase vis-à-vis other assets as the asset becomes relatively safer, relatively more salable, and relatively more profitable. In other words, demand is directly correlated to safety (inversely correlated to risk), liquidity, and expected return. Although demand is difficult to observe directly, the Theory of Portfolio Choice is empirically testable because, ceteris paribus, demand and price are directly related. In other words, increased (decreased) demand leads to increased (decreased) market prices. Securities that become relatively less risky or more easily salable, or that are expected to bring higher returns, therefore, should appreciate in price. Securities that become more risky, that are less salable, or that are expected to bring lower returns, relative to other assets, should depreciate. The prices of securities in early U.S. capital markets moved according to the predictions of the Theory of Portfolio Choice, further evidence of the efficiency of those capital markets. U.S. government bonds, for instance, always traded at a premium (lower yield) compared with municipal (state, county, city) bonds of the same term to maturity and coupon rate. After adjusting for tax considerations, the same is true today: the U.S. government is much less likely to default than a municipality because it had, and has, more comprehensive powers to tax, borrow abroad, and create money than the lower levels of government do.

The securities market of Charleston, South Carolina, is a good place to look for evidence that early securities markets behaved according to the Theory of Portfolio Choice because it was relatively small. While the prices of equities generally moved together in response to changes in macroeconomic conditions, such as interest rates and price levels, which affected all assets of the same class in essentially the same manner, prices moved in opposite directions when firm-specific information became available to the market. For example, in late September 1804 the market learned that the South Carolina Bank was not doing as well as anticipated. The expected return for its shares dropped, causing the market price of its shares to drop from $78 to $73 per share. That same week, shares in the BUS increased from $584 to $600, as some investors liquidated South Carolina Bank shares in order to purchase BUS stock. Similarly, a poorer than expected dividend announcement by the South Carolina Bank in January 1822, when many financial institutions were rebounding from the aftermath of the Panic of 1819, caused South Carolina Bank shares to drop from $62 to $58. Shares of the SBUS and Union Bank (of South Carolina) simultaneously increased $.50, just as the theory predicts.

It is also possible to trace sectoral shifts between bonds and equities. Bond prices and yields (interest rates) were, of course, inversely related. As market interest rates increased, bond prices sank, and vice versa. Banks, on the other hand, typically did quite well during periods of high nominal interest rates and moderate or low inflation or, in other words, during periods of relatively high real interest rates. Prevented by law from charging interest above a certain rate, around 6 or 7 percent in most states, banks could not directly benefit from interest rate increases by charging higher rates. When market rates increased, however, demand for bank loans almost invariably increased, allowing bankers to be more selective and to receive more collateral and concessions from borrowers. When real interest rates increased, therefore, investors eschewed bonds in favor of bank stock. In early July

1830, for example, the price of U.S. Five Percents slipped from $106 to $104 and South Carolina Six Percents dropped from $118 to $117. At the same time, the prices of Union Bank shares jumped to $64 per share from $62, and State Bank shares appreciated from $86 to $90.

The opposite trend also occurred, as investors sometimes fled equities for the relative safety of bonds. Bondholders, after all, are paid before equity holders in case of a downturn in profitability or default. During panics, therefore, investors preferred bonds to stocks, ceteris paribus.

Equities also moved in opposite directions according to the market's evaluation of each issuer's or sector's relative outlook. Between March and August 1810, BUS shares dropped from 125 percent of par to 116 percent of par due to uncertainty over its bid for recharter. Over that same period, Union Bank shares increased from 117.5 to 118.5 percent of par. Other bank shares fluctuated in a narrow range. The real winners of the uncertainty in the banking sector were insurance stocks. During the late spring and summer of 1810, Fire and Marine Insurance shares rose from 115 to 118.5, and Boston Marine insurance shares increased from 120 to 125.

In the early stages of the War of 1812, the opposite trend took place in the Philadelphia market. Shares of marine insurance companies, such as the Insurance Company of Philadelphia and the Insurance Company of North America, plummeted, while shares in solid banks, such the BNA, increased substantially. Marine insurance had become riskier, while banks stood to profit from increased loan demand.

The market also correctly valued risk. The Baltimore market, for instance, correctly placed risk premiums on certain corporate bonds. A number of railroads issued bonds in tranches with different risk levels. Central Ohio Railroad issued four types of bonds, the first class or tranche of which held a first mortgage on the corporation's real estate. The second and third tranches held second and third mortgages, respectively. That meant that, in the event of the corporation's bankruptcy, the holders of such bonds would have received nothing until the holders of the bonds of higher tranches received payment. The fourth and final tranche held claims only to the corporation's revenues. Holders of those fourth-class bonds, in other words, held no lien on real estate at all. The prices of the bonds of the first tranche were *always* higher than the prices of the second tranche, and so on, just as the Theory of Portfolio Choice predicts. The Baltimore and Ohio Railroad (B&O) also issued bonds in classes with varying risks and the market likewise correctly priced them according to risk level. Similarly, the market always priced bonds that some state or city "guaranteed" higher than the unguaranteed bonds of the same issuer. Unbacked bonds of the Northern Central railroad, for instance, were always priced below the Northern Central's guaranteed bonds.

The prices of equities also lagged below the prices of bonds of the same issuer. In June 1853, for instance, B&O equities sold at around 70 percent of par, while B&O bonds of the first class sold for 97.50 percent of par. Why would the market price securities from the same issuer differently? In this case, it did so because in the event of the B&O's bankruptcy, the bondholders of the first tranche would be repaid far before the stockholders, who were invariably residual claimants or the last paid out of the firm's assets.

Evidence of Efficiency: Bid-Ask Spreads

If a financial market is efficient, the spread between the bid price (buyer's price, or dealer's buying price) and the ask price (seller's price, or dealer's selling price) will be low.[42] Unlike brokers, who match buyers with sellers, securities dealers buy and sell securities at stated prices for their own account. In so doing, they make the market for the securities in which they deal liquid. In most circumstances, dealers can accommodate buyers or sellers immediately, though at the cost of a slightly disadvantageous price. Dealers attempting to "make a market" for a particular security, in other words, buy from investors at the bid price and sell to investors at the ask price, pocketing the difference or spread. For example, if an investor wishes to sell 100 shares of a certain bank stock, he or she might use a broker to seek an investor or investors desirous of buying 100 shares of that stock. The matching process might take some time, days or even weeks, to occur, but the seller will pay only a small brokerage fee. An alternative is for the seller immediately to sell the shares to a dealer (market maker) at the market maker's bid price. The market maker then holds the shares, for minutes, hours, days, or longer, until an investor seeks to buy them at the dealer's ask price.

Unlike brokers, who earn a slow but steady commission, dealers or market makers take on significant price risk. They can suffer huge losses if caught holding a large portfolio of a depreciating security. On the other hand, they can also make huge gains if they acquire numerous shares of a security that experiences a rapid appreciation. At any given moment, however, the market maker's gross profit is simply the difference, or spread, between his bid and ask prices.

The smaller the bid-ask spread, therefore, the smaller the gross profits of the market maker and the better the prices for investors. If a market maker attempts to keep the bid-ask spread for a particular security artificially high, other dealers, in the absence of barriers to entry or other anticompetitive factors, will begin to make a market in the security and drive the bid-ask spread down to natural levels.

[42] This section is based on Garg 2000.

What were those natural spread levels? Like the natural price of any other good or service, the natural bid-ask spread is a function of the efficiency of the market. If financial markets are inefficient, subject to wild price swings and high degrees of information asymmetry, market makers will need considerable compensation (a large bid-ask spread) in order to be induced to make a market in specific securities. If, on the other hand, securities markets are stable and fulsome, the natural bid-ask spread can decrease and still induce dealers to act as market makers.

After about 1830, when exchanges began to supplant brokers as the primary sources of securities price data in business newspapers, the bid-ask spreads in early U.S. securities markets are easily observable and measurable. Sonali Garg has calculated the mean bid-ask spread of each security using this formula: Ask price − bid price/[(ask price + bid price)/2]. She then averaged the results for all securities to calculate a mean spread per day for each of three major markets, New York, Boston, and Philadelphia, over the period 1832–56.

Average bid-ask spreads over that period were consistently below 15 percent in all three markets and, save Philadelphia in 1842, were always below 20 percent. Indeed, in the 1830s, bid-ask spreads in New York and Boston were almost always below 5 percent, and in Philadelphia below 10 percent. After the financial and economic disruptions of the late 1830s and 1840s, bid-ask spreads in the three major markets converged and trended lower, averaging well below 5 percent, until 1852. By way of comparison, bid-ask spreads on the New York Stock Exchange in the late twentieth century averaged about .50 percent for the equities of large corporations, 1 percent for medium-sized firms, and 3 percent for small firms. Bid-ask spreads on NASDAQ were about .65 percent for large issuers, 2 percent for medium firms, and 4 percent for small companies.[43] Off the major exchanges, including the new after-hours trading venues,[44] spreads for equities between 1 and 2 percent are common, but spreads as high as 12 percent are not unknown.[45] The imminent decimalization of stock prices may reduce bid-ask spreads further in the near future,[46] but until that occurs, today's stock markets have not significantly improved efficiency over their antebellum ancestors. The corporate bond market, on the other hand, is much more efficient today than 200 years ago, with spreads between .13 and .26 percent for investment-grade

---

[43] Bessembinder and Kaufman 1997.

[44] Ruth Simon, "After Hours Trading Carries Sizable Costs for Investors," *Wall Street Journal*, 9 February 2000.

[45] Lynn Doran, "Market-Making in the Third Market for NYSE-Listed Securities," *Financial Review*, 1 November 1999.

[46] Larry Bauman, "Decimal Prices Devotees Ask: Do Pieces of Eight Make Cents?" *Wall Street Journal*, 29 April 1997.

debt and at least .19 percent for high-yield bonds, though some complain that even those relatively tiny spreads are much larger than they need be.[47]

Geographical Distribution of Stockholders:
Maine and Beyond

To recap briefly, early U.S. securities prices were rational and followed the predictions of the Theory of Portfolio Choice. The markets were transactionally efficient, offering investors a choice between a low commission but potentially slow sale through a broker, or a higher cost but immediate transaction through a market maker. Additionally, prices for identical securities in different markets were synchronous and close. How integrated were the markets in the sense of ownership of securities by investors who lived at a distance from the issuer? In other words, did nonlocals often own securities? Did, say, Bostonians own the shares of Philadelphia region turnpikes? Did New Yorkers own the bonds of Massachusetts's railroads or Virginia's banks? Alternatively, did the United States merely possess a series of localized capital markets not strongly linked to the others?

A unique set of records from antebellum Maine helps to begin to answer such questions. Maine banks tended to be owned about half by locals and about half by nonlocal Maine citizens, out-of-state investors, and institutions. Those figures suggest a high degree of capital mobility. Stockholder evidence from other states suggests that Maine was not unusual in this regard. Regional or local U.S. capital markets, in other words, were clearly part of a larger, national capital market.

Sources and Methods

Beginning in the late 1830s, Maine required all state-chartered banks to report, annually, the name, residence, and par value of stock held of each of their shareholders. An 1843 law required nonbank state business corporations to do likewise. The secretary of state collected and printed the reports as pamphlets. Only some of the pamphlets survive, in the American Antiquarian Society. The 1839, 1841, and 1853 pamphlets, reflecting stock ownership on 1 January of those years, were used for banks, and the 1845 pamphlet was used for nonbank business corporations.[48]

---

[47]Ian Springsteel, "Uncovering the Spread," *CFO, The Magazine for Senior Financial Executives*, 1 February 1999.

[48]The following pamphlets were used to create the tables upon which this section is based: Asaph R. Nichols, *List of Stockholders, With Amount of Stock Held by Each, in the Banks of Maine* (Augusta, Maine: Smith & Robinson, 1839); Samuel P. Benson, *List of*

TABLE 5.1. Number of Banks (Corporations) and Total Capital for
Sampled Years

Year	No. of Banks (Corporations)	Total Par Capitalization ($)
1839	50	4,595,000
1841	47	4,459,000
1845	(19)	3,273,200
1853	44	4,281,747

Sources: Asaph R. Nichols, *List of Stockholders, With Amount of Stock Held by Each, in the Banks of Maine* (Augusta, Maine: Smith & Robinson, 1839); Samuel P. Benson, *List of Stockholders, (With Amount of Stock Held by Each,) in the Banks of Maine* (Augusta, Maine: Severance & Dorr, 1841); [Secretary of State of Maine], *An Abstract of the Returns of Corporations, Made to the Office of the Secretary of State, in January, 1845, for the Year 1844* (Augusta, Maine: William T. Johnson, 1845); John G. Sawyer, *List of Stockholders, (With Amount of Stock Held by Each Jan. 1 1853,) in the Banks of Maine* (Augusta, Maine: William T. Johnson, 1853).

I transcribed the place of residence and par value of ownership for each stockholder but did not track individual stockholder's names. I also coded each stockholder for gender and corporate status. For coding purposes corporations include both business corporations, such as commercial banks, savings banks, insurance companies, and bridge companies, and nonbusiness corporations, such as towns, states, charities, churches, and schools.

Table 5.1 overviews the number of banks (or nonbank business corporations in the case of 1845) and their total par capitalization.[49] The economic and financial disruptions that followed in the wake of the Panic of 1837 caused the number of banks and total bank capitalization to decrease between 1839 and 1841. Additional bank failures reduced the number of Maine banks to 35, and total capitalization to just over $3 million, in 1844. A slow expansion in bank numbers and capitalization then ensued, with the size of the banking system by 1853 almost matching its 1841 figures.[50]

Stockholders, (With Amount of Stock Held by Each,) in the Banks of Maine (Augusta, Maine: Severance & Dorr, 1841); [Secretary of State of Maine], *An Abstract of the Returns of Corporations, Made to the Office of the Secretary of State, in January, 1845, for the Year 1844* (Augusta, Maine: William T. Johnson, 1845); John G. Sawyer, *List of Stockholders, (With Amount of Stock Held by Each Jan. 1 1853,) in the Banks of Maine* (Augusta, Maine: William T. Johnson, 1853).

[49]The par price of a stock reflects the extent of the corporation's indebtedness to the stockholder per share. The par price should not be confused with the market price, the price that investors paid in the secondary market to purchase shares. The market price was sometimes equal to, sometimes higher than, and sometimes lower than the par price, depending on the supply of and demand for a particular stock.

[50]Chadbourne 1936:54.

TABLE 5.2. Distribution of Shares in Selected Years

Year	No. of Stockholders	Mean Holding $	Mode Holding $	Highest Holding $	Lowest Holding $
1839	3,079	1,609.46	500	36,750	35
1841	2,902	1505.96	500	48,700	50
1845	1,240	2641.94	500	63,500	53
1853	3,452	1,233.12	500	50,000	40

Sources: Asaph R. Nichols, *List of Stockholders, With Amount of Stock Held by Each, in the Banks of Maine* (Augusta, Maine: Smith & Robinson, 1839); Samuel P. Benson, *List of Stockholders, (With Amount of Stock Held by Each,) in the Banks of Maine* (Augusta, Maine: Severance & Dorr, 1841); [Secretary of State of Maine], *An Abstract of the Returns of Corporations, Made to the Office of the Secretary of State, in January, 1845, for the Year 1844* (Augusta, Maine: William T. Johnson, 1845); John G. Sawyer, *List of Stockholders, (With Amount of Stock Held by Each Jan. 1 1853,) in the Banks of Maine* (Augusta, Maine: William T. Johnson, 1853).

Overview of Stock Ownership

Stock ownership patterns per year are detailed in Table 5.2. Between 1839 and 1841 the mean par holding of bank stock per investor decreased about $100. Over those same years, however, the minimum holding increased $15 while the largest holding jumped almost $12,000. By 1853 the mean holding had decreased by some $250 to $1,233. The minimum holding moved down $10 to just $40, while the largest holding increased slightly to $50,000. Shares of nonbank business corporations, sampled in 1845, were much more closely held. The mean holding of nonbank shares was more than $1,000 higher than that of bank shares. The $53 minimum holding was 6 percent higher than the highest minimum bank holding, while the largest nonbank holding was a whopping $13,500 more than the largest bank holding. Interestingly, in every case the most common (mode) investment size was exactly $500, which in most cases represented five shares (at $100 par per share). Those findings suggest that corporate shares, especially bank stocks, were widely held among the wealthy and business classes.

A simple categorical breakdown of the owners confirms the view that bank stocks were widely held. Table 5.3 presents the ownership of stock by women, corporations, and "foreigners" or out-of-state residents, be they from other countries or merely other parts of the Union. Generally, the percentage of women shareholders, corporate stockholders, and foreign stockholders grew over time, as did the percentage share of the par dollar value of those groups' holdings. Women, for example, owned 9 percent of Maine's bank capital in

TABLE 5.3. Distribution of Shares by Shareholder Type

Year	Percentage of Women Stockholders	Women's Share of Capital	Percentage of Corporate Stockholders	Corporations' Share of Capital	Percentage of Foreign Stockholders	Foreigner's Share of Capital
1839	15.33	8.93	7.15	13.94	8.99	13.83
1841	17.33	9.55	6.69	15.77	11.44	15.79
1845	7.5	4.02	2.18	2.97	57.18	78.82
1853	24.71	16.00	3.48	5.96	11.94	20.82

Sources: Asaph R. Nichols, *List of Stockholders, With Amount of Stock Held by Each, in the Banks of Maine* (Augusta, Maine: Smith & Robinson, 1839); Samuel P. Benson, *List of Stockholders, (With Amount of Stock Held by Each,) in the Banks of Maine* (Augusta, Maine: Severance & Dorr, 1841); [Secretary of State of Maine], *An Abstract of the Returns of Corporations, Made to the Office of the Secretary of State, in January, 1845, for the Year 1844* (Augusta, Maine: William T. Johnson, 1845); John G. Sawyer, *List of Stockholders, (With Amount of Stock Held by Each Jan. 1 1853,) in the Banks of Maine* (Augusta, Maine: William T. Johnson, 1853).

1839 but 16 percent in 1853. An exception was the percentage of corporate stockholders and their share of bank capital, which shrank from about 7 percent and 14 percent, respectively, to just 3.5 percent and 6 percent, respectively, between 1841 and 1853.

A huge difference in the nonbank sample of 1845 is again discernible. Relatively few women and corporations owned nonbank stock. Foreign nonbank stockholders, on the other hand, outnumbered domestic stockholders close to 6 to 5 and accounted for almost 4 out of every 5 par investment dollars.

Maine's banks appear, on balance, to have done a good job of inducing domestic investment. The low level of corporate investment suggests that stock ownership was genuine investment and not the mere pyramiding of financial assets. The sizable, persistent, and growing presence of female stockholders too suggests that stock ownership was often made for investment, and not speculative, purposes. In other words, most shareholders used their accumulated wealth, not loans, to purchase stock and they sought regular dividend payments, not large capital gains.

Bank Stock Ownership Patterns by Bank Size

A look at the ownership patterns of individual banks, detailed in Tables 5.4, 5.5, and 5.6, reinforces the view that Maine's banks attracted significant domestic investment. In all three sampled years, most banks were small ($50,000 to $75,000 par capitalization) and widely held by investors with mean holdings of less than $1,000. Investors in most medium banks ($100,000 to $150,000 par capitalization) and investors in some large banks (par capitalization greater than $200,000) held, on average, stock with a par value of between $1,000 and $1,500. Some small, medium, and large banks were relatively closely held, with average stakes amounting to over $1,750. A few large banks, such as the Maine Bank and Veazie Bank, were very closely held, with mean holdings over $10,000. Some of those banks were "speculative" affairs controlled by "foreigners."[51] Others, however, were simply closely held banks created to finance the activities of specific industrial families and firms.[52]

A Geographical Analysis of Bank Stockholdings

Tables 5.7, 5.8, and 5.9 describe the geographical spread of stockholders in Maine's banks. Most stockholders lived in Maine, in a swath extending from the state's southeastern border with New Hampshire to its northeastern border with New Brunswick, along the coastal

[51] Ibid., 55–68.   [52] Lamoreaux 1994.

TABLE 5.4. Stock Distribution by Bank, 1839

Bank Name	Capital Stock	No. of Stockholders	Mean Holding	Women's Share of Capital	Corporations' Share of Capital	Foreigners' Share of Capital
Lime Rock	50,000	84	595.24	9	0	0
Belfast	50,000	83	602.41	7	0	14
Megunticook	49,000	78	628.21	5	0	0
Medomak	50,000	67	746.27	17	0	28
Thomaston	50,000	67	746.27	17	4	0
Mariners'	50,000	61	819.67	29	1	26
Sagadahock	50,000	61	819.67	18	0	0
Commercial	50,000	59	847.46	12	0	0
Manufacturers'	100,000	104	961.54	24	11	44
Skowhegan	75,000	76	986.84	9	10	0
Freeman's	50,000	48	1,041.67	6	1	8
Union	50,000	47	1,063.83	8	8	0
St. Croix	50,000	45	1,111.11	12	25	0
South Berwick	50,000	43	1,162.79	11	21	20
Frankfort	50,000	39	1,282.05	1	8	29
Merchants'	150,000	115	1,304.35	10	21	8
Brunswick	75,000	55	1,363.64	0	1	2
Frontier	100,000	72	1,388.89	5	0	27
Bank of Westbrook	50,000	35	1,428.57	5	9	9
Exchange	100,000	68	1,470.59	8	32	2
Washington County	50,000	34	1,470.59	0	21	10
Ticonic	75,000	50	1,500.00	5	0	0
Bank of Portland	225,000	149	1,510.07	18	22	10
Androscoggin	50,000	33	1,515.15	5	0	0
Franklin	50,000	32	1,562.50	8	1	0

Bank	Capital	Stockholders		Avg. stock		
Granite	100,000	64	2	1,562.50	4	2
Manufacturers' & Traders'	150,000	95	20	1,578.95	28	12
Northern	75,000	46	10	1,630.43	10	11
Citizens'	60,000	36	2	1,666.67	19	0
Kenduskeag	100,000	60	4	1,666.67	20	24
Stillwater Canal	50,000	29	0	1,724.14	30	17
York	100,000	58	0	1,724.14	0	14
City	200,000	114	9	1,754.39	23	0
Lincoln	100,000	57	2	1754.39	5	0
Negeumkeag	50,000	28	1	1,785.71	4	16
Bank of Cumberland	250,000	136	11	1,838.24	27	10
Canal	400,000	217	15	1,843.32	19	8
Calais	100,000	54	6	1,851.85	36	69
Bangor Commercial	100,000	49	2	2,040.82	33	38
Gardiner	100,000	47	6	2,127.66	4	21
Casco	300,000	130	15	2,307.69	20	6
Agricultural	50,000	20	0	2,500.00	0	0
Globe	100,000	40	0	2,500.00	9	22
Mercantile	100,000	39	2	2,564.10	14	11
Augusta	110,000	41	12	2,682.93	21	33
Eastern	100,000	28	2	3,571.43	7	29
Central	85,000	23	1	3,695.65	13	52
Lafayette	100,000	25	16	4,000.00	0	64
Bank of Bangor	100,000	16	0	6,250.00	0	14
Maine	230,000	22	5	10,454.55	7	0

Sources: Asaph R. Nichols, *List of Stockholders, With Amount of Stock Held by Each, in the Banks of Maine* (Augusta, Maine: Smith & Robinson, 1839); Samuel P. Benson, *List of Stockholders, (With Amount of Stock Held by Each,) in the Banks of Maine* (Augusta, Maine: Severance & Dorr, 1841); [Secretary of State of Maine], *An Abstract of the Returns of Corporations, Made to the Office of the Secretary of State, in January, 1845, for the Year 1844* (Augusta, Maine: William T. Johnson, 1845); John G. Sawyer, *List of Stockholders, (With Amount of Stock Held by Each Jan. 1 1853,) in the Banks of Maine* (Augusta, Maine: William T. Johnson, 1853).

TABLE 5.5. Stock Distribution by Bank, 1841

Bank Name	Capital Stock	No. of Stockholders	Mean Holding	Women's Share of Capital	Corporations' Share of Capital	Foreigners' Share of Capital
Lime Rock	50,000	84	595.24	6	0	2
Megunticook	49,000	82	597.56	6	4	13
Belfast	50,000	81	617.28	9	0	22
Medomak	50,000	68	735.29	15	0	13
Thomaston	50,000	65	769.23	10	18	3
Mariners'	50,000	61	819.67	10	1	10
Sagadahock	50,000	60	833.33	2	0	0
Commercial	50,000	59	847.46	12	0	1
Skowhegan	75,000	86	872.09	10	6	8
Manufacturers'	100,000	108	925.93	19	11	41
Freeman's	50,000	52	961.54	7	1	0
Union	50,000	50	1,000.00	7	16	0
South Berwick	50,000	44	1,136.36	18	19	36
St. Croix	50,000	40	1,250.00	2	28	64
Merchants'	150,000	117	1,282.05	16	24	9
Brunswick	75,000	57	1,315.79	0	11	7
Bank of Portland	225,000	163	1,380.37	18	23	12
Frontier	100,000	72	1,388.89	4	0	30
Citizens'	60,000	43	1,395.35	7	0	0
Ticonic	75,000	53	1,415.09	8	3	6
Bank of Cumberland	200,000	141	1,418.44	11	27	12
Bank of Westbrook	50,000	35	1,428.57	11	20	0
Granite	100,000	68	1,470.59	10	5	11
Manufacturers' & Traders'	150,000	102	1,470.59	23	33	14

Bank						
Androscoggin	50,000	33	1,515.15	5	0	0
Kenduskeag	100,000	65	1,538.46	3	24	25
Northern	75,000	48	1,562.50	9	10	7
Washington County	50,000	32	1,562.50	3	1	7
York	100,000	64	1,562.50	21	4	24
Franklin	50,000	31	1,612.90	6	1	0
Negeumkeag	50,000	31	1,612.90	0	0	16
Frankfort	50,000	29	1,724.14	1	0	73
Lincoln	100,000	57	1,754.39	2	5	0
Canal	400,000	220	1,818.18	13	21	9
Calais	100,000	54	1,851.85	7	28	74
Lafayette	50,000	26	1,923.08	4	0	19
Stillwater Canal	50,000	25	2,000.00	4	57	13
Gardiner	100,000	48	2,083.33	6	4	22
Casco	300,000	131	2,290.08	16	29	0
Agricultural	50,000	21	2,380.95	3	4	0
Augusta	110,000	45	2,444.44	15	12	36
Mercantile	100,000	35	2,857.14	2	62	8
Eastern	100,000	28	3,571.43	18	10	39
Central	85,000	23	3,695.65	0	0	54
Globe	100,000	27	3,703.70	0	53	33
Bank of Bangor	100,000	13	7,692.31	0	0	34
Maine	230,000	25	9,200.00	5	8	0

Sources: Asaph R. Nichols, *List of Stockholders, With Amount of Stock Held by Each, in the Banks of Maine* (Augusta, Maine: Smith & Robinson, 1839); Samuel P. Benson, *List of Stockholders, (With Amount of Stock Held by Each,) in the Banks of Maine* (Augusta, Maine: Severance & Dorr, 1841); [Secretary of State of Maine], *An Abstract of the Returns of Corporations, Made to the Office of the Secretary of State, in January, 1845, for the Year 1844* (Augusta, Maine: William T. Johnson, 1845); John G. Sawyer, *List of Stockholders, (With Amount of Stock Held by Each Jan. 1 1853,) in the Banks of Maine* (Augusta, Maine: William T. Johnson, 1853).

TABLE 5.6. Stock Distribution by Bank, 1853

Bank Name	Capital Stock	No. of Stockholders	Mean Holding	Women's Share of Capital	Corporations' Share of Capital	Foreigners' Share of Capital
Georges	30,247	121	249.98	8	0	13
Lime Rock	50,000	136	367.65	14	0	3
Medomak	50,000	93	537.63	13	2	37
Mariners'	50,000	82	609.76	13	1	8
Thomaston	50,000	74	675.68	31	12	5
Union	50,000	72	694.44	12	0	2
Ellsworth	50,000	71	704.23	27	0	34
Waterville	50,000	71	704.23	3	0	4
Biddeford	150,000	189	793.65	16	14	48
Manufacturers' & Traders'	100,000	126	793.65	15	17	11
Rockland	75,000	94	797.87	9	0	2
Belfast	75,000	93	806.45	14	0	29
Manufacturer's	100,000	124	806.45	28	6	17
Skowhegan	75,000	93	806.45	12	9	12
Bank of Cumberland	100,000	121	826.45	20	8	1
Commercial	100,000	116	862.07	13	2	5
York	75,000	82	914.63	24	8	28
Freeman's	50,000	52	961.54	12	1	21
Frontier	75,000	75	1,000.00	5	0	36
Northern	75,000	73	1,027.40	22	5	21
Calais	50,000	48	1,041.67	0	10	73
Ticonic	100,000	94	1,063.83	28	2	9

Brunswick	60,000	51	1,176.47	24	3	6
Sagadahock	100,000	84	1,190.48	3	0	1
South Berwick	100,000	83	1,204.82	25	4	48
Granite	100,000	82	1,219.51	25	0	18
Merchants'	150,000	122	1,229.51	9	14	9
Androscoggin	50,000	39	1,282.05	29	2	2
Merchants'	50,000	39	1,282.05	5	0	42
Augusta	110,000	73	1,506.85	22	23	26
Canal	400,000	263	1,520.91	28	11	3
Casco	300,000	179	1,675.98	19	17	10
Lincoln	200,000	112	1,785.71	8	1	2
Lewiston Falls	50,000	27	1,851.85	2	0	37
Lumberman's Bank	31,500	15	2,100.00	38	0	0
Gardiner	100,000	44	2,272.73	19	4	31
Exchange	50,000	19	2,631.58	3	0	65
Bank of Hallowell	50,000	12	4,166.67	0	0	0
Mercantile	50,000	12	4,166.67	0	10	40
Atlantic Bank	100,000	18	5,555.56	0	15	16
Bank of the State of Maine	250,000	44	5,681.82	9	0	86
Eastern	100,000	16	6,250.00	7	0	0
Kenduskeag	100,000	9	11,111.11	0	0	10
Veazie Bank	200,000	10	20,000.00	30	0	30

Sources: Asaph R. Nichols, *List of Stockholders, With Amount of Stock Held by Each, in the Banks of Maine* (Augusta, Maine: Smith & Robinson, 1839); Samuel P. Benson, *List of Stockholders, (With Amount of Stock Held by Each,) in the Banks of Maine* (Augusta, Maine: Severance & Dorr, 1841); [Secretary of State of Maine], *An Abstract of the Returns of Corporations, Made to the Office of the Secretary of State, in January, 1845, for the Year 1844* (Augusta, Maine: William T. Johnson, 1845); John G. Sawyer, *List of Stockholders, (With Amount of Stock Held by Each Jan. 1 1853.) in the Banks of Maine* (Augusta, Maine: William T. Johnson, 1853).

TABLE 5.7. Bank Stockholders by Location, 1839

Location Name	No. of Stockholders	Percentage of All Stockholders	Dollar Value of Stocks	Average Dollar Holding	Percentage of All Capital
Alna	10	0.32	19,100	1,910.00	0.39
Augusta	128	4.16	248,200	1,939.06	5.01
Bangor	140	4.55	371,800	2,655.71	7.50
Belfast	43	1.40	31,200	725.58	0.63
Biddeford	18	0.58	12,200	677.78	0.25
Bowdoinham	10	0.32	32,500	3,250.00	0.66
Brewer	15	0.49	44,900	2,993.33	0.91
Brunswick	98	3.18	192,550	1,964.80	3.89
Calais	29	0.94	50,800	1,751.72	1.03
Cumberland	21	0.68	13,975	665.48	0.28
Eastport	43	1.40	55,300	1,286.05	1.12
Farmington	10	0.32	14,700	1,470.00	0.30
Frankfort	26	0.84	18,600	715.38	0.38
Gardiner	41	1.33	62,300	1,519.51	1.26
Gorham	27	0.88	33,725	1,249.07	0.68
Hallowell	57	1.85	106,300	1,864.91	2.15
Kennebunk	36	1.17	48,425	1,345.14	0.98
Machias	11	0.36	17,225	1,565.91	0.35
Maine	15	0.49	41,750	2,783.33	0.84
Norridgewock	10	0.32	10,200	1,020.00	0.21
North Yarmouth	14	0.45	13,525	966.07	0.27

Orono	16	0.52	26,800	1,675.00	0.54
Pittston	10	0.32	26,200	2,620.00	0.53
Portland	539	17.51	1,017,235	1,887.26	20.53
Saco	72	2.34	89,725	1,246.18	1.81
Sidney	12	0.39	10,200	850.00	0.21
Topsham	45	1.46	63,200	1,404.44	1.28
Unknown residence	866	28.13	1,073,375	1,239.46	21.66
Vassalborough	22	0.71	34,100	1,550.00	0.69
Waldoboro	43	1.40	34,400	800.00	0.69
Warren	17	0.55	15,175	892.65	0.31
Waterville	21	0.68	35,200	1,676.19	0.71
Westbrook	14	0.45	17,125	1,223.21	0.35
Wiscasset	31	1.01	29,900	964.52	0.60
Towns (105) with fewer than 10 stockholders each	277	9.00	322,725	1,165.07	6.51
Deceased, no residence given	15	0.49	35,500	2,366.67	0.72
Out of state	277	9.00	685,400	2,474.37	13.83

Sources: Asaph R. Nichols, *List of Stockholders, With Amount of Stock Held by Each, in the Banks of Maine* (Augusta, Maine: Smith & Robinson, 1839); Samuel P. Benson, *List of Stockholders, (With Amount of Stock Held by Each,) in the Banks of Maine* (Augusta, Maine: Severance & Dorr, 1841); [Secretary of State of Maine], *An Abstract of the Returns of Corporations, Made to the Office of the Secretary of State, in January, 1845, for the Year 1844* (Augusta, Maine: William T. Johnson, 1845); John G. Sawyer, *List of Stockholders, (With Amount of Stock Held by Each Jan. 1 1853,) in the Banks of Maine* (Augusta, Maine: William T. Johnson, 1853).

TABLE 5.8. Bank Stockholders by Location, 1841

Location Name	No. of Stockholders	Percentage of All Stockholders	Dollar Value of Stocks	Average Dollar Holding	Percentage of All Capital
Augusta	109	3.76	189,580	1,739.27	4.34
Bangor	105	3.62	306,525	2,919.29	7.01
Bath	40	1.38	33,540	838.50	0.77
Belfast	43	1.48	28,300	658.14	0.65
Biddeford	19	0.65	12,500	657.89	0.29
Bloomfield	31	1.07	30,300	977.42	0.69
Brewer	18	0.62	46,350	2,575.00	1.06
Brunswick	86	2.96	158,500	1,843.02	3.63
Calais	43	1.48	63,800	1,483.72	1.46
Camden	51	1.76	31,500	617.65	0.72
Cumberland	18	0.62	9,345	519.17	0.21
Eastport	41	1.41	48,600	1,185.37	1.11
Frankfort	17	0.59	13,900	817.65	0.32
Gardiner	44	1.52	75,600	1,718.18	1.73
Gorham	29	1.00	32,675	1,126.72	0.75
Hallowell	45	1.55	93,500	2,077.78	2.14
Kennebunk	42	1.45	47,500	1,130.95	1.09
Lincolnville	11	0.38	4,800	436.36	0.11
Maine	18	0.62	54,300	3,016.67	1.24
Norridgewock	16	0.55	14,400	900.00	0.33

North Yarmouth	19	0.65	12,350	650.00	0.28
Portland	517	17.82	876,800	1,695.94	20.06
Saco	68	2.34	76,005	1,117.72	1.74
Skowhegan	10	0.34	10,200	1,020.00	0.23
South Berwick	21	0.72	26,850	1,278.57	0.61
Thomaston	87	3.00	66,800	767.82	1.53
Topsham	53	1.83	68,200	1,286.79	1.56
Unknown	382	13.16	646,215	1,691.66	14.79
Vassalborough	27	0.93	36,800	1,362.96	0.84
Vinalhaven	12	0.41	6,100	508.33	0.14
Waldoborough	46	1.59	39,300	854.35	0.90
Warren	38	1.31	21,975	578.29	0.50
Waterville	20	0.69	37,500	1,875.00	0.86
Westbrook	16	0.55	14,110	881.88	0.32
Wiscasset	36	1.24	30,000	833.33	0.69
Towns (127) with fewer than 10 stockholders each	381	13.13	400,975	1,052.43	9.17
Deceased, no residence given	11	0.38	14,440	1,312.73	0.33
Out of state	332	11.44	690,165	2,078.81	15.79

Sources: Asaph R. Nichols, List of Stockholders, With Amount of Stock Held by Each, in the Banks of Maine (Augusta, Maine: Smith & Robinson, 1839); Samuel P. Benson, List of Stockholders, (With Amount of Stock Held by Each,) in the Banks of Maine (Augusta, Maine: Severance & Dorr, 1841); [Secretary of State of Maine], An Abstract of the Returns of Corporations, Made to the Office of the Secretary of State, in January, 1845, for the Year 1844 (Augusta, Maine: William T. Johnson, 1845); John G. Sawyer, List of Stockholders, (With Amount of Stock Held by Each Jan. 1 1853,) in the Banks of Maine (Augusta, Maine: William T. Johnson, 1853).

TABLE 5.9. Bank Stockholders by Location, 1853

Location Name	No. of Stockholders	Percentage of All Stockholders	Dollar Value of Stocks	Average Dollar Holding	Percentage of All Capital
Alfred	10	0.29	13,225	1,322.50	0.31
Augusta	101	2.93	133,240	1,319.21	3.14
Bangor	60	1.74	316,150	5,269.17	7.45
Bath	196	5.69	279,005	1,423.49	6.57
Belfast	49	1.42	41,275	842.35	0.97
Biddeford	70	2.03	37,500	535.71	0.88
Bloomfield	30	0.87	30,460	1,015.33	0.72
Bowdoinham	20	0.58	30,140	1,507.00	0.71
Bremen	11	0.32	4,400	400.00	0.10
Brunswick	100	2.90	115,840	1,158.40	2.73
Calais	16	0.46	11,450	715.63	0.27
Camden	31	0.90	12,800	412.90	0.30
Cumberland	11	0.32	6,160	560.00	0.15
Eastport	32	0.93	27,000	843.75	0.64
Ellsworth	29	0.84	22,000	758.62	0.52
Fairfield	19	0.55	14,200	747.37	0.33
Farmington	21	0.61	14,200	676.19	0.33
Gardiner	31	0.90	55,980	1,805.81	1.32
Gorham	38	1.10	36,490	960.26	0.86
Hallowell	33	0.96	26,300	796.97	0.62
Jefferson	14	0.41	10,700	764.29	0.25
Kennebec	13	0.38	11,440	880.00	0.27
Kennebunk	62	1.80	51,260	826.77	1.21
Lewiston	16	0.46	23,100	1,443.75	0.54
Norridgewock	20	0.58	15,240	762.00	0.36
Oldtown	14	0.41	31,000	2,214.29	0.73
Portland	462	13.42	677,345	1,466.11	15.96

Portsmouth	12	0.35	15,800	1,316.67	0.37
Richmond	11	0.32	9,100	827.27	0.21
Rockland	94	2.73	67,950	722.87	1.60
Saco	131	3.80	95,375	728.05	2.25
Sidney	12	0.35	8,820	735.00	0.21
Skowhegan	16	0.46	12,320	770.00	0.29
South Berwick	31	0.90	34,950	1,127.42	0.82
South Thomaston	10	0.29	4,300	430.00	0.10
St. George	13	0.38	2,050	157.69	0.05
Standish	18	0.52	18,090	1,005.00	0.43
Thomaston	74	2.15	27,750	375.00	0.65
Topsham	70	2.03	95,300	1,361.43	2.24
Union	16	0.46	7,500	468.75	0.18
Unknown	259	7.52	385,150	1,487.07	9.07
Vinalhaven	17	0.49	10,450	614.71	0.25
Waldoborough	48	1.39	20,500	427.08	0.48
Warren	108	3.14	41,917	388.12	0.99
Waterville	75	2.18	80,260	1,070.13	1.89
Westbrook	11	0.32	23,140	2,103.64	0.55
Westport	15	0.44	10,100	673.33	0.24
Winslow	11	0.32	7,000	636.36	0.16
Wiscasset	36	1.05	20,160	560.00	0.47
Woolwich	23	0.67	19,000	826.09	0.45
Towns (149) with fewer than 10 stockholders each	421	12.23	306,830	728.81	7.23
Out of state	412	11.97	886,535	2,151.78	20.88

Sources: Asaph R. Nichols, *List of Stockholders, With Amount of Stock Held by Each, in the Banks of Maine* (Augusta, Maine: Smith & Robinson, 1839); Samuel P. Benson, *List of Stockholders, (With Amount of Stock Held by Each,) in the Banks of Maine* (Augusta, Maine: Severance & Dorr, 1841); [Secretary of State of Maine], *An Abstract of the Returns of Corporations, Made to the Office of the Secretary of State, in January, 1845, for the Year 1844* (Augusta, Maine: William T. Johnson, 1845); John G. Sawyer, *List of Stockholders, (With Amount of Stock Held by Each Jan. 1 1853,) in the Banks of Maine* (Augusta, Maine: William T. Johnson, 1853).

lowlands and interior river valleys. (Most of the communities lay near current right-of-ways of Interstate 95 and Route 1.) Major towns in that swath with more than 10 stockholders included, from south to north, Kennebunk, Biddeford, Saco, Portland, Brunswick, Bath, Gardiner, Augusta, Skowhegan, Brewer, Bangor, Machias, and Calais. More than 100 other towns in Maine were also home to stockholders, though usually ones with smaller than average holdings.

Portland was by far the most important source of bank capital, far outstripping all other Maine towns and even the combined investments of all foreign investors. Portland's share, however, declined from 17.5 percent of stockholders to just 13.5 percent of stockholders between the early 1840s and the early 1850s. Portland's share of the par dollar value of bank capital over that same period also slipped, from 20 percent to 16 percent. Those figures suggest that the capital market grew broader, and hence less reliant on Portland, during the 1840s.

Most of Maine's "foreign" bank capital came from investors in Boston, eastern New Hampshire, and major towns in Canada's Maritime Provinces, such as Halifax, St. John, St. Stephen, and St. Andrews. Some investors lived in commercial towns in Rhode Island, Connecticut, and Vermont. Other investors lived in major money centers, such as New York, Philadelphia, Baltimore, New Orleans, and London. Share owners in Maine banks lived as far west as Buffalo, New York; Akron and Cincinnati, Ohio; Crawfordsville, Indiana; St. Louis, Missouri; Stillwater, Minnesota; and, by 1853, California.

Importantly, none of the banks appeared to have suffered from having too many "foreign" or nonlocal stockholders. Enough local stockholders remained to monitor the activities of bank directors and cashiers to prevent inordinate amounts of fraud. Depositors and noteholders, most local, also had some incentive to watch Maine's banks for signs of perfidy or excessive risk taking. As the percentage of nonlocal stockholders grew, the stock would have become increasingly less desirable for additional nonlocal stockholders to buy or hold (if inherited), effectively capping "foreign" bank ownership.

Evidence from Elsewhere

Maine appears not to have been unique; other states successfully raised domestic investment without choking off capital mobility. Take, for example, the case of the Permanent Bridge Company of Philadelphia. Almost all of the subscribers to its two public offerings, which ran between 1798 and 1803, were local residents.[53] As the company established a track record, however, nonlocal investors began to buy shares in the active secondary market for the stock.

[53]Schuylkill Permanent Bridge Co. Stock Books, HSP.

Between 1799 and 1815, 32,153 Permanent Bridge Company shares traded hands in 716 transactions. Investors from Bucks, Montgomery, Delaware, Lancaster, and Northumberland counties, Pittsburgh, and other places in Pennsylvania began to buy shares by early 1801. By 1804 investors in New Jersey had purchased shares. Later, investors from as far away as Baltimore, Boston, and Washington, D.C., as well as North Carolina, New York, and Connecticut, purchased significant amounts of the stock.

Bank of Newburgh shares traded in New York City as early as 1812.[54] As early as 1829 it was "pretty generally conceded, that a good portion of [New York's] banking capital has been furnished by foreigners, and men of wealth residing in other states in the Union."[55]

The Worcester Bank and Central Bank, both of Worcester, Massachusetts, also succeeded in attracting local, regional, and national investors between 1812 and 1846.[56] While most investors lived in Worcester proper or in surrounding communities in central Massachusetts, some Worcester Bank investors resided in eastern Massachusetts, and others lived as far away as Philadelphia and Princeton. By 1850 the Central Bank boasted of investors from San Francisco, California, to Bangor, Maine. Much the same story can be told of the Bank of Concord, Massachusetts, chartered in 1832.[57] The 164 initial stockholders came from 22 communities, mostly from Concord's Middlesex County. However, investors also hailed from near by Boston, as well as from New Hampshire and Maine.

Investors in inland cities purchased shares in big-city corporations, especially banks. Robert Vaux of Reading,[58] Samuel Emlen of Westhill,[59] and James Hamilton of Carlisle,[60] Pennsylvania, were avid investors in Philadelphia and national securities. Philadelphians also invested in inland companies. In 1813, for example, the brokerage firm of Thomas A. Biddle and J. Wharton Company handled the sale of 20 shares of Lancaster and Susquehanna Turnpike stock to David Lewis and Henry Drinker of Philadelphia.[61] Philadelphia capitalists also invested heavily in Pennsylvania's railroads.[62] Baltimoreans were

[54]Samuel Tooker to John Humm, 4 January 1813, Bank of Newburgh Papers, NYHS.
[55] *Report of the Committee on Banks and Insurance Companies, Made to the Senate, January 19, 1829* (Albany: Croswell & Van Benthuysen, 1829), 5.
[56]Worcester Bank Records, folders 7 and 8, Stock Certificates and Transfers, 1812–29, 1844–46, AAS; Central Bank of Worcester Business Records, Stock Record Book, 1830–64, AAS.
[57]Patterson 1971:14–34.
[58]Joseph Hiester to Robert Vaux, Reading, 5, 25 July 1823, Vaux Papers, HSP.
[59]Samuel Emlen to Robert Vaux, 17 January, 3 February, 15, 16, 30 March 1813, ibid.
[60]Mark Prager to James Hamilton, 21 February, 1 March, 6 March 1824, James Hamilton Papers, HSP.
[61]Thomas A. Biddle and J. Wharton Company to James Houston, Esq., 20 August 1813, Thomas A. Biddle and J. Wharton Company Letter Book, HSP.
[62]Majewski 2000.

known to invest in banks in northern Virginia and Washington D.C.[63]
By the 1830s western banks, such as the Bank of Kentucky, established
share transfer agencies in major cities, including Philadelphia, New
York, and New Orleans, to accommodate investor demand for their
shares in those cities.[64]

Why Nonbank Stock Ownership Patterns Differed

As noted earlier, the ownership of nonbank business corporations differed radically from that of Maine's banks. Table 5.10 details the ownership pattern by corporation, and Table 5.11 by stockholder residence.
Maine's nonbank corporations were, on average, much more closely
held than its banks. The mean shareholder stake was much larger than
for most banks; women and corporations each owned just a small fraction of the nonbank capital. Most stockholders lived out-of-state and
those stockholders owned a majority of the capital. A closer look by
corporation type, however, yields some interesting variations. To begin with, the stockownership patterns of local companies (e.g., bridge
companies and short railroads), some small manufacturing companies
(e.g., the Sanford and Saccarappa companies), and the state's two insurance companies looked more like that of the state's banks. Mean
stakes and foreign ownership were low in each; corporate ownership
was similar to that of banks. Additionally, women's investments, though
lower than that in banks, was higher than that in other nonbank corporations.

Large manufacturing concerns and long railroads, on the other
hand, were more closely held. Foreigners owned most of the stock,
and investments by women and corporations were few and tiny. One
reason for the difference is that some of those large nonbank corporations were, unlike the banks, essentially interstate businesses. The
Portsmouth, Saco, and Portland Railroad, for example, linked Maine
to Portsmouth, New Hampshire, with its sea and land links to Boston,
the region's entrepôt. Boston capitalists, therefore, invested heavily
in the line. Although probably more a *reflection* of investors' prefer-
ences than a *cause* of stock ownership patterns, the fact that the market
prices of shares of Maine's large, nonbank corporations were regularly
published in Boston commercial newspapers certainly helped to maintain high "foreign" investment levels.[65]

Another factor is that the largest nonbank corporations were huge
compared with even the largest Maine banks. The York Manufacturing

[63] *Federal Gazette & Baltimore Daily Advertiser,* 4 January 1804.
[64] Duke, 1895:66; Sylla, Wilson, and Wright 2002.
[65] See, for example, the *Boston Shipping List, Prices Current, Commercial and Underwriters'
Gazette* for the market prices of shares in the Portland, Saco, and Portsmouth Railroad.

TABLE 5.10. Stock Distribution by Nonbank Corporation, 1845

Corporation Name	Capital Stock	No. of Stockholders	Mean Holding	Women's Share of Capital	Corporations' Share of Capital	Foreigners' Share of Capital
Norridgewock Bridge	5,300	30	176.67	4	0	0
Norridgewock Falls Bridge	10,000	35	285.71	5	5	0
Cumberland Marine Railway Co.	2,000	5	400.00	0	0	15
Jay Bridge Corp.	7,900	16	493.75	0	0	5
Georges Insurance Co.	60,000	99	606.06	0	0	0
Ocean Insurance Co.	100,000	95	1,052.63	9	5	10
Maine Stage Co.	60,000	56	1,071.43	0	10	1
Sanford Manufacturing Co.	24,000	17	1,411.76	0	17	22
Laconia Co.	240,000	147	1,632.65	2	0	92
Winslow Bridge Corp.	10,000	6	1,666.67	0	0	0
Saccarappa Manufacturing Co.	60,000	30	2,000.00	0	26	3
Saco Water Power Co.	300,000	140	2,142.86	5	3	82
Portsmouth, Saco and Portland Rail Road	868,500	315	2,757.14	3	3	86
Casco Manufacturing Co.	24,000	8	3,000.00	0	0	3
Kennebec Fire Co.	16,000	3	5,333.33	0	0	0
York Manufacturing Co.	1,000,000	175	5,714.29	8	3	97
Palmer and Machiasport Rail Road	50,000	7	7,142.86	0	0	100
Machias Water Power and Mill Co.	350,000	47	7,446.81	1	1	69
Mousam Manufacturing Co.	85,500	9	9,500.00	0	0	94

Sources: Asaph R. Nichols, *List of Stockholders, With Amount of Stock Held by Each, in the Banks of Maine* (Augusta, Maine: Smith & Robinson, 1839); Samuel P. Benson, *List of Stockholders, (With Amount of Stock Held by Each,) in the Banks of Maine* (Augusta, Maine: Severance & Dorr, 1841); [Secretary of State of Maine], *An Abstract of the Returns of Corporations, Made to the Office of the Secretary of State, in January, 1845, for the Year 1844* (Augusta, Maine: William T. Johnson, 1845); John G. Sawyer, *List of Stockholders, (With Amount of Stock Held by Each Jan. 1 1853.) in the Banks of Maine* (Augusta, Maine: William T. Johnson, 1853).

TABLE 5.11. Nonbank Stockholders by Location, 1845

Location Name	No. of Stockholders	Percentage of All Stockholders	Dollar Value of Stocks	Average Dollar Holding	Percentage of All Capital
Anson	12	0.96	2,800	233.33	0.09
Biddeford	10	0.8	4,705	470.50	0.15
Brunswick	18	1.44	27,200	1,511.11	0.89
Camden	17	1.36	8,900	523.53	0.29
Machias	12	0.96	92,300	7,691.67	3.03
Madison	12	0.96	3,618	301.50	0.12
Norridgewock	26	2.08	5,856	225.23	0.19
Portland	141	11.28	191,317	1,356.86	6.28
Saco	33	2.64	54,917	1,664.15	1.80
Sanford	10	0.8	17,400	1,740.00	0.57
Thomaston	62	4.96	37,900	611.29	1.25
Unknown	32	2.56	60,512	1,891.00	1.99
Westbrook	10	0.8	28,600	2,860.00	0.94
Towns (127) with fewer than 10 stockholders each	136	10.88	138,943	1,021.64	4.56
Out of state	709	56.72	2,360,641	3,329.54	77.55

Sources: Asaph R. Nichols, List of Stockholders, With Amount of Stock Held by Each, in the Banks of Maine (Augusta, Maine: Smith & Robinson, 1839); Samuel P. Benson, List of Stockholders, (With Amount of Stock Held by Each,) in the Banks of Maine (Augusta, Maine: Severance & Dorr, 1841); [Secretary of State of Maine], An Abstract of the Returns of Corporations, Made to the Office of the Secretary of State, in January, 1845, for the Year 1844 (Augusta, Maine: William T. Johnson, 1845); John G. Sawyer, List of Stockholders, (With Amount of Stock Held by Each Jan. 1 1853,) in the Banks of Maine (Augusta, Maine: William T. Johnson, 1853).

Company, for instance, had a par capitalization of $1 million, several times the size of Maine's largest bank. The Portsmouth, Saco, and Portland Railroad was almost as large. Even the Saco Water Power Company and the Laconia Company were huge compared with most of Maine's banks. The companies attracted a considerable number of investors, well over 100 each, but to fill out their capitalizations they had to tap each investor more deeply than the relatively small banks had to. The par value of each share was therefore set much higher than the $35 to $100 par value of the typical bank share. The par value of each share in a large manufacturing company, for example, usually ran between $300 and $1,000. Portland, although the most important source of domestic nonbank business capital, was simply not large enough to supply the huge demands for capital such large companies made.

Additionally, in the 1840s investors considered banks (and insurance companies to some extent) much safer investments than railroad or manufacturing stocks. The banking sector, for one thing, had a longer history; the first bank began operation in the Maine district in 1799,[66] and the first bank in New England began operation fifteen years before that. Second, banks, especially small, local ones, were easier for small investors to monitor. Most bank liabilities in the early nineteenth century were banknotes that circulated as money; if stockholders perceived too many banknotes in circulation, they could pressure directors to lend more prudently. The Suffolk Bank system also imposed discipline on bank directors.[67] Additionally, regular dividends acted as clear, public signs of bank profitability. Large manufacturing concerns, or long railroads, on the other hand, were much more difficult to monitor and their dividends at first were much more erratic than those of most banks. Those forces colluded to keep many small investors out of the nonbank business corporation capital market in the 1840s.

Conclusions

In the 1840s and 1850s Maine was, economically, one of the least advanced states in New England. It had achieved statehood, after all, relatively late, in the early 1820s, and did not firmly establish its border with Canada until the 1840s. To this day, large portions of the state remain unpopulated. Despite this seeming backwardness, however, Maine, well before the Civil War, had an indigenous market capable of raising capital, mostly from state residents, for over two score banks, with a total capitalization approaching $9 per capita.

[66]Chadbourne, 1936:13–14.   [67]Bodenhorn 2002; Rolnick, Smith, and Weber 1998.

Importantly, those investments were not immobile; investors outside of Maine could and did buy and sell shares. When corporations sought more capital, or riskier investments, than Maine citizens could provide, as in the case of large, nonlocal, nonfinancial corporations, substantial "foreign" investment took place. The relatively advanced state of Maine's capital market appears to have been typical of the capital markets in the north at least by the beginning of the antebellum period.

The early U.S. securities markets were also price-integrated. Prices of similar securities in different markets rose and fell together. Similarly, prices of identical securities were usually very close; differences were largely a function of transaction costs. Additionally, prices of individual securities moved rationally according to the Theory of Portfolio Choice. In other words, all other factors being equal, safer, more liquid, more remunerative securities garnered higher prices. Finally, the early securities markets were also transactionally efficient. Brokerage commissions, as we will see, were low even by today's standards. Bid-ask spreads, though higher than today's, were not unduly large. In short, like the securities markets that developed in postrevolutionary Holland and Britain, the early U.S. securities market was remarkably modern.

6

Expansion of the Securities Services Sector, 1790–1850

In the previous chapter, we learned that the early U.S. securities sector was modern in the sense that it was price-integrated and transactionally efficient. But was it large enough to matter? Scholars know precious little about the trading patterns of America's early "stock" – corporate equities and government debt, such as U.S. Sixes. There are several reasons why, until just a few years ago, the early U.S. securities sector received very little scholarly attention. First, intensive archival research was necessary to show that the early securities markets were broader (more issues) and deeper (more trades) than hitherto believed. Those trained in archival research, primarily historians, were little interested in the actual functioning of the economy, preferring instead to explore the public policy debates, most of which concerned banks and banking. Those interested in the functioning of the economy, mostly economists, did not have the archival temperament necessary to find relevant sources, which were often deeply buried in disintegrating newspapers, crusty account books, and giant, filthy bank ledgers. The topic, in other words, fell into the crevice between two disciplines. Second, and just as important, until recently there was little theoretical reason to jump into that Great Divide to see what could be found. Finance was thought to follow, rather than to lead, economic growth. Many now argue otherwise, so there is incentive to explore the early securities sector in detail.

This chapter first addresses the brokerage industry, describing the functions, commission rates, and numbers of brokers. It next describes the IPO market. The third section assesses the depth and breadth of the Philadelphia secondary securities market. In other words, it tries to determine, roughly, the number and types of securities traded and the frequency and size of the trades. The fourth and final section suggests that we may be seeing only the tip of a much larger secondary securities market. In short, the securities sector was certainly large enough to matter.

Brokers: Their Role and Numbers

We know that financial intermediaries, especially commercial banks, served as conduits that channeled excess funds into productive pursuits. Financial markets provided an alternative, more direct method of matching investors and entrepreneurs. Early corporations regularly sold equity stakes in themselves, called shares of stock, directly to investors. When investors wished to invest elsewhere, or to consume their wealth, they sold their shares to other investors in the stock, or secondary securities, market.

Securities brokers aided in those transactions by matching those who wished to sell stock with those who wished to buy stock. Sometimes they were middlemen who simply gathered information about buyers and sellers and literally matched them. At other times, they acted as "dealers," buying and holding securities on their own account with the hope of profiting from price changes. At such times, early brokers acted like today's "market makers," buying and holding inventories of securities for resale in the near future in order to increase market liquidity and make additional profits.

Because the relative ease with which stocks could be bought and sold, or in other words their "liquidity," helped in large measure to determine the stocks' general market values, and hence the cost of corporate borrowing, stockbrokers played an important economic role. In other words, effective brokerage makes secondary securities markets more efficient. If there was too little brokerage, fewer trades would be made, liquidity would suffer, and securities would be less valuable. That would increase the cost of obtaining long-term financing, which, in turn, would reduce the economy's total output.

Scholars have completed only a few studies of stockbrokers, most of which were primarily concerned with individual firms.[1] Luckily, ample sources exist to create a fuller picture of early American stockbrokerage. Some brokers, such as Philadelphians Clement Biddle and Mark Prager, have left us detailed letter and account books. Many brokers and dealers placed lengthy, descriptive advertisements in newspapers. Finally, city directories invariably listed occupations in their alphabetical lists of inhabitants. Sometimes, directories even provided compiled lists of brokers.

One of the most interesting aspects of early stockbrokers is that they worked as pure brokers, matchers of buyers and sellers, very inexpensively. Commissions generally ranged between .25 and .50 percent, or in other words between $2.50 and $5.00 per $1,000 worth of securities traded. That range compares very favorably with management fees for late second-millennium U.S. mutual funds, which exceeded

[1] Henrietta Larson's excellent study (1931) of S&M Allen is a prime example.

.60 percent for stock funds and hovered around .60 percent for bond funds.[2] That rate range, which appears to have continued until at least the 1830s, began as early as 1791, when Philadelphia broker Clement Biddle informed London banker John Lloyd that "the Brokerage which I charge on purchase of registered Stock is one quarter per Cent & where I purchase unregistered Stock & procure the same to be registered... half a percent brokerage."[3] Biddle himself maintained those rates at least through 1792,[4] and probably long beyond that because those rates were very durable. George Nelson of Charleston mentioned a commission of .25 percent in March 1794.[5] Philadelphia broker James Glentworth charged .25 percent commission in December 1794.[6] On 23 May 1799 Leonard Bleecker of New York charged investor Henry Remsen $3.00 "brokerage" for arranging the sale of $1,466.66 face value of U.S. Sixes at 89 percent of par, or $1,085.59, or just over .25 percent.[7] A year later, Ebenezer Hazard of Philadelphia informed Jedediah Morse of Massachusetts that "our Brokers charge a Quarter P Ct. Commissions for purchasing."[8] During the War of 1812, Thomas A. Biddle and J. Wharton Company of Philadelphia charged just .25 percent commission.[9] Biddle, Wharton, and Brothers did likewise in 1817.[10] In 1818 Mark Prager charged Edward Burd .25 percent commission on the sale of $1,000 par value of U.S. Sixes.[11] Prager did likewise for a sale of U.S. Sixes in 1824.[12] In 1828 the New York Chamber of Commerce *capped* commission rates on the sale or purchase of stocks at 1 percent.[13]

There is no evidence that brokers charged higher commissions for matching buyers to sellers of infrequently traded stocks. Brokers making a market in a less liquid stock, however, did receive a larger "spread," or difference between their bid and ask prices. This makes perfectly good economic sense as it did not cost the broker any more to tell other brokers that he had a client who wished to buy (sell)

[2]British brokers received only .125 percent in the 1840s, however. Dr. D. McCauley, "Interest, Exchange, and Stock-Jobbing," *DeBow's Review*, April 1846, 373. Ken Brown, "GAO Urges Funds to Reveal Fees: Shift Could Spur Improved Prices," *Wall Street Journal*, 6 July 2000.

[3]Clement Biddle to John Lloyd, 22 April 1791, Clement Biddle Letter Book, HSP.

[4]Clement Biddle to William Campbell, 13 May 1791; to William Rogers, 20 June 1791; to George Lewis, 18 January 1792, Clement Biddle Letter Book, HSP.

[5]George Nelson to Mr. Bell, 19 March 1794, George Nelson Letter Book, UNCSC.

[6]Mark Prager to Mark Prager Sr., 17 December 1794, Prager Letter Book, HSP.

[7]Henry Remsen Papers, 1797–1846, NYPL.

[8]Ebenezer Hazard to Jedediah Morse, 11 April 1800, Ebenezer Hazard Papers, Gratz – American Miscellaneous, HSP.

[9]21 September 1813, Thomas A. Biddle and J. Wharton Company Letter Book, HSP.

[10]Biddle, Wharton & Bros. Stock Book, 1817, HSP.

[11]Mark Prager to Edward Burd, 24 November 1818, under Burd, AM 03494, HSP.

[12]Mark Prager to James Hamilton, 6 March 1824, HSP.

[13]*Philadelphia Public Sales Report*, 19 January 1828.

security X than it did to tell them he had a client who wished to buy (sell) security Y. A broker-dealer who bought a less liquid stock, however, suffered a risk of loss that had to be compensated.

For similar reasons, pure brokers had little incentive to monitor issuers, except insofar as to provide their clients with sound advice. Brokers who also acted as dealers, that is to say most brokers, on the other hand, had tremendous incentive to monitor issuers. At any given time, after all, a market maker might be the largest investor in a given issuer. It is little wonder then that brokers maintained extensive information networks.[14]

Low commissions were great for investors but probably not so good for brokers, almost all of whom supplemented their incomes. Most if not all brokers, therefore, also acted as dealers. Brokers routinely visited each other in order to find appropriate matches. They did not always, however, immediately find one. If a customer did not wish to wait for the broker to find a counterparty, the broker would serve as the customer's counterparty, buying a security that the customer wished to unload or selling the customer a security out of the broker's own inventory. The investor paid more, in the form of a lower sale price or higher purchase price, than he or she would have in a brokered deal but received immediate gratification. The brokers, for their part, hoped to resell or repurchase the security soon at a more advantageous price. The profit from the spread could be much higher than the mere commission rate but could also be a losing proposition if prices moved contrary to the broker's expectation. (This is the usual trade-off between risk and return.) By acting as dealers, early stockbrokers kept the market for the bond and equity issues liquid.

Securities brokers also acted as private banks of discount and deposit. They collected their customers' dividend and coupon payments and held the proceeds of securities sales as deposits in their account books, subject to their customers' orders and drafts. The brokers, in other words, effectively had control of their customers' money and could, just like any bank, safely lend a fraction of those funds.[15] Some brokers, such as William Newton and Company, even paid interest for lodged deposits.[16] The similarities between those procedures and the cash management accounts offered by today's brokerages are clear.

Brokers lent much like banks, on the security of various forms of commercial paper like promissory notes, inland drafts, bills of exchange, or on hypothecated securities. Unlike most banks, however, they could also lend on the security of commodities. They also made

[14]Larson 1931; Martin and Barron 1975.
[15]Thomas A. Biddle and J. Wharton Company Letter Book, HSP.
[16]*Political and Commercial Register*, 12 November 1805.

lending decisions much more quickly than banks, which usually had fixed discount days. In 1799, for instance, Philadelphia broker Jonas Phillips advertised that he discounted notes and advanced money "on Public securities or merchandize which will be executed at the shortest notice."[17]

Brokers also borrowed from commercial banks, sometimes heavily and to their peril. In 1799, for example, "a Yankee money Broker of the name of B.F. Haskins failed some little Time since and has taken in both the Banks pockets roundly by overdrawing,"[18] a clear case of moral hazard. As early as 1789, commercial banks' loans to brokers affected securities prices.[19] "The Bank not discounting freely," Seth Johnson informed Andrew Craigie in 1791, "causes a want of money, & tends to keep down the price of paper."

Combinations of stock and exchange brokering, added of course to private banking, were very common.[20] Boston's William Cleland, for example, advertised in 1796 that he "purchased and sold, on Commission ... United States Stocks, Shares in the National and other Banks, State Notes, Shares in Bridges, Real Estates, Vessels, &c. &c.," in addition to negotiating "Foreign and Inland bills of exchange."[21] Similarly, Philadelphia broker James McCurach bragged that "he has always bills of exchange, for sale – Buys and sells all kinds of stock, furnishes money on the shortest notice for negotiable paper, &c."[22]

Early brokers also engaged in a variety of other money-related activities. New York's James Griffiths, for example, advertised in 1796 that he "continues to procure and let monies on loan, purchases and sells stock, procures freights and charters of vessels, purchases and sells cargoes, and negociates every species of Commission Business."[23] Another popular side business, then as now, was lottery ticket retailing.[24]

Many early brokers conducted business in public taverns, which were often hubs of local commercial activity. Occasionally, a broker would purchase the tavern in which he operated. Broker James H. Lynch of Richmond, Virginia, for example, established his own coffeehouse, "Lynch's Coffee-House."[25] Early brokers, like their modern descendants, also served as information clearinghouses. The early brokers conducted extensive correspondence with other

[17] *Philadelphia Aurora and General Advertiser*, 16 January 1799.
[18] Nicholas Low to Rufus King, 8 May 1799, Rufus King Papers, vol. 37, NYHS.
[19] Seth Johnson to Andrew Craigie, 20 December 1789; Seth Johnson to Andrew Craigie, 2, 6, March 1791, Andrew Craigie Papers, AAS.
[20] *Political and Commercial Register*, 25 February 1807.
[21] *Boston Columbian Centinel*, 6 January 1796.
[22] *Political and Commercial Register*, 3 October 1805.
[23] *Argus, or Greenleaf's New Daily Advertiser*, 25 March 1796.
[24] *Political and Commercial Register*, 19 March 1805; Perkins 1994.
[25] *Richmond Enquirer*, 4 March 1841.

brokers, major investors, and anyone who expressed an interest in investing.[26] Indeed, many brokers referred to their offices as "intelligence offices."[27]

When it came to brokering securities, brokers did not specialize,[28] although they sometimes advertised very specific securities for purchase or sale. In 1810, for example, Charles Ghequiere of Baltimore offered "for Sale, Several well secured ground rents,[29] amount to about $100 per annum" and stock in the Frederick & Reistertown Turnpike. He also sought to purchase stock in several banks.[30] Most advertisements were more general. Francis White of Philadelphia, for example, advertised in 1787 that he "wanted to Purchase, Loan-Office Certificates of Pennsylvania Continental Certificates, of any State or Kind, Shilling and Dollar Money, and all other Kinds of Public Securities, for which the Highest Price will be Given. Country People and others, May be supplied with Certificates, and Shilling Money, to pay for their Warrants and Patents at the land Office, at as low a Prices as the Market will admit. Money borrowed or lent on approved Notes or Deposits, and negociated so as to accommodate People with the Kind that may best suit them."[31] Similarly, in 1792, Baltimore broker Elkin Solomon dealt in "Ground-Rents...Final Settlements; Indents; Continental Money; Maryland Convention; North Carolina Certificates; Virginia Continental State Money; Black, State and Red Money, of the State of Maryland; Maryland Depreciation Certificates, as well as the Funded Debt, viz. Six per Cents, Three per Cents, and Deferred."[32]

The "Intelligence and Broker's Office" of Cavanaugh and Hart brokered just about everything. In addition to buying and selling "certificates and paper money of every denomination, bills of exchange on England, Holland, France, &c. bank stock, and all other kinds of transferable property," and discounting "bills and notes," the brokers offered to match "persons wanting to purchase or sell any kind of goods, lands, farms, lots or houses, horses and carriages of any sort." They also provided a job service, promising to match employees and employers for $.25. Renters and tenants were also matched. The office also dealt in slaves.[33] Similarly, in 1814, Baker's General Intelligence Office bought and sold "bound Servants...Foreign Notes...Bank

[26]Thomas A. Biddle and J. Wharton Company Letter Book, HSP.
[27]Pennsylvania Gazette, 15 March 1786.
[28]Ibid., 27 July 1785, 15 March 1786, 7 March 1787.
[29]For a description of ground rents, see Wright 1998b, 1999b.
[30]Baltimore American and Commercial Daily Advertiser, 11 April 1810.
[31]Pennsylvania Gazette, 26 August 1787. Other examples include the advertisements of George Taylor Jr., William Blackburn, and John Donnaldson, Political and Commercial Register, 30 July, 23 November 1804, 4 March 1805.
[32]Baltimore Daily Repository, 28 May 1792.
[33]Pennsylvania Gazette, 12 November 1788.

Stock and Treasury Notes." It also procured "substitutes" for those wishing to avoid military service.[34]

Sometimes brokers also sold dry goods.[35] Occasionally, truly bizarre combinations appeared. At his "Universal Intelligence and Exchange Office," Simon Fishbaugh bought and sold, in addition to "all kinds of public securities... Virginia land warrants, [and] ... tracts of Pennsylvania patented lands, in Bucks, Berks, Chester, Lancaster and Westmoreland counties... a quantity of best Boston mackerel, and a few barrels of limes, in prime order, &c."[36] Charles Young was a stock and exchange broker, notary public, accountant, scrivener, and conveyancer.[37] One Philadelphia broker also adjusted "insurance losses" for a time.[38]

The great diversity of brokers' activities makes drawing any conclusions about their numbers difficult. Brokers could simply shift their business emphasis to counter securities volume fluctuations. When volumes were low, they could sell more lottery tickets, or fish. When volumes were high, they could concentrate on securities sales.

As a general trend, though, the number of brokers should have increased over time, if only to keep up with the growing population and increased breadth and depth of the securities markets. Indeed, this appears to have been the case in Philadelphia. In 1800 Philadelphia was home to 28 securities brokers,[39] up from 22 late in the eighteenth century.[40] By 1810 the number of brokers had receded slightly to 26,[41] but in 1820 there were 27 Philadelphia brokers with surnames beginning with the letters A through M alone.[42] The 1820s and 1830s witnessed little change in the number of brokers, which appears to have stabilized around 45.[43] The number of brokers exploded to 111 by 1850.[44]

Other cities also experienced growth in the number of brokers over the period of this study. Newspapers, letter books, and directories reveal the existence of securities brokers in Albany, New York; Alexandria, Virginia; Annapolis, Maryland; Baltimore, Maryland;

[34] *Political and Commercial Register*, 15 August 1814.   [35] Ibid., 16 May 1805.

[36] *Pennsylvania Gazette*, 9 August 1786.   [37] Ibid., 25 August 1790.

[38] *Political and Commercial Register*, 9 July 1813, 17 March 1814.

[39] *The New Trade Directory for Philadelphia, Anno 1800... Containing a Complete List of all the Occupations and Trades... Practised in the City and Liberties.*

[40] Barnes 1911:5.   [41] *Robinson's Directory.*

[42] *Whitely's Directory.* The figures for 1810, 1820, and 1830 were derived by compiling lists from the directories' "white pages," the alphabetical listings of occupants by last name. The number of names in the 1810 directory was only 12,936. The 1820 directory, by contrast, contained 25,920 names, and the 1830 directory many more than that, so only A–M was scanned for brokers.

[43] *Desilver's Directory*, 1830; *O'Brien's Pocket Directory*, 1838–39.

[44] *Bywater's Directory.* Only 56 of those 111 were members of the newly formed stock exchange.

Boston, Massachusetts; Charleston, South Carolina; Hartford, Connecticut; New York, New York; Norfolk, Virginia; Pittsburgh, Pennsylvania; and Richmond, Virginia.[45]

Initial Public Offerings

Early brokers were engaged exclusively in the secondary market. In other words, they brokered or bought and sold securities already issued. Companies also completed equity IPOs. Basically, companies sold their shares directly to investors, without the aid of intermediaries like today's investment banks. The first securities that required underwriting were federal, state, and later corporate debt obligations. During the War of 1812, a syndicate of private bankers underwrote an issue of U.S. Treasury bonds.[46] In the antebellum period, private bankers began to underwrite state and railroad bond issues, a function that they also fulfilled with federal debt issues during the Civil War.[47] It was only in the postbellum era that underwriting of equities, preferred and common, began in earnest, though even then stocks continued to reach market through private sales and insiders' sales through brokers.[48] All early IPOs, in other words, were what analysts today call DPOs, or direct public offerings.

The Bank of North America: America's First IPO

America's first IPO went smoothly, considering that at the time, 1781–82, the new nation was engulfed in the darkest part of the American Revolution. Newly appointed superintendent of finance, Robert Morris, hatched the plan for a commercial bank in the spring of 1781. Morris, a Philadelphia merchant with close connections to the young nation's wealthiest and most enterprising entrepreneurs,[49] believed he needed to call in the aid of private credit to help bolster the weak central government's flagging finances. Many others agreed, but Morris faced several obstacles. Precious few Americans, for example,

---

[45]Important specific sources for supplementing city directories include: Larson 1931; *Philadelphia Public Sales Report*, various dates in 1827 and 1828; *Finance and Industry, New York and Philadelphia Stock Exchanges: Banks, Bankers, Business Houses, and Moneyed Institutions of the Two Great Cities of the United States* (New York: Historical Publishing, 1886); Jacob Barker, *Third Trial of Jacob Barker, for Conspiracy* (New York: Clayton and Van Norden, 1827); Andrew Craigie Papers, AAS; John Delafield Letter Book, NYPL; Clement Biddle Letter Book, HSP; Mark Prager Letter Book, HSP; James O. Wettereau Collection, Columbia University, New York. Important newspapers for brokerage advertisements include: *Alexandria Gazette; Baltimore American; Baltimore Telegraph; Boston Columbia Centinel; Charleston Courier; New York Independent Journal; New York Public Advertiser; Philadelphia Political and Commercial Register; Richmond Enquirer.*
[46]Adams 1978a.   [47]Carosso 1970:1–28.   [48]Carosso 1970:29–50.
[49]Wright 1996.

had experience with joint-stock corporations. Colonial America had been home to only six domestic business corporations and a handful of joint-stock associations.[50] Due to that lack of experience, Morris did not know how to price the shares of the proposed bank. In his "Plan for Establishing a National Bank in the United States of North America," Morris noted that "it is not possible to determine what is the highest Sum that could speedily be obtained by Subscription." He reasoned that "to ask more than could be obtained wou'd have a fatal effect, to ask less is a partial Evil. It is an Evil which admits of a Remedy by opening a New Subscription and that remedy is provided in the plan."[51] Morris realized that it would be easier to sell additional shares after the Bank had established itself, paid some dividends, and helped to stabilize the weak republic's shaky fiscal situation.[52]

Morris also realized that the offer of limited liability would attract much passive investment. Although its charters did not specifically grant limited liability, Morris clearly believed that stockholder liability was limited to the par value of the stock.[53] Finally, Morris knew that the likely existence of a secondary market would fuel demand for shares. He therefore added to the fifth clause of his national bank plan a marginal notation allowing each subscriber to "sell and transfer his share or shares at his pleasure." By mid-June Morris reported that subscriptions to the new bank "go on pretty well" but a dearth of "hard Money," driven out of circulation by "depreciated paper, Tender and Penal Laws," slowed the process.[54] Morris attempted to sell shares to investors throughout the thirteen colonies, Cuba, and Europe.[55] Predictably, there was little demand from areas "where the Inhabitants are little acquainted with commerce"[56] but considerably more from merchants, millers,[57] and politicians.[58] By November, when the bank's stockholders voted for directors, $70,000, in shares of $400 each, had been subscribed, but some of that figure was sold to government creditors and hence represented an equity for debt conversion rather than new investment.[59] A huge influx of specie, the proceeds of a French loan to the Continental Congress, helped the bank considerably, allowing it to open in early January 1782, though its IPO was still in progress.[60] The continuation of the subscription, of course, capped the bank's stock price in the secondary market at par. News of a definitive peace treaty arrived in March 1783. By 30 June 1783 nongovernment subscriptions stood at $215,200.[61] After a 6.5 percent semiannual dividend was announced in July 1783, the subscription books, just as Morris had predicted two years earlier, filled rapidly, after which the price of the stock in the secondary market rose above

[50]Baldwin 1903.   [51]*PRM*, 1:70.   [52]*PRM*, 1:71, 146, 288, 295.   [53]*PRM*, 1:361.
[54]*PRM*, 1:144–45.   [55]*PRM*, 1:319, 357.   [56]*PRM*, 2:69.   [57]*PRM*, 2:152.
[58]*PRM*, 2:367.   [59]*PRM*, 3:167.   [60]*PRM*, 3:121, 497, 503.   [61]*PRM*, 5:797.

par.[62] Continued high dividends attracted much attention, allowing for the sale of additional shares in 1784. With considerable Dutch investment,[63] this second offering did quite well. "You cannot imagine with what rapidity the Subscriptions filled, after the books were open," Philadelphia Samson Fleming wrote William Edgar of New York.[64] At about the same time, the IPO of a second Philadelphia bank filled in just 10 days. The new bank merged with the BNA before it began operation.[65]

Better Times, Better Results: An Overview of Early National IPOs

The BNA IPO was one of the rockiest in early American history. Subsequent subscriptions, particularly for banks, filled extremely quickly.[66] For example, the subscription to the Union Bank of New London filled with "rapidity" in early 1792, with subscribers from New London, Norwich, and "the neighbouring towns."[67] The 1803 Bank of Philadelphia IPO filled immediately, with 198 investors taking shares.[68] The IPO of the North River Bank of New York filled five times over in 1821.[69] Even smaller markets could fill subscriptions quickly. In 1824 the first bank to be established in Rochester, New York, then a mere town of slightly more than 3,000 souls, attracted five times the amount of capital that it sought.[70] Because early corporate charters stated the exact price at which shares could be sold, the stock commissioners, agents in charge of the IPO, could not raise the share price to decrease the quantity demanded, engaging instead in nonprice rationing that often took on political overtones.[71] Indeed, a riot almost broke out when the subscription books for Alexander Hamilton's brainchild, the BUS, opened in 1791. Stockbrokers in Philadelphia grossly underestimated the demand for shares in the new national bank. At least one broker told correspondents that it would take at least one month for the subscription to fill.[72] When the books opened on 5 July a mad rush for the door ensued; "In about an hour the subscription was declared to be closed."[73] (Predictably, there was a tremendous "pop" in share prices in the after market.) To reduce the likelihood of the repetition of such scenes, state legislatures often limited the number of shares that any one person, or in some cases

---

[62]*PRM*, 9:639.   [63]*PRM*, 8:813, 9:644.
[64]Samson Fleming to William Edgar, 9 February 1784, William Edgar Papers, NYPL.
[65]Rappaport 1996:160.   [66]Perkins 1994.
[67]*Massachusetts Columbian Centinel*, 18 February 1792.   [68]Wainwright 1953:6.
[69]*Richmond Enquirer*, 13 April 1821.   [70]*Rochester Telegraph*, 11 May 1824.
[71]Wright 1997a:986.
[72]Clement Biddle to William Campbell, 19 June 1791; to David Finlay, 1 July 1791, Clement Biddle Letter Book, HSP.
[73]Clement Biddle to William Rogers, 5 July 1791, ibid.

any one town or occupation, could subscribe to early banks.[74] The appointment of stock commissioners, who had power to apportion shares when the demand for shares exceeded the fixed supply, was highly politicized.[75]

Nor was the enthusiasm for early IPOs solely a northern phenomenon. In 1785 a Potomac River improvement company raised £4,300, "a sum far beyond what was requisite to incorporate the company," in a single afternoon.[76] In 1792 a bank in Alexandria, Virginia, subscribed in "less than two hours," leaving many would-be stockholders "disappointed." In 1804 the Potomac Bank of Virginia, which then did not even have a government charter, filled its subscription within 24 hours.[77]

Generally speaking, early corporations, especially banks and insurance companies, did not engage in elaborate marketing schemes to ensure a rapid IPO. In large seaport cities, they published advertisements in major papers. The Insurance Company of North America, for example, which was headquartered in Philadelphia, published a column-long prospectus. Such advertisements were the forerunners of today's "tombstones," minus the list of underwriters, of course.[78] Others solicited banks and other financial intermediaries directly, through private letter[79] or pamphlet prospectus.[80] Corporations in less densely populated areas spread word of their IPOs via word of mouth, public meetings, and printed bulletins.[81] Others, such as the inland navigation companies of upstate New York, managed to obtain good publicity; a news article proclaiming that the companies would "immediately realize a handsome annual dividend" allowed the companies to obtain funds from as far away as Philadelphia.[82]

Very few early IPOs were made by corporations actually in business; most occurred during the planning stage. This makes the relative ease with which subscriptions filled even more interesting. It also explains why some early IPOs in emerging sectors were slow. It took several months for the Society for the Establishment of Useful Manufacturers (SEUM) to fill up its subscription books in 1791, for example, because the company had no track record and textile manufacturing concerns

[74]Wright 1997a:443, 486, 544, 547.
[75]Chaddock 1910; Wright 1997a:791, 838, 875–76.
[76]*Pennsylvania Gazette*, 1 June 1785.
[77]*Columbian Mirror and Alexandria Gazette*, 5, 8 December 1792, as quoted in Crothers 1999:16–17, 34–37.
[78]*Gazette of the United States*, 15 August 1798.
[79]See, for example, Directors' Minutes, Bank of Philadelphia, 14 September 1826, 8 January 1827, 23 June 1831, Philadelphia National Bank Records, HSP. See also the Directors' Minutes, Philadelphia Insurance Company, HSP.
[80]Philadelphia Insurance Company, 1803, Fire and Marine Insurance, Society Collection, HSP.
[81]Majewski 2000.   [82]*Pennsylvania Gazette*, 24 October 1792.

were few and far between in America at that time.[83] The nation's first life insurance company also had difficulty raising equity capital. It took a pamphlet by Thomas Willing, the first president of the BNA and the first president of the BUS, to fill the books.[84]

The first corporations priced their shares at $400 and even $500 each, over $4,000 in today's dollars. Soon, corporations discovered that they could raise the same amount of capital but fill their subscriptions more rapidly by issuing more shares at a lower price per share. By 1800 par share prices for most new corporations dropped to between $10 and $100, allowing far wider participation in IPOs. The Manhattan Company, a joint-stock water company (with secret aspirations of functioning as a bank), was heavily oversubscribed on the first day because of its low offering price per share.[85] Stock ownership in early America, recent studies have shown, was much wider than previously assumed.[86]

New Data on Early IPOs

Continuing research bolsters those findings. In 1810 the Commercial and Farmers Bank of Baltimore sold more than $500,000 worth of its stock in just a few days.[87] The 239 subscribers took an average of more than $2,000 each, but some investors purchased as little as $20 and one bought $31,000 worth of stock. Institutions, insurance companies, savings banks, government treasurers, schools, and other commercial banks, not individuals, placed the largest subscriptions. Most subscriptions, however, were small ones made by individuals; indeed, the mode subscription was $200.

Even local internal-improvement concerns found that they could raise equity capital without the help of intermediaries. The upstate New York Inland Navigation companies overfilled their subscription books by almost half.[88] The Permanent Bridge Company of Philadelphia was another successful early internal-improvement company. From April 1798 until April 1800, 427 different investors subscribed for an average of 35.13 shares.[89] The lowest subscription was for one share; the largest, shares given to the City of Philadelphia in consideration for real estate, was for 2,000 shares. The largest private investment was for 310 shares. The mode subscription was just 10 shares. Trading in the secondary market was extremely limited until the subscription closed. In a few weeks in 1803, the bridge firm sold an additional 5,477 shares. Most subscribers lived in the City of Philadelphia but considerable numbers lived in nearby counties. The size of the offering seems to have slowed the IPO; a much smaller offering about the

---

[83]Wright 1997a:184–85.   [84]Wright 1996.   [85]Wright 1997a:260.
[86]Crothers 1999; Karmel 1999; Majewski 2000; Wright 1999a, 2000.
[87]Directors' Minutes, Commercial and Farmers' Bank, MHS.
[88]*Pennsylvania Gazette*, 13 June 1792.   [89]Permanent Bridge Stock Books, HSP.

same time by the Schuylkill River Bridge Company closed much more quickly.[90] In that IPO, each of the 59 investors purchased on average just over 5 of the $50 shares. The largest investor bought only 50; the mode purchase was 2 shares. In 1795, "the shares in the projected Causeway" between Boston and Dorchester Point "were immediately filled up." In other words, subscribers purchased all £20,000 worth of stock when the books opened.[91] In 1825 the IPO of the Staunton and James River Turnpike Company filled quickly.[92] About the same time, "Jersey Blues were seen struggling in unwonted competition with our Wall Street regulars, for priority" in the Morris Canal Company IPO. The issue was quickly subscribed 10 times over.[93] A few days later, the IPO of the Blackstone Canal of Rhode Island oversubscribed by 1 P.M. on the first day and the IPO of the New York Water Works Company was oversubscribed 4.5 times.[94] In 1833 the IPO of the Utica and Schenectady Railroad Company brought in $14 million, "seven times the amount of the [authorized] Capital."[95]

The IPOs of "country banks," banks outside of the major seaport cities, sometimes went slowly but rarely faltered. For example, in 1814–15 the Bank of Chester County needed six months to fill its books,[96] though investors took up almost half of the offering in the first week.[97] The delay, which contemporaries thought was caused by "local jealousy," appears not to have hurt the bank materially, however; eventually 167 investors bought an average of 11.5 shares. The largest stockholder took 100 shares; the mode purchase was two shares.[98] In 1830 the Central Bank of Worcester, Massachusetts, was able to sell 1,000 shares of its stock to 89 different investors (11.25 average, 5 mode) in Worcester and surrounding communities.[99] In 1832 the Concord Bank of Massachusetts oversold its subscription on the first day. A total of 164 investors subscribed for 1,084 shares; only 1,000 shares had been authorized.[100]

Trading Volumes in the Secondary Securities Markets: The Case of Philadelphia

The available sources offer a provocative glimpse at both the depth and breadth of securities trading in the secondary market in Philadelphia

[90]Schuylkill Bridge Subscription List, HSP.   [91]*Boston Columbian Centinel*, 1 July 1795.
[92]*Richmond Enquirer*, 3 May 1825.
[93]*New York National Advocate*, as quoted in the *Richmond Enquirer*, 6 May 1825.
[94]*New York National Advocate*, as quoted in the *Richmond Enquirer*, 10 May 1825.
[95]*Richmond Enquirer*, 28 June 1833.
[96]Bank of Chester County, Stock Ledger, 1814–22, CCHS.
[97]*American Republic*, 14 June 1814.
[98]Bank of Chester County, Stock Transfer Ledger, 1814–72, CCHS.
[99]Central Bank of Worcester Records, Stock Record Book, 1830–64, AAS.
[100]Patterson 1971:14–34.

throughout the early national period. For the earlier years, when only letter book information is available, a narrative exposition is necessary. The discussion becomes briefer and more analytical when brokers' account books and newspaper volume information become available.

At one level, the volume of securities trading matters much less than liquidity, the *ability* of holders to sell securities for fair market prices at will, a key attraction of financial securities. As long as buyers stand ready to purchase any securities offered for sale, the markets can be said to be "liquid" because investors can divest when they see fit. If it happens that few investors desire to divest, trading volumes will be low, but the markets will still be liquid as long as buyers remain ready to purchase. Strong anecdotal evidence suggests that such was the case in early American securities markets, including Philadelphia's. When a stock did not trade, in other words, it was usually because no one wanted to sell it, not because no one wanted to buy it. This seems to have been especially true after 1800. Unfortunately, there is no direct way to measure liquidity. The volume of trades, however, can serve as a rough gauge of liquidity – if a security is actively traded, it is likely also to be liquid. We cannot conclude, however, that an inactively traded stock is illiquid because it may just be that no one wants to sell it. Stock of the BNA, for example, rarely appeared for sale although investors from London to St. Croix clamored for it.[101]

Philadelphia's stock market, though initially perhaps larger than that of New York, probably represented only one-quarter of the securities trades in the nation in the 1790s and early 1800s. Over the decades Philadelphia's share of trading diminished significantly. By the late 1830s the number of shares traded in Philadelphia amounted to only about 15 percent of that in New York alone.[102] By that time, stock trading in Philadelphia and all of the other markets probably totaled only half of New York's impressive volume. Thus, the volume figures discussed here are a mere fraction of total U.S. stock market volume. It seems clear, then, that despite the repeated assertions of "moral economy" historians,[103] early Americans, even if they might have thought or wished otherwise, were clearly part of a capitalist economy.

Indications of Early Trading Activity, 1789–1798

American securities dealers set to work quickly after the ratification of the Constitution, beginning arbitrage operations even before the

---

[101] Mark Prager to James St. Ferrall, 9 February 1797; Mark Prager to Thomas Geise, 13 May 1797, Mark Prager Letter Book, HSP.
[102] Werner and Smith 1991: appendix B.
[103] Henretta 1998; Merrill and Wilentz 1993.

implementation of Hamilton's funding system. Clement Biddle of Philadelphia, for example, was already filling orders for New York dealers William Rogers and Robert Gilchrist by early 1789.[104] Within a few months Biddle was also corresponding with brokers in Maryland[105] and making sales to investors in Switzerland and England.[106] Biddle's letters make clear that by late spring 1789 brokers carrying "gluts" of securities shuttled between New York, Philadelphia, and Baltimore seeking higher prices.[107] By the end of July, Philadelphia brokers had concluded that "Demand from Europe" also influenced local prices.[108] The supply and demand of the many securities also waxed and waned with news of national political developments linked to the funding issue.[109] Many of Biddle's letters clearly indicate that securities were changing hands, but Biddle was rarely precise about the dollar amounts of the various "large parcels"[110] and "brisk demand"[111] he mentioned to correspondents. Similarly, it is difficult to quantify statements like "little is done in [the] Paper [securities] Business here"[112] or "very few have been bought and sold."[113]

Biddle often conducted business in the "The Merchants' Coffee-House & Place of Exchange." Started by Edward Moyston on 12 January 1789, the exchange conducted business from 12 noon until 2 P.M. and from 6 to 8 P.M.[114] I have found no evidence indicating that the persons trading on the exchange entered into any sort of trading contract like the famous Buttonwood agreement made by New York brokers in 1792. However, the Philadelphia Stock Exchange, which still exists, claims to have formed in 1790 with Biddle as a leading member. If an agreement existed, it presumably did not attempt to monopolize securities trading, because Biddle traded freely and extensively "out of doors."

Despite the existence of a central trading location, brokers found it difficult to track the market value and future prospects of a plethora of debt securities under the control of a dozen different governments. The dearth of information made efficient trading difficult. For instance, when several New York brokers came into Philadelphia by stage in December 1789 a "General alarm" practically ended trading. The Philadelphians believed that the New Yorkers must have been privy

[104]Clement Biddle to William Rogers, 5, 8, 12, 16 February 1789; to Robert Gilchrist, 5 March 1789, Clement Biddle Letter Book, HSP. Unless specified otherwise, the following letters are from Clement Biddle, Clement Biddle Letter Book, HSP.
[105]To William Deakins Jr., 4 March 1789; to Luther Martin, 18, 23 April 1789.
[106]To Brother & Sister Tellier, 24 April 1789; to Richard Smith, 25 April 1789.
[107]To Robert Gilchrist, 15, 25 May 1789.   [108]To Robert Gilchrist, 27 July 1789.
[109]To George Joy, 9 September 1789.   [110]To Robert Gilchrist, 20 July 1789.
[111]To Col. MacGregor, 19 November 1789.
[112]To Robert Gilchrist, 2 September 1789.   [113]To George Joy, 9 September 1789.
[114]*Pennsylvania Packet*, 21 February 1789; Business Card of Edward Moyston, 18 August 1789, Society Miscellaneous, Business Cards, HSP.

to important secret information and rushed south to take advantage of their neighbors' ignorance. "For some days past there has been so violent a push from N York for Finals & Indents," Biddle explained, "that most people have been afraid to sell."[115] Biddle for one complained that increased prices for certain securities must have been "occasioned" by New York speculators "more than by real Demand."[116] He could not believe that foreign demand had spurred the "Rise" because he had heard that "many sums limitted at about 6/ were offered on the Exchange at Amsterdam & unsold."[117] In early 1790, Biddle noted that "the scarcity of Certificates makes it difficult to lay out a large Sum with Dispatch."[118] Buyers of indents and finals flooded the market, so frightening holders that Biddle could buy few "parcels."[119] Trading slowed further as investors digested news of Hamilton's proposed funding plan.[120] By the end of January, however, the situation reversed; many offered securities for sale but "few" purchasers had "Cash to any amount."[121]

In the last few days of January the price of finals "gradually fell" from 8/3 to 7/6,[122] first in New York, then in Philadelphia. Political news regarding Hamilton's funding plan, Biddle implied, was the reason for the fall. Philadelphians feared that funding would meet "warm opposition" in Congress and perhaps would be replaced with a "less favourable Plan."[123] Trading continued "not brisk" and "dull" in February because news of James Madison's funding plan, which would have discriminated between initial holders and speculators, made investors skittish.[124] Convinced that the rejection of Madison's motion would make securities "certainly rise," Biddle repeatedly beseeched his New York correspondents to send him more, faster, and more accurate information regarding "Congress Debates."[125] Biddle was right; Congress's rejection of Madison's motion gave "spirits to the holders of Certificates" and increased prices, and apparently transaction volumes, in both New York and Philadelphia.[126] But the brief euphoria soon gave way to another lull, which Biddle attributed to the fact that there was not "any Real Demand" for securities in Europe "at the present

[115]To William Rogers, 17 December 1789.
[116]To William Rogers, 3 December 1789; to Robert Gilchrist, 10, 14 December 1789.
[117]To William Rogers, 17 December 1789.   [118]To Luther Martin, 16 January 1790.
[119]To Robert Gilchrist, 7, 11 January 1790.
[120]To Robert Gilchrist, 17, 24 January 1790; to William Rogers, 21 January 1790; to William Deakins, 24 January 1790.
[121]To Robert Gilchrist, 28 January 1790.
[122]That is to say, from 8 shillings 3 pence on the pound to 7 shillings 6 pence on the pound, or from 41.25 percent of par to 37.50 percent of par.
[123]To Robert Gilchrist, 31 January 1790.
[124]To John Groves; to Luther Martin, 16 February 1790.
[125]To Robert Gilchrist, 18, 25 February 1790.
[126]To William Campbell, 28 February 1790.

high Price Especially at the Current low Exchange."[127] During the first week of this "stagnant" period, Biddle appears to have brokered thousands of dollars worth of transactions per week.[128] By the middle of March, however, Biddle would not quote prices because there had been no recent transactions upon which to base an estimate.[129] Cash and information from New York, and hence demand for securities, remained limited until the end of April[130] when prices jumped because of orders from New York.[131]

By early May 1790 Biddle was again doing thousands of dollars worth of business per week.[132] He mentioned that another Philadelphia broker, Mathew McConnell, sold $10,000 worth of Finals in a single transaction in early May.[133] At the end of May, Biddle told a London investor that he had purchased $15,000 of Finals in the past month.[134] Shortly thereafter, the price of Finals rose on news that the funding bill would soon pass Congress. Three British agents offered $30,000 worth for sale at 50 percent of their face value.[135] By mid-June, however, the market reversed again as Congress set the funding bill aside in order to debate "the place of adjournment," the location of the next temporary national capital. Trading so slowed that Biddle was, again, unable to offer price quotations to his correspondents.[136] Conditions loosened slightly in late June because some entered the market to sell "from extreme necessity." Biddle saw the opportunity to purchase "some Bargain[s]" but lacked the cash to make large purchases.[137] Prices and demand continued upward in early July; Biddle's weekly transaction figures probably topped $10,000.[138]

The roller coaster ride of prices and volumes continued throughout July as Congress continued to dawdle with the funding bill[139] and brokers worked together to calculate the rational prices for the various types of the proposed federal debt instruments.[140] Early August witnessed a major increase in prices and volumes.[141] When a sudden jolt in late August sent prices spiraling downward in New York, prices in Philadelphia followed suit until "the advices of Mr. Hamilton's proposition for laying out a million of Dollars in purchase of Finals began to operate on price."[142] Prices vacillated for over a week as investors

[127]To Robert Gilchrist, 4 March 1790.   [128] To Robert Gilchrist, 7, 9 March 1790.
[129]To Robert Gilchrist, 14 March 1790.
[130]To Robert Gilchrist, 1, 13, 16 April 1790; to William Rogers 15, 20, 26 April 1790.
[131]To John Dougherty, 29 April 1790; to William Rogers, 29 April 1790.
[132]To William Rogers, 2, 6, 10 May 1790.   [133]To William Rogers, 10 May 1790.
[134]To Richard Smith, 23 May 1790.   [135]To William Rogers, 30, 31 May, 6 June 1790.
[136]To William Rogers, 15, 18, 20 June 1790.   [137] To William Rogers, 22 June 1790.
[138]To William Rogers, 4, 7 July 1790; to Robert Gilchrist, 4 July 1790.
[139]To William Rogers, 27 July 1790.   [140]To William Rogers, 29 July 1790.
[141]To William Rogers, 3, 4, 5, 6, August 1790.
[142]To William Rogers, 8, 11, 13 August 1790.

awaited Hamilton's appearance in the market.[143] Hamilton's ploy worked; the mere news that he would buy securities bolstered confidence until demand again picked up.[144]

Late September and early October 1790 brought another minor crisis. This time Hamilton did make purchases, but his first effort actually depressed prices because he bought only $50,000 of some $300,000 worth of securities offered for sale.[145] Lower prices did not bring reduced trading volume this time, however, as bulls, and even bears like Biddle, tried to affect prices through purchases.[146] Hamilton made purchases in Philadelphia again in November causing "very brisk" demand for Finals.[147] In late November a number of New York brokers visited Philadelphia and caused "a great Bustle and Rore" and some increase in the price of Finals. Biddle believed, however, that "little was really done."[148]

In December 1790 prices again rose and volumes remained steady as news of a European loan, and a European peace, reached the States. Peace in Europe, Biddle argued, would leave "much money in Holland & England without Employment & [therefore] tend to Raise the price of American Funds."[149] Although European investors preferred to place securities orders with New York brokers at that time, the effect on the Philadelphia market, which, as we have seen, was closely integrated with the New York market, was the same – prices and volumes increased.[150] European investment, however, was not strong enough to keep the market going. By the end of December prices and trade volume slumped.[151] "Our Coffee house [is] quite still in the Evening," Biddle lamented on 7 January 1791.[152] An order for $70,000 of securities from Amsterdam helped to pick the market up in mid-January.[153]

Apparently too busy with his job as head census enumerator, Biddle largely withdrew from securities trading in February 1791. He probably did not miss much as his late January, limited February, and early March letters indicate that there was but little demand.[154] The slow

[143]To William Rogers, 16, 18, 19 August 1790.
[144]To William Rogers, 23, 24, 26, 31 August, 13 September 1790.
[145]To William Rogers, 27, 30 September, 7 October 1790; to Adam Gilchrist, 7 October 1790.
[146]To William Rogers, 7, 17, 21, 24 October 1790; to Alexander Macomb, 24 October 1790.
[147]To William Rogers, 11, 19 November 1790.
[148]To William Rogers, 25 November 1790.
[149]To William Deakins Jr., 5 December 1790; to William Rogers, 25 November, 8 December 1790.
[150]To Robert Gilchrist, 11 December 1790; to William Rogers, 12 December 1790.
[151]To William Rogers, 28, 29 December 1790; to Robert Gilchrist, 29 December 1790.
[152]To George Lewis, 7 January 1791.   [153]To George Lewis, 19 January 1791.
[154]To George Lewis, 31 January, 8 February, 7 March 1791.

market continued through mid-April.[155] Interestingly, Biddle during this lull defined "very dull" as "hardly 5000 Ds done in one Evening."[156] With a six-day trading week then the norm, it appears the securities volume in Philadelphia was at least $1.5 million per year in the early 1790s. Biddle himself did at least $15,000 of securities per week in early April[157] and more than $20,000 per week in mid-April.[158] About that time, Biddle reported the sale of $120,000 of Sixes, apparently to Dutch capitalist Theophile Cazenove.[159] Other orders from Europe, via New York, caused securities prices and volumes in Philadelphia to take "a gradual but considerable rise."[160] Although prices quickly stabilized, Biddle continued to conduct more than $20,000 of business per week.[161] About this time he bragged to London banker John Lloyd that he was "daily executing very extensive Commissions" in the brokerage line.[162]

By early May, volumes shrank again, this time because of a supply shortage. "On the whole," Biddle informed a correspondent, "there are more buyers than sellers."[163] Biddle thought the situation arose because "most cautious monied men" were holding securities in anticipation of using them to purchase stock in the BUS while "frequent & steady orders from different parts of Europe" continued to come in.[164] His analysis may have been incorrect, however, because by mid-May he reported a glut of sellers of Six Percents and a dearth of buyers.[165] Yet at the end of May he again reported a shortage of sellers, noting, in fact, that he had never before "found every kind of paper so scarce."[166] He attributed the scarcity to "there being really little Stock to sell."[167] Biddle responded to the dearth by dispatching "2 or 3 Runners" to the "Country" to round up New Loans and Finals.[168] Based on the activities of "timid" Philadelphia broker Mark Prager, Biddle believed a number of "Dutch orders" had recently been placed.[169] Throughout June 1791 volumes remained low and on some days ceased, but there was enough activity for Biddle to send regular price quotations to his correspondents.[170] According to Biddle, prices at Philadelphia remained "nearly at par" with those at New York.[171] But despite some movement in the market in early July, it quickly ceased because of

[155]To William Rogers, 10, 11 March 1791; to George Lewis, 11, 13 March 1791; to William Campbell, 13 March 1791.
[156]To George Lewis, 13 March 1791.   [157]To William Rogers, 7 April 1791.
[158]To William Rogers, 12, 18 April 1791.   [159]To William Rogers, 13 April 1791.
[160]To William Campbell, 15 April 1791; to Robert Gilchrist, 15 April 1791.
[161]To William Rogers, 22 April 1791.   [162]To John Lloyd, 22 April 1791.
[163]To William Rogers, 7 May 1791.   [164]To William Campbell, 9 May 1791.
[165]To William Rogers, 17 May 1791.   [166]To William Rogers, 31 May 1791.
[167]Ibid.; to James Williams, 2 June 1791; to Jesse Dewees, 2 June 1791.
[168]To William Rogers, 2 June 1791.   [169]Ibid.
[170]1 June to 1 July 1791, Clement Biddle Letter Book, HSP.
[171]To George Lewis, 15 June 1791; to William Rogers, 20 June 1791.

TABLE 6.1. New Federal Debt
Subscribed to the Philadelphia Transfer
Books, 1791–1793

When Subscribed	Dollar Value
Before June 1791	6,827.94
June 1791	31,948.97
July 1791	180,466.97
August 1791	104,654.39
September 1791	348,306.12
June 1792	120,975.62
July 1792	18,074.89
After July 1792	29,468.16
TOTAL	840,723.06

Sources: Abstract of Certificates of the State
Debt of Pennsylvania received by Thomas
Smith Commissioner of Loans for the said State
on account of a Loan to the United States,
RG-4, Records of the Comptroller General,
State Debt, 1780–97; Abstracts of Continental
Certificates, 1791–97, box 1, folder 1, Pennsyl-
vania State Archives, Harrisburgh.

the excitement of the subscription to the BUS.[172] Thereafter securities prices and trade volumes rose,[173] partly because of relatively heavy
subscriptions to the new federal debt in Philadelphia (see Table 6.1),
and partly because of an influx of dealers from Boston and New York
who had descended on Philadelphia "in great numbers" for the bank
subscription.[174] Trading in bank script was heavy, and Biddle, who
professed some disbelief that there was "enough money to spare in
America" for the bank,[175] began almost immediately to try to interest
British investors in the new equities.[176] Debt trade volumes, however,
soon sank back to its low June level[177] only to increase when "the
highest yet known" prices were reached on the night of 23 July.[178]

Prices, and apparently volumes too, of securities, especially bank
script, continued steadily upward. On 11 August, Biddle informed a
correspondent that "the present madness cannot last." "A revultion
must take place,"[179] he argued, because the amount of foreign demand did not warrant the current prices[180] and because the "Rage" for
script brought other securities trading "almost [to] a stand."[181] The

[172] 1 July to 6 July 1791, Clement Biddle Letter Book, HSP.
[173] To various recipients, 11 July 1791.   [174] To Jonathan Williams Jr., 11 July 1791.
[175] To William Rogers, 11 July 1791.   [176] To John Heathcote and Co., 13 July 1791.
[177] To William Rogers, 13 July 1791.   [178] To William Patterson, 24 July 1791.
[179] To William Rogers, 11 August 1791.   [180] To William Deakins Jr., 29 July 1791.
[181] To Forrest & Stoddert, 11 August 1791; to David Finlay, 12 August 1791; to Michael
Heathcote & Co., 14 August 1791.

prices of debt began to slip but Hamilton entered the market and, more through the easing of "apprehentions" than through purchases, stabilized securities prices a few pence above his purchase rates.[182] By 21 August, Biddle thought he knew what was driving the market – rampant futures speculation in New York. "I can no other way account for the rise which is above any calculation I can make for the profit from the bank & the quantity of money in the Country," he informed a correspondent.[183] By the end of August, however, script volume fell off to next to nothing while debt volumes remained "Remarkably Dull."[184] At the end of the first week of September, Biddle informed correspondents that he thought securities prices were right where they should be, given limited foreign demand. "They are quite equal to their value for Citizens," he argued.[185] Nevertheless, prices fell again in light trading, and again Hamilton bolstered the market with his purchases.[186] Volumes continued light and prices relatively stable through September. For reasons unknown, in early October there was a "brisk demand" for Deferred stock, Hamilton's new zero-coupon bonds.[187] At the end of October, trading picked up significantly "owing to the Numbers of Persons in th[e brokerage] line assembled" in Philadelphia for the first election of the directors of the BUS.[188]

By early November, Philadelphia brokers began to use forward and futures contracts more extensively.[189] The speculations included U.S. debt but seemed focused on BUS script, the price of which "varied in New York very repeatedly within a fortnight from 138 to 150 D[ollar]s" and in Philadelphia "from 139 to 149."[190] Express messengers kept dealers informed of price movements in both markets.[191] On the evening of 17 November 1791, Biddle traded $10,000 of Six Percents in a single transaction.[192] Volumes declined in late November,[193] only to pick up in early December, presumably because of a large order from Europe.[194] Biddle sold as many as 64 BUS scripts in a single day in early December. News of St. Clair's loss to Native American forces, which arrived in Philadelphia on the evening of 8 December,

[182]To David Finlay, 17 August 1791; to Buchan Patton & Co., 18 August 1791; to James Williams, 19 August 1791; to William Rogers, 21 August 1791.
[183]To Robert Gilchrist, 21 August 1791.
[184]To A. Campbell, 28 August 1791; to William Rogers, 30 August, 1 September 1791; to Ms. Wilson, 4 September 1791.
[185]To Buchan, Patton and Co., 7 September 1791.
[186]To Robert Gilchrist, 9 September 1791; to George Gray, 11 September 1791; to William Campbell, 13 September 1791.
[187]To William Rogers, 6 October 1791; to J. B. Dandridge, 10 October 1791.
[188]To Forrest and Stoddert, 23 October 1791.
[189]To George Lewis, 2, 7 morning, 7 evening, 9, 11, 14 November 1791.
[190]To William Campbell, 17 evening November 1791.
[191]To George Lewis, 17 November 1791.   [192]To George Lewis, 18 November 1791.
[193]To George Lewis, 22 November 1791; to Robertson, Saunders, and Co., 24 November 1791.
[194]To Forrest and Stoddert, 4 December 1791; to William Campbell, 4 December 1791.

slowed sales of U.S. debt.[195] Philadelphians understood that the defeat would not impair the ability of the United States to service its debt, but they believed the news would adversely affect the views of "the monied men of Europe to whom the Business will be magnified & the consequences less understood."[196] Except for Mondays, which Biddle noted were traditionally light,[197] trading volume slowly rose through December as brokers from across the nation poured into Philadelphia for the opening of the BUS.[198] That bank "discounted very liberally," pleasing all and keeping transaction volumes high.[199]

In January 1792 the prices of securities in New York rose, forcing Philadelphia prices upward. Philadelphia investors nevertheless remained skittish, especially when packet letters showed that prices for American securities in London were somewhat lower than expected.[200] In mid-January "there was a Run . . . for large Sums" of Six Percents that died when word of the formation of a new bank in New York reached Philadelphia.[201] Except for "sham sales" and exchange of a few small parcels, little was done.[202] Interestingly, prices in Philadelphia in January finally rose slightly above those in New York. The flow of money from New York to Philadelphia quickly reversed with Biddle sending over $13,000 in gold to New York to fund his purchases there.[203] By the end of January, Biddle was trading scores – and, in some instances, hundreds – of BUS half shares almost every trading day.[204] In early February, Biddle noted that he had $30,000 to $40,000 of Six Percents to sell.[205] He disposed of as many as $25,000 worth of Six Percents a day.[206] For the most part,[207] volumes in the first two weeks of February remained high as what Biddle perceived as a speculative bubble grew.[208] In mid-February, however, both the BNA and the BUS began "withholding discounts," making both prices and volumes suffer.[209] The failure of the New York bank schemes and somewhat more liberal discounts loosened the market

---

[195]To George Lewis, 9 December 1791.
[196]To William Campbell, 11 December 1791.
[197]To George Lewis, 22 November, 21 December 1791.
[198]To James Williams, 11 December 1791.
[199]To William Rogers, 21 December 1791.
[200]To George Lewis, 12, 13 January 1792; to William Rogers, 15 January 1792; to George Gray, 15 January 1792.
[201]To George Lewis, 16 January 1792; to William Campbell, 17 January 1792.
[202]To George Lewis, 18, 19, 21 January 1792; to Captain Campbell, 22 January 1792.
[203]To Robert Gilchrist, 21, 23 January 1792; to Captain Campbell, 22 January 1792.
[204]To George Lewis, 25, 29 January 1792.   [205]To George Lewis, 5 February 1792.
[206]To George Lewis, 6, 7 February 1792.
[207]An exception was 13 February when only $5,000 to $6,000 worth of securities were sold on time. To George Lewis, 13 February 1792.
[208]To William Rogers, 5 February 1792.
[209]To George Lewis, 16, 19 February 1792; to William Rogers, 17, 25 February 1792; to Captain Campbell, 19, 21, 23 February 1792.

TABLE 6.2. A Week of Trading, Monday, 20
February through Saturday, 25 February 1792

Security	Volume	
	No. of Shares	Par Value
BNA	14	
Bank of United States	416	
Canal prizes	29	
Pennsylvania Debt		7,620.29
U.S. Deferred		22,433.33
U.S. Sixes		107,060.40
U.S. Threes		72,354.80

Source: *Pelosi's Marine List and Price Current.*

in late February,[210] but still, according to Biddle, there was "not much done."[211] A mercantile paper defined that phrase precisely for each day from Monday, 20 February, through Saturday, 25 February. During that trading week, 459 shares changed hands in 106 transactions. Most were BUS half shares, but BNA shares and canal prizes also traded. Also that week, investors traded just over $210,000 (par value) of U.S. Sixes, Threes, Deferred, and Pennsylvania debt in 96 transactions. Some trades were immediate but many were forward or futures contracts[212] (see Table 6.2).

Bank discounts and securities volumes remained relatively low in the first week of March,[213] but the latter picked up considerably on the seventh, when Biddle sold 85 BUS half shares and $6,000 of Three Percents.[214] Two days later Biddle reported that "advises from New York of a fall & our Banks discounts being very limited indeed, occasioned a great Bustle amongst the dealers in Stocks of every kind."[215] "Five per cent a month with good deposits," Biddle noted, "would be given for money."[216] After news of the failure of William Duer reached Philadelphia on 11 March, prices and volumes plummeted.[217] The Panic of 1792 had begun in earnest. "The demand for money and general alarm," Biddle told a correspondent, "was beyond any thing I have known." "Borrowing at any rate is out of the question," he claimed. Securities could not be turned into cash, only into promissory notes, which the banks would not discount.[218] On 18 March Biddle instructed a correspondent to borrow money in Maryland because the going rate in Philadelphia then stood at 10 to 12 percent per month.[219] A few

[210] To Robert Gilchrist, 26 February 1792.   [211] To Philip R. Fendall, 28 February 1792.
[212] *Pelosi's Marine List and Price Current*, 27 February 1792.
[213] To William Rogers, 4 March 1792.   [214] To George Lewis, 7 March 1792.
[215] To William Campbell, 9 March 1792.   [216] Ibid.
[217] To George Lewis, 11 March 1792.   [218] To George Lewis, 12, 17 March 1792.
[219] To William Campbell, 18 March 1792.

TABLE 6.3. Trading Activity, Schuylkill and Susquehanna Navigation
Company, 1792

Time Period	No. of Transactions	No. of Shares Traded
25 February – 28 February	8	10
March	314	430
April	91	135
May	19	34
June	47	76
July	12	23
August	30	65
September	18	48
October	8	10
November	4	4
December	8	10
TOTALS	559	845

Source: Schuylkill and Susquehanna Navigation Co. Stock Transfer Book, 1792, Union
Canal Co. Records, HSP.

days later prices stabilized and volumes increased, probably on orders
from bargain hunters in Philadelphia and southern markets.[220] The
failure of Alexander Macomb in early April initiated a second wave
of panic that stopped trading for almost a week.[221] Again bargain
hunters from the South stepped in to make purchases.[222] In a brilliant
move, Hamilton added considerable liquidity to the system by selling
guilder bills on liberal terms.[223] On 22 April Biddle correctly noted
that "Prices are Recovering."[224] By the 25 April sales of securities were
"brisk."[225] Prices vacillated but volumes remained strong throughout
May.[226] The stock transfer book of the Schuylkill and Susquehanna
Navigation Company, shown in Table 6.3, reinforces the pattern described by Biddle. Interestingly, despite its high trading volume of
almost 85 percent turnover in 1792, the newspapers rarely quoted the
price of Schuylkill and Susquehanna shares. The stock transfer books
of the BUS also indicate that the market recovered quickly. Between
26 April and 12 June 1792, some 4,300 BUS shares changed hands in
just under 500 transactions.[227]

[220]To George Lewis, 20, 21, 25 March 1792.
[221]To George Lewis, 12 April 1792; to Forrest and Stoddert, 17 April 1792.
[222]To R. M. Scott, 18 April 1792.　　　[223]To George Lewis, 18 April 1792.
[224]To William Rogers, 22 April 1792.　　　[225]To George Lewis, 25 April 1792.
[226]To Captain Campbell, 26 April 1792; to William Campbell, 2, 4 May 1792; to George
Lewis, 6 May 1792.
[227]Precis of "Stock Transfer Book," April 26–June 12, 1792, folder 64, box 6, James O.
Wettereau Papers, Columbia University, New York.

The 1792 correction worked to keep prices in line with those in Europe.[228] Except for a few minor aftershocks in early June caused by the protesting of some of Macomb's bills in London,[229] the effects of the panic were short-lived and actually salutary. Besides bringing prices into line with those of Europe, which fell only 6 percent on news of the panic,[230] the disruption showed that the various U.S. stock markets were tightly integrated. In other words, upon any great fall in prices in one market, money from more liquid markets would pour in to take advantage of arbitrage opportunities.

Little volume information is available for 1793, but we do know that in February of that year money was "very – very – very scarce indeed! – So say all,"[231] and that in the fall a yellow fever epidemic that raged "with great violence" brought "business of all kinds . . . at a stand."[232] When the record picks up again in January 1794, demand for stocks was rather strong.[233] When the price of stocks, and trade volumes, dipped in March, Philadelphia broker Mark Prager immediately wrote to Europe seeking investors. U.S. funds, he claimed, were a "great Speculation in Case there is a peace in Europe they must unavoidably rise very much as the interest is paid very punctually every quarter, and our resources are very great."[234] Prager continued his efforts into April.[235] European investors, including some living in the West Indies[236] and even India, readily purchased American securities.[237] By May the price and trade volume of securities rebounded because the "Course of Exch[ange]" between the United States and Britain was "so exhorbitant[ly] high" and "good Bills" so scarce that Americans began to "remit Stocks" to their British creditors.[238] The situation persisted through the middle of November 1794.[239] By the first of December prices increased because of large Dutch purchases of American debt, the victory of General "Mad Anthony" Wayne, the bloodless suppression of the Whiskey Rebellion, and improved diplomatic relations

---

[228]To George Lewis, 22 May 1792; to William Campbell, 24 May 1792; to William Rogers, 27 May 1792.
[229]To William Hodgson, 1 June 1792; to George Lewis, 3, 9, 15 June 1792; to Captain Campbell, 6 June 1792.
[230]To Captain Campbell, 27 June 1792.
[231]Richard S. Smith to Joseph Smith, 7 February 1793, Gratz Manuscripts, HSP.
[232]Benjamin Bankson to Henry Remsen Jr., 3 October 1793, Henry Remsen Papers, NYPL.
[233]To Mark Prager Sr., 24 January 1794. Unless specified otherwise, the following letters are from Mark Prager, Mark Prager Letter Book, 1794–98, HSP.
[234]To Mark Prager Sr., 22 March 1794.   [235]To Mark Prager Sr., 12 April 1794.
[236]See the certificate of deferred debt, 21 July 1792, North Carolina Loan Office, due to "Henry Jennings of St. Eustatia" for $62.73. box 9c, Society Miscellaneous Collection, HSP.
[237]To Robert Wilson, 29 May 1794.   [238] To Mark Prager Sr., 8 May 1794.
[239]To unknown, 9 August 1794; to Mark Prager Sr., 20 October, 12 November 1794.

with Britain. Trade volumes continued strong because it was "the general opinion, that stocks will rise much more."[240] In the first half of December, Prager purchased $20,000 of Three Percents for sale in Britain alone.[241]

The first four or five months of 1795 witnessed a different pattern – high prices but little trading. Restrictions of bank discounts and apprehensions of higher prices appear to have been the main culprits.[242] By June "great orders" from England increased prices and trade volumes of all major securities except BUS stock.[243] From July 1795 to July 1796 however, volumes sagged because the money market again tightened and prices of American securities in England dropped.[244] In late July 1796 trading stopped for a time[245] but seems to have picked up again soon thereafter. In December 1796 the "Scandalous Conduct" of some of the directors of the Bank of Pennsylvania created a "critical situation" in the Philadelphia money market and dampened equities trading into the first months of 1797.[246] By early February Prager sought to interest investors in the West Indies in Philadelphia bank stock.[247] Matters improved in April. Prager sought to help Biddle sell $20,000 of Six Percents by writing to friends in Wilmington, Delaware. By the time the Delawareans responded, Biddle had already disposed of the lot.[248] Late April 1797 news that the Bank of England had stopped paying specie helped prices and volumes to increase.[249] By late August, trading slowed again due to a yellow fever epidemic.[250] The contagion spread quickly; by mid-September Philadelphia was "entirely deserted" and "all the brokers" moved "out [of] the town" and refrained from business.[251] It was not until March 1798 that Prager again began quoting securities prices for his correspondents.[252]

Trading Volumes: Evidence from Brokers' Account Books, 1798–1819

More complete, though hardly comprehensive, evidence of trading volumes comes from the surviving account books of some of

[240]To Mark Prager Sr., 1 December 1794.   [241]To Mark Prager Sr., 17 December 1794.
[242]To Mark Prager Sr., 4, 26 February, 1 April 1795; to Patrick Ferrall, 16 February 1795.
[243]To Mark Prager Sr., 4 June 1795.
[244]To Benjamin and Abraham Goldsmid, 18 July 1795, 20 January 1796; to Mark Prager Sr., 18 July, 8, 22 August, 10 October, 28 November 1795, 20 January, 25 May 1796; to Thomas Giese, 12 September, 3 October 1795, 14 January, 27 February 1796.
[245]To Mark Prager Sr., 28 July 1796.   [246] To Thomas Giese, 14 December 1796.
[247]To James St. Ferrall, 9 February 1797.
[248]To John William Irwin, 25, 27 April 1797.
[249]To Salomans and Elliot, 29 April 1797.
[250]To Arnold Henry Dohrman, 22 August 1797.
[251]To John William Irwin, 15, 25 September 1797.
[252]To Salomons and Elliot, 5 March 1798.

TABLE 6.4. Andrew Summers's Securities Trading Activity, 1798–1806

Name of Security	Average Price in Dollars[a]	Par Value Traded	No. of Shares Traded	Market Value Traded
Deferred Sixes	72.65	20,589.24		15,089.98
Eights	105.37	77,319.61		81,472.75
Four and a halfs	63.75	382.50		243.84
Navy Sixes	87.72	500.00		438.60
Sixes	90.58	4,640.22		3,880.00
Threes	52.86	47,973.61		26,878.37
TOTALS	–	151,405.18		128,003.54
Bank of Pennsylvania	534.32		13	7,028.00
Bank of Philadelphia	106.11		129	13,637.73
BUS	519.68		10	5,195.00
Delaware Bridge	15.00		40	600.00
Delaware Insurance Co.	24.31		260	6,285.00
East India Company of North America scrip	1.00		7,000	7,000.00
Frankford Turnpike	107.70		5	538.50
Germantown Pike	116.25		51.50	5,987.00
Germantown to Perkiomen Turnpike	107.74		218.50	19,174.50
Lancaster to Susquehanna Turnpike	313.84		9	2,823.36
Lancaster Turnpike	290.25		18	5,397.00
North America Insurance Co.	9.99		12,080.50	115,181.15
Pennsylvania Insurance	507.72		158	78,974.00
Philadelphia Insurance Company	117.79		288	35,752.84
Phoenix Insurance Co.	54.27		424.50	18,487.36
Schuylkill Bridge	1.00		50	50.00
Union Insurance Co.	59.41		1,061.17	59,582.13
Water Loan	100.00		6	600.00
TOTALS	–		21,822.17	382,293.57

[a] Debt in dollars per $100.

Source: Andrew Summers & Co. Daybook, 1798–1806, HSP.

Philadelphia's securities brokers. Bill and note broker Andrew Summers traded in public securities as a mere sideshow. With his efforts concentrated on negotiating bills of exchange and discounting promissory notes, Summers rarely traded in government debt or corporate equities, sometimes going months without executing a single trade.[253] In the eight years between 1798 and 1806, he bought or sold only $510,297.12 worth of such securities (see Table 6.4). What his business lacked in volume, however, it made up in breadth. Over

[253] Andrew Summers Account Books, HSP.

TABLE 6.5. Andrew Summers's Securities Trading Activity, 1806–1808

Name of Security	Average Price in Dollars[a]	Par Value Traded	No. of Shares Traded	Market Value Traded
Deferred Sixes	96.88	14,874.70		14,413.05
Eights	104.52	21,900.00		22,936.00
Sixes	95.75	11,420.18		10,947.47
TOTALS	—	48,194.88		48,296.52
BNA	570.68		18	10,300.00
Bank of Pennsylvania	528.00		2	1,056.00
Bank of Philadelphia	122.72		1,030	127,452.75
BUS	528.68		8	4,186.00
Delaware Insurance Co.	71.39		1,920	136,518.25
Frankford Turnpike	6.00		5	30.00
Germantown to Perkiomen Turnpike	62.00		18	1,116.00
Lancaster Turnpike	225.00		1	225.00
North America Insurance Co.	9.42		2,772	25,479.40
Pennsylvania Insurance	629.00		10	6,312.00
Philadelphia Insurance Co.	152.11		190	24,020.90
Phoenix Insurance Co.	86.86		4,929.50	406,493.55
Schuylkill Bridge	6.95		50	347.50
Trenton Bank	37.69		360	13,500.00
Union Insurance Co.	75.07		1,077	80,693.00
United States Insurance Co.	17.40		2,125	37,850.50
TOTALS	—		14,515.5	875,580.85

[a] Debt in dollars per $100.

Source: Andrew Summers & Co. Daybook, 1806–8, HSP.

those years, Summers traded 24 different types of securities, 7 varieties of government debt securities, and the equities of banks, insurance companies, and transportation concerns. Over one-fifth of the dollar volume of his business involved trading more than 12,000 shares, at an average price just under $10 per share, of the Insurance Company of North America. Apparently, he was a leading market maker in that security. He also traded, at an average price of about $59 per share, more than 1,000 shares of the Union Insurance Company. He dealt in other equities, especially pricier ones, less frequently.

Between February 1806 and December 1807, the volume of Summers's stock business grew tremendously. In a little less than two years, Summers traded almost $900,000 worth of securities (see Table 6.5).

Three of those securities were forms of government debt, seven were the equities of insurance companies, five the equities of banks, and four the equities of transportation companies. Most of those securities Summers had traded to some extent before 1806, but a few, such as Trenton Bank shares, were new. Unfortunately, it remains unclear whether Summers took significant market share from other brokers or whether the years 1806 and 1807 witnessed a major increase in securities trading.

Reliable trade volume figures are not available for 1808. The blotter of Biddle and Company, however, shows that an active market for at least 22 different types of securities existed in Philadelphia in that year. The traded securities were: Eights, Sixes, Deferred Sixes, Converted Sixes, Exchanged Sixes, and Threes (federal debt securities); BUS, Bank of Pennsylvania, Farmers' and Mechanics' Bank, and the Bank of Philadelphia (bank equities); Insurance Company of North America, Philadelphia Insurance Company, Phoenix Insurance Company, Delaware Insurance Company, Union Insurance Company, Pennsylvania Insurance Company, United States Insurance Company (insurance company equities); Frankford Turnpike Company, Germantown Pike Company, Lancaster Turnpike Company, Flower Town Turnpike Company, and the Cheltenham Turnpike Company (transportation company equities).

In 1809 Biddle and Company traded over $1.3 million dollars worth of securities (see Table 6.6). Securities traded included six types of government debt instruments, a municipal water bond, and the equities of six banks, nine insurance companies, and seven transportation companies. Federal debt accounted for just over $670,000, or slightly more than half of Biddle's trading activity that year.

Following the banner year of 1809, Biddle and Company traded just over $812,000 in the first 11 months of 1810 (see Table 6.7). The types of securities traded were almost identical to those traded in 1809 and included 5 types of government debt instruments, a municipal water bond, the debt instrument of a fraternal society, and the equities of 8 banks, 10 insurance companies, and 6 transportation companies. Federal securities accounted for just over $300,000, or slightly more than one-third, of the firm's trading volume. Again, it is difficult to determine whether those changes represent wider changes in the market or only in Biddle and Company's market share. If we assume, however, that Biddle and Company's share of BNA trading, the total number of shares traded of which are known through the firm's internal records, was the same as its share of other securities, Biddle and Company's market share appears to have grown fourfold. In 1809, 286 BNA shares traded hands in 87 transactions. Biddle and Company handled 5, or 5.7 percent, of those transactions. In 1810 Biddle and Company handled 16 of 66, or 24.3 percent, of BNA trades.

TABLE 6.6. Biddle and Company's Securities Trading Activity, 1809

Name of Security	Average Price in Dollars[a]	Par Value Traded	No. of Shares Traded	Market Value Traded
Converted Sixes	102.63	111,687.14		114,441.24
Deferred Sixes	102.49	128,899.85		132,396.17
Exchanged Sixes	102.13	53,229.55		54,375.011
Louisiana Sixes	103.63	27,450.00		28,492.50
Sixes	106.35	272,458.41		278,121.97
Threes	65.59	94,498.79		61,772.69
TOTALS	–	688,223.74		669,599.581
BNA	589.60		6	3,536.00
Bank of Pennsylvania	566.28		34	19,348.32
Bank of Philadelphia	132.70		548	72,980.63
BUS	509.16		227	115,578.00
Chestnut Hill &c. Turnpike Co.	97.50		20	1,950.00
Delaware Insurance Co.	73.15		383	27,109.34
Eagle Insurance Co.	111.00		30	3,320.00
Farmers' and Mechanics' Bank	66.63		2,148	14,2397.88
Flower Town Turnpike Co.	97.50		25	2,437.50
Frankford Turnpike Co.	102.20		242	24,842.00
Germantown Pike Co.	92.65		151	13,558.50
Lancaster Turnpike Co.	222.51		14	3,165.00
Marine Insurance Co.	58.25		64	3,726.00
North America Insurance Co.	10.51		10,731	114,410.85
Old York Road Turnpike	89.00		12	1,068.00
Pennsylvania Insurance Co.	693.28		24	16,690.00
Philadelphia Insurance Co.	163.22		57	9,410.00
Phoenix Insurance Co.	88.61		289	25,986.00
Schuylkill Bridge	6.34		150	1,092.75
Trenton Bank	40.80		396	14,688.50
Union Insurance Co.	69.70		503	35,380.25
United States Insurance Co.	46.90		218	10,197.50
Water Loan	102.71		9	925.00
TOTALS	—		16,281	663,798.02

[a] Debt in dollars per $100.
Source: Biddle Daybook, 1809–10, HSP.

TABLE 6.7. Biddle and Company's Securities Trading Activity, 1810

Name of Security	Average Price in Dollars[a]	Par Value Traded	No. of Shares Traded	Market Value Traded
Converted Sixes	101.56	27,036.86		47,947.81
Exchanged Sixes	100.63	47,610.41		47,931.27
U.S. Deferred Sixes	101.98	43,793.51		44,516.35
U.S. Sixes	101.97	97,058.63		98,828.05
U.S. Threes	65.68	101,808.04		63,845.21
TOTALS	—	317,307.45		303,068.69
American Fire Insurance	48.00		10	480.00
BNA	594.52		44	26,012.00
Bank of Pennsylvania	562.36		13	7,277.40
Bank of Philadelphia	133.82		153	20,480.50
BUS	475.08		247	116,635.00
Columbia Insurance	59.50		25	1,487.50
Commercial Bank scrip	19.83		40	790.00
Delaware Insurance Co.	64.36		102	6,484.25
Farmers' and Mechanics' Bank	70.87		1150	81,207.05
Flower Town Turnpike	100.00		5	500.00
Frankford Turnpike	102.50		35	3,587.50
Germantown Turnpike	100.29		61	6,114.00
Lancaster Turnpike	240.99		18.50	4,258.50
Marine Insurance	59.60		160	9,499.50
Masonic Lodge	102.00		15	1,530.00
Mechanics Bank scrip	5.50		50	275.00
North America Insurance Co.	10.53		2,134	23,317.08
Pennsylvania Insurance	704.00		22	15,606.00
Philadelphia Insurance. Co.	177.52		30	5,339.25
Phoenix Insurance Co.	82.22		1,317	107,356.25
Schuylkill Bridge	8.00		100	800.00
Trenton Bank	36.79		104	3,830.50
U.S. Insurance Co.	48.26		1,198	57,418.75
Union Insurance Co.	73.54		56	4,161.50
Water Loan	103.69		49	5,019.25
Willow Grove Turnpike	96.00		17	1,632.00
TOTALS	—		7,155.5	511,098.78

[a] Debt in dollars per $100.

Source: Biddle Daybook, 1809–10, 1810, HSP.

Systematic records for the Philadelphia securities market again become scarce until 1817. In that year, Biddle, Wharton and Company traded 72,534 corporate shares, with a total market value of just over $5.2 million, in 728 transactions. They also engaged in 927 transactions involving debt instruments totaling more than

$5.7 million par value and $5.4 million market value. Debt instruments included: U.S. Threes, Sixes, and Sevens, "Old" Sixes, Deferred Sixes, and Exchange Sixes, as well as two municipal loans and "Mississippi Stock," which was actually a bond. Traded equities, excluding some minor trading in New York banks, included the BUS, seven local banks, six insurance companies, and four internal improvement corporations.[254] In the final six months of 1819, that same company dealt in just $900,000 worth of securities (market value) and only $254,000 worth of equities (market value).[255] Again, it is not clear if the drop indicates a wider market decline in the volume of trading or merely represents a lull in this particular firm's business. The firm's trading in shares of the BNA, however, can again be used to approximate its market share. In 1817, Biddle, Wharton, and Company engaged in 26 BNA-related transactions, out of 85 total, or about 30 percent. In half of 1819 the firm was involved in 10 BNA transactions or about 20 percent (there were 100 BNA transactions in 1819 divided by 2 = 50 for the half year). So part of the drop in trade volumes may simply represent a decrease in the firm's market share (see Tables 6.8 and 6.9).

Evidence from Newspapers and Stock Exchanges, 1833–1842

Records indicating the extent of securities trading in Philadelphia in the 1820s have not been found. A very good set of data, the published sales of the Philadelphia Board of Exchange, begins in 1833. Those records show that the Philadelphia market grew markedly broader and deeper in the years between the Panic of 1819 and the Panic of 1837. In 1834, the first full year of trading for which we have records, 100,789 equities traded hands in 2,164 transactions. In addition, 376 bond transactions took place. The market value of trades of both types topped $7.3 million, while the par value of those trades amounted to nearly $6.9 million. U.S., Pennsylvania, Philadelphia, and corporate bond transactions worth about $1.5 million (a little more in market terms, a little less at par value) accounted for about 20 percent of the dollar value of all trades. The bulk (15 percent of the dollar value of all transactions or 75 percent of the bond transactions) of those transactions involved various forms of Pennsylvania state debt. Corporate debt instruments came in a strong second, accounting for 7 percent of the par value of all trades. Because some corporate debt instruments sold at considerable discount, however, they accounted for only about 3 percent of the market value of all trades.

Bank equities accounted for about 55 percent of the dollar value (market and par) of all trades. Delaware Valley banks accounted for

[254]Biddle Stock Book, 1817, HSP.   [255]Biddle Journal, 1819, HSP.

TABLE 6.8. Biddle and Company's Securities Trading Activity, 1817

Name of Security	Average Price in Dollars[a]	Par Value Traded	No. of Shares Traded	Market Value Traded
Fairmount Loan	102.5	4,000		4,100
Louisiana Sixes	100.35	62,867.00		62,765.92
Mississippi Stock	77.49	662,339.3		512,274.48
U.S. Deferred	99.60	254,135.10		251,412.43
U.S. Exchanged Sixes	102.75	2,978.61		3,060.52
U.S. Sevens	106.73	133,306.80		141,440.54
U.S. Sixes, New	102.05	3,771,691.00		3,859,680.21
U.S. Sixes, Old	99.68	80,092.19		79,812.30
U.S. Threes	66.18	756,740.20		499,065.97
Water Loan	101.75	805.00		820.11
TOTALS	—	5,728,955.20		5,414,432.48
BNA	513.35		117	59,682.00
Bank of Pennsylvania	524.65		100	51,726.00
Bank of Philadelphia	103.58		97	10,186.00
SBUS	108.60		61,668	4,727,948.66
Camden Bank	48.00		61	3,006.00
Commercial Bank	54.08		1,620	87,546.88
Delaware Bridge	61.67		71	4,425.00
Delaware Insurance	44.00		48	2,073.00
Farmers' and Mechanics' Bank	61.75		1,086	69,571.75
Fire Insurance Co.	42.40		218	8,690.00
First Bank of the U.S. "remnants"	10.80		584	7,486.00
Frankfort and Bristol Turnpike	81.67		13	1,055.00
Germantown Turnpike	67.5		31	2,455.00
North America Insurance Co.	10.45		4,248	47,501.90
Pennsylvania Insurance Co.	539.56		27	14,260.00
Philadelphia & Lancaster Turnpike	300.00		3	900.00
Philadelphia Insurance Co.	168.67		27	4,510.00
Phoenix Insurance Co.	75.50		67	5,272.00
Schuylkill Bank	21.63		1,046	22,026.00
Trenton Bank	34.33		88	3,060.00
Union Insurance Co.	55.38		149	8,382.75
TOTALS	—		71,369	5,141,763.94

[a] Debt in dollars per $100.

Source: Biddle Journal, 1817, HSP.

TABLE 6.9. Biddle and Company's Securities Trading Activity, 1819

Name of Security	Average Price in Dollars[a]	Par Value Traded	No. of Shares Traded	Market Value Traded
Deferred Sixes	100.00	39,037.37		39,037.37
Exchanged Sixes	102.75	700.00		719.25
Louisiana Sixes	100.93	48,202.02		48,782.22
Mississippi Stock	82.53	26,825.00		22,215.13
Sevens	105.40	36,464.47		38,569.87
Sixes	100.25	1,500.00		1,503.75
Sixes of 1812	101.78	112,710.90		114,658.30
Sixes of 1813	102.14	441,618.20		451,305.70
Sixes of 1814	102.32	94,964.52		97,403.80
Sixes of 1815	102.12	30,099.43		30,740.37
Threes	64.36	86,461.40		56,172.25
Yazoo Stock	83.50	2,400.00		2026.50
TOTALS	—	920,983.31		903,134.51
BNA	469.00		68	31,710.00
Bank of Pennsylvania	468.54		53	24,812.00
Bank of Philadelphia	82.50		129	10,905.00
SBUS	96.55		1,685	161,410.00
Commercial Bank	41.69		390	16,311.75
Delaware Insurance Co.	50.00		6	300.00
Farmers' and Mechanics' Bank	54.93		78	4,282.75
First Bank of the U.S. "remnants"	10.50		33	361.00
North America Insurance Co.	11.65		44	523.00
Philadelphia Insurance Co.	180.00		4	720.00
Schuylkill Bank	19.00		139	2,677.50
TOTALS	—		2,629	254,013

[a] Debt in dollars per $100.

Source: Biddle Journal, 1819, HSP.

about 23 percent of the trade activity, while out-of-region banks spanning from Pittsburgh to Cincinnati to Kentucky to New Orleans accounted for about 22 percent of the dollar trade activity, both in terms of par and market value. Shares of the SBUS made up the remaining 10 percent of the bank equity trading activity. Insurance company equities composed about 2.5 percent of the dollar value of the trades, while various miscellaneous corporations, including the Chestnut Street Theatre and the shares of the exchange itself, made up only about 1 percent of the dollar value of the trades. The equities of various transport companies composed the final 21 percent of the trades. Railroads (15 percent) and canal companies (5.5 percent) account for the bulk of the transport sector with steam, bridge, and turnpike companies barely registering in the data.

The capital market in Philadelphia in 1834 was as broad as it was deep. In that year the major financial paper listed the weekly prices of some 75 securities, including about two dozen forms of debt and the equities of 28 banks, 15 insurance companies, and 20 transportation companies. Additionally, the exchange's members traded significant numbers of nonlisted securities.

Stock market volume boomed in 1835, jumping to more than 500,000 shares, a level matched in 1836. The panic cut stock trading volumes in half in 1837, and fewer than 200,000 shares changed hands in each of the next four years. The market almost completely collapsed in 1842, when only slightly more than 33,500 shares changed hands. The bond market's fortunes were just the opposite as the number of par dollars traded and the number of transactions grew during the panic years. That finding is not surprising. Bonds are less risky than stocks in several respects; most investors undoubtedly found stocks too risky during the volatile panic years. Table 6.10 details the yearly fluctuations in equities and bond volumes, and average trade sizes, in the Philadelphia market from 1834 until 1842.

Conclusions

The Philadelphia stock market, the second largest of America's half-dozen major early securities markets, grew broader and deeper each successive decade. From distant banks to local insurance companies, from transportation companies to coal concerns, Philadelphia investors backed a variety of enterprises safe in the knowledge that they could liquidate their investments at fair market prices at just about any time.

The biggest knock against the early securities markets, that they were not liquid enough to have made much contribution to economic growth, simply is not true. The early markets were not as liquid as the market for treasury securities today, but given the constraints and expectations of the era, they performed admirably. The implications of liquid secondary markets for early American economic growth are clear. The liquidity of corporate securities induced investors to prefer

TABLE 6.10. Trading Volumes on the Philadelphia Stock Exchange, 1835–1842

Year	No. of Shares	No. of Transactions	Average of Shares/Transactions	Par Volume of Bonds in $	No. of Transactions	Average of Volume/Transactions
1834	100,789	2,164	46.58	1,439,427	376	3,828.26
1835	506,656	5,773	87.76	1,330,051	360	3,694.59
1836	505,345	5,110	98.89	485,802	251	1,935.47
1837	244,289	3,504	69.72	581,972	306	1,901.87
1838	127,187	4,976	25.56	584,525	452	1,293.20
1839	163,841	6,119	26.78	633,538	554	1,143.57
1840	191,697	4,154	46.15	1,242,901	817	1,521.30
1841	141,254	3,137	45.03	1,406,609	1127	1,248.10
1842	33,593	1,134	29.62	1,306,798	871	1,500.34

Sources: Philadelphia Price Current, Philadelphia Commercial List, various dates.

them over less liquid assets, thereby driving the prices of the securities up (and their yields down). Cheaper access to long-term capital allowed corporations (the issuers of the securities and hence the beneficiaries of their higher prices and lower yields) to engage in more wealth-producing projects, such as the purchase of new technology and the reorganization of production processes creating a more specialized division of labor. Those changes, in turn, helped the corporations to produce more output from a given amount of input or, in other words, to cause real productivity increases.

Additionally, the rate of investment surged in the nineteenth century. Although that surge had many causes, the liquidity of the secondary markets was certainly a major one. There is little incentive to invest in illiquid assets. (What is the sense of owning something of great value that cannot be sold at a fair price?) The plethora of liquid stocks and bonds, therefore, very likely increased the aggregate rate of investment by inducing people to save who otherwise would not have done so for lack of liquid investment opportunities.

Nonlisted Securities

By the nation's fiftieth birthday, the lists of securities prices published in the major commercial newspapers were truly impressive. Those lists grew even more impressive in the 1830s and 1840s. Large amounts of anecdotal evidence, combined with what we know of the rapid growth in the number of corporations in the early United States, strongly suggest that we have yet to appreciate the full size and complexity of early U.S. securities markets. For each security listed in the newspapers, many more were not. Although many, if not all, of those unlisted or nonlisted securities traded infrequently, they still traded easily enough to induce long-term investment.

Growth in the Number of Business Corporations

The growth of bank corporations alone was explosive. In 1782 the United States possessed only 1 incorporated commercial bank. By 1800 there were 28. In 1810, 102 incorporated commercial banks were in operation, a number that more than trebled to 327 by 1820. In 1830 the United States boasted 381 incorporated banks. By 1837 that number almost doubled, to 729. Authorized capitalization also soared, from $400,000 in 1782, to $17,420,000 in 1800, to almost $160 million in 1820, to just over $471.5 million in 1837.[256]

Unfortunately, complete figures for other types of U.S. corporations are not yet available. The best estimates to date can be found in the

[256]Fenstermaker 1965: appendix A.

work of George Evans, who mined the statute books of Connecticut, Maine, Maryland, Massachusetts, New Jersey, New York, Ohio, and Pennsylvania in search of business corporations. The total number of business corporations chartered each year in just those eight states is revealing. There were two trends. The most noticeable was a long-term upswing in the number of corporations created per year, which blossomed from 7 in 1800, to 42 in 1805, to 71 in 1810, to 77 in 1815, to 102 in 1830. The second trend was a series of short-term dips in charter activity related to downturns in the business cycle. In 1819, for instance, which witnessed a financial panic, the number of new incorporations dropped to 28 from 59 in 1818. Similarly, the number of new charters dropped in 1837, another panic year, to 253 from 348 in 1836.

Data on exit rates, the number of corporations that ceased functioning for any reason, are not currently available. Before the panic of the late 1830s, few corporations exited through bankruptcy. Some, however, voluntarily wound up their affairs and terminated. Most early corporate charters were of limited duration, from a few years to a few decades. Some, such as both banks of the United States, were denied recharter and were forced to exit. Most, however, received new charters. Evans's figures presumably represent only new corporations, not recharters.[257]

We can, therefore, very roughly calculate the total number of U.S. business corporations in any given year simply by adding Evans's yearly totals, multiplying by some factor to account for states that Evans ignored, and making some allowance for exit. Rather than pick arbitrary numbers for the extension and the exit figures, let us think of this issue in broader terms. We can say with certainty that in the 1790s the United States possessed dozens of business corporations. In the first decade of the 1800s there were scores of U.S. corporations. By the 1810s hundreds of corporations existed and by the 1820s, thousands. By the end of the 1830s, there must have been close to 10,000 U.S. business corporations, close to 1,000 of which were banks. Other major types of corporations included other financial services companies (life, fire, and marine insurance, loan companies, savings banks, stock exchanges), transportation firms (canal, railroad, turnpike, bridge, steamboat, and ferry companies), utilities (water, gas), service (hotels, taverns), education (libraries, museums, technical associations), and manufacturing and mining companies. Pennsylvania alone granted at least 819 corporate business charters between 1780 and 1837 (see Table 6.11). By way of comparison, in 1844 England and Ireland had only about 1,000 corporations.[258]

[257]Evans 1948.   [258]Hunt 1936.

TABLE 6.11. Number and Type of
Corporations Chartered by Pennsylvania,
1780–1837

Type	Number
Agricultural societies	5
Banking institutions	78
Bridge	52
Canal and navigation	52
Chamber of commerce	1
Charitable	18
Coal	12
Coal and navigation	1
Fire	22
Hotel	1
Ice	2
Insurance	41
Literary institutions	116
Loan companies	3
Manufacturing companies	22
Medical societies	4
Museum	1
Navigation and railroad	1
Navigation, railroad, and coal	2
Railroad	78
Railroad and coal	1
Railway and dock	1
Road	2
Savings institutions	11
Trading companies	2
Turnpike companies	248
Water companies	19
Scientific associations	7
Art societies	3
Miscellaneous	13
TOTAL	819

Source: *Baltimore American*, 23 November 1837.

The vast majority of American business corporations issued equities. A few were organized as mutuals. In addition, some of the joint-stock corporations were closely held. If the following analysis is any indication, however, even shares of closely held corporations were at least occasionally traded. Each of those corporations represented major advances on mere partnerships. Most offered limited liability; even some unincorporated associations did that. The joint-stock structure, as we have seen, helped to decrease information asymmetry. Additionally, joint-stock companies could grow considerably larger, and hence more efficient, than partnerships or sole proprietorships.

Evidence of Trading in Nonlisted Stocks

Importantly, large numbers of nonlisted securities, securities not normally listed in newspapers, also traded in the secondary markets. Because data on such securities are difficult to come by, we can only offer a largely narrative description of the trading of nonlisted securities.

Corporate record books are the best source for such data but very few survive; however, they offer a provocative picture. For example, a careful study showed that fully half of the Bank of Concord's original investors in 1832 had sold out their positions within one decade.[259] By the late 1830s, over half a dozen institutional investors regularly bought the shares of those who wished to sell. In nearby Worcester, 2,818 shares of the Central Bank changed hands in 297 transactions between 1830 and 1848, when there were 1,000 Central Bank shares outstanding. In other words, about 15.5 percent of that bank's shares traded each year over that span.[260]

Remnants of the stock transfer book of the Chester County Silk Company, based in West Chester, Pennsylvania, have also been found.[261] In 70 transactions between June 1837 and May 1840, 190 shares traded hands. Unfortunately, the total number of shares outstanding is unknown. Shares in another West Chester company, the Bank of Chester County, clearly were actively traded. Between 1814 and 1845, exactly 15,500 shares traded hands in 1,167 transactions, an average of 500 shares per year.[262] The bank had 4,500 outstanding shares, so the share turnover rate of the bank was about 11 percent per year.

A more anecdotal source of information about nonlisted stock trading is old stock certificates.[263] The survival of such certificates was probably not random, so the only conclusion we can draw from them is that securities did not have to be listed in order to trade. Surviving stock certificates, for example, tell us that at least 827 shares of Worcester Bank stock changed hands in 111 transactions between 1812 and 1846.[264]

We also know from stock certificates that the Insurance Company of North America purchased 10 shares in the Susquehanna and Lehigh

[259]Patterson 1971:14–34.
[260]Central Bank of Worcester Business Records, Stock Record Book, 1830–64, AAS.
[261]Chester County Silk Company Stock Transfer Book, CCHS.
[262]Bank of Chester County, Record of Stock Transfers, 1814–72, ms. 78010, CCHS.
[263]See, for example, Stock Certificates, box 9b, Society Miscellaneous Collection, HSP.
[264]Worcester Bank Records, Stock Certificates and Transfers, 1812–29, 1844–46, AAS.

Turnpike Road, a nonlisted security, in July 1804.[265] In May 1809 Joseph Ball purchased 1 share in the Pennsylvania Academy of the Fine Arts, a nonlisted security.[266] The Union Insurance Co. purchased 5 shares in the nonlisted Downingtown, Ephrata, and Harrisburg Turnpike Road in October 1810.[267] That same insurance firm bought 10 shares in the Falmouth Turnpike, another nonlisted corporation, in 1811.[268] Also in 1811, the BNA acquired 40 shares in the Permanent Bridge, which was usually a nonlisted security.[269] Thomas Biddle bought 2 shares in the nonlisted Philadelphia, Dover and Norfolk Steamboat Transportation Company in 1825.[270] Thomas Biddle and Company purchased 10 shares of the Manayunk Flat Rock Turnpike, a nonlisted security, in July 1831; about the same time, it bought 100 shares of the nonlisted New Castle Manufacturing Company of New Castle, Delaware.[271] Surviving certificates also tell us that several shares of the Harrisburg Bridge Company stock traded hands in 1813 and 1823.[272]

Rothenberg showed that probate records are excellent sources for determining the extent and depth of securities ownership. In her extensive analysis of Middlesex County, Massachusetts, a largely rural county just west of Boston, she found ownership of a wide range of government and corporate bonds and the equities of large, listed corporations and numerous small, unlisted ones. More than 1 in 10 decedents owned some form of public security; investors hailed from Cambridge and Charlestown, the most urban areas of the county, but also from rural communities, such as Framingham, Dunstable, Stow, Chelmsford, Weston, Woburn, Groton, and Tewksbury.[273]

The will of President George Washington, while perhaps not typical, showed the importance of financial securities in some investors' portfolios as early as 1800.[274] At his death, Washington owned almost $10,000 worth of U.S. bonds, 24 shares in the nonlisted Potomac Company, 5 shares in the nonlisted James River Company, 170 shares in the seldomly listed Bank of Columbia, 20 shares in the nonlisted Free School, and shares in the Bank of Alexandria. Washington advised his legatees to retain their stock, "there being a moral certainty of a great and increasing profit arising from them, in the course of a few years."

The third major source for nonlisted securities is newspaper articles and advertisements.[275] Brokers and auctioneers often advertised

---

[265]Susquehanna and Lehigh Turnpike Road, Thomas A. Biddle Stock Certificates, 31 July 1804, HSP.
[266]Ibid., 18 May 1809.   [267]Ibid., 11 October 1810.   [268]Ibid., 1 March 1811.
[269]Ibid., 30 December 1811.   [270]Ibid., 1 November 1825.   [271]Ibid., 18 July 1831.
[272]Box 9c, Society Miscellaneous Collection, HSP.   [273]Rothenberg 1992:120–22.
[274]*Pennsylvania Gazette*, 26 February 1800.
[275]For other examples, see the *Baltimore Telegraph and Mercantile Advertiser*, 25 April, 26 June, 17 August 1815.

specific, nonlisted securities for sale. In 1811, for example, C. Hayward offered 588 shares in the nonlisted Rhode Island Coal Company for "cash down only."[276] Similarly, in 1813 John Dorsey of Philadelphia advertised for sale 3 shares in the Lehigh Coal Mining Company and 5 shares in the Chesapeake and Delaware Canal, both nonlisted securities.[277] Advertisements for stockholder meetings, while not direct evidence of securities trading, certainly do suggest that corporate governance was important even in nonlisted firms. In January 1811, for instance, newspaper advertisements summoned to a meeting the stockholders of two companies with nonlisted securities, the Boylston Market Association and the Ashby Turnpike Corporation.[278]

Local histories sometimes mention the prices of nonlisted securities. According to one local historian, for example, shares of the Bank of Albany were 45 to 50 percent above par in the local market in 1797.[279] Similarly, Majewski's recent study lists a considerable number of nonlisted securities, mostly issued by local transportation firms.[280]

Occasionally, letters mentioning the trading of nonlisted securities are discovered. In 1829, for example, Chester Patterson of Union, New York, wrote to John Hum concerning the sale of Patterson's stock in the Bank of Newburgh. "In your offer of 95 per cent," Patterson complained, "you did not tell me whether it must be subject to the next dividend and I pay interest on the note at the same time or not."[281]

Some securities were not listed because the issues were simply too small, or the issuers too unimportant. The shares of the Society for the Manufacture of Sugar from the Sugar Maple Tree fall into that category. A stock certificate entitled the owner to "one Share in the Property of said Society."[282] The debt issues of Richmond, Norfolk, Petersburg, and other Virginia cities were generally small, so the prices of their debt instruments did not always make the newspaper lists.[283]

Some securities simply did not change hands very often. The Philadelphia Library shares likely fell into that category,[284] as did Dismal Swamp Land Company shares.[285] Some securities apparently were not listed because most stockholders lived far from commercial centers. Virginia's Bank of the Valley and G. H. Creek Bridge likely fit

[276] Boston Columbian Centinel, 30 January 1811.
[277] Philadelphia Political and Commercial Register, 8 November 1813.
[278] Boston Columbia Centinel, 19 January 1811.   [279] Munsell 1850, 1:31.
[280] Majewski 2000.
[281] Chester Patterson to John Hum, 20 September 1829, Bank of Newburgh Papers, NYHS.
[282] Stock Certificate of the Manufacture of Sugar from the Sugar Maple Tree, 8 March 1793, Wilson Manuscripts, 4:37, HSP.
[283] Richmond Enquirer, 22 June 1838.
[284] Grotjan's Philadelphia Prices Current, 16 November 1812.
[285] Norfolk American Beacon and Commercial Diary, 20 May 1818.

that category.[286] Nonlisted shares often changed hands only via auction, suggesting that volume was too light even for brokers to match buyers with sellers. Manchester Turnpike shares, for example, sold by auction in Petersburg, Virginia, in 1804.[287]

Auctions were also used to dispose of relatively large lots of listed securities, as when James H. Lynch auctioned off $25,000 of U.S. Six Percent bonds in $250 lots in Richmond in 1816.[288] An even larger lot ($40,000) of U.S. Sixes, however, was later sold directly to investors, via a newspaper advertisement, apparently without the aid of brokers.[289] Auctioneers also disposed of equities, usually of deceased persons. For example, in 1824 Lynch sold more than 500 shares of Bank of Virginia and Farmers' Bank stock, formerly the property of Dr. George Cabell of Lynchburg, Virginia.[290]

Some securities were unlisted because the issuer was merely an association, not a corporation, making liability issues a concern. In 1816 there were 7 unchartered banking companies in Washington, D.C., alone, and 12 others spread throughout in Virginia.[291] It is not known how many associations there were or how many issued transferable equities.

Some unlisted securities come to our attention only because the company reissued shares when stockholders did not keep up with their installment payments. Such was the case of the Roanoke Navigation Company, which sold more than 400 shares of some 34 different delinquent investors to new investors in Halifax, North Carolina, in 1820.[292] The nonlisted New Bedford and Bridgewater Turnpike did likewise in 1812,[293] as did the James River and Kanawha Company in 1842.[294]

Sometimes, greatly undervalued securities remained unlisted. The stock of the South Carolina Rail Road, which traded between 60 and 70 percent of par, remained unlisted until late May 1833, when it finally reached par.[295] Other shaky railroad stocks also remained off the newspaper lists until they attained some stability.[296] Occasionally, highly overvalued securities were not listed. Shares in the nonlisted Tredegar Rolling Mill, for example, were considered "very valuable Stock" that always sold, when offered for sale, at a premium.[297]

As the Civil War neared, the number of unlisted securities grew rapidly, even in the upper South. In one auction in Virginia in 1850, for example, the following unlisted equities sold: Richmond Fire Association, Virginia Fire and Marine Insurance Company, Virginia

---

[286] *Alexandria Gazette*, 8 November 1816, 22 October 1817.
[287] *Richmond Enquirer*, 20 June 1804.   [288] Ibid., 29 June 1816.
[289] Ibid., 10 December 1816.   [290] Ibid., 28 September 1824.   [291] Ibid., 11 May 1816.
[292] Ibid., 12 May 1820.   [293] *Boston Columbia Centinel*, 8 July 1812.
[294] *Richmond Enquirer*, 3 June 1842.
[295] Ibid., 28 June 1833; *Charleston Courier*, 27 May 1833.
[296] *Richmond Enquirer*, 30 May 1837.   [297] Ibid., 6 June 1839.

Towing Company, Belle Isle Manufacturing Company, Virginia Woolen Company, Exchange Hotel Company, and Fauquier White Sulphur Springs Company.[298] A year later, the estate of Anderson P. Miller of Nottoway sold, by auction, shares in the unlisted Manchester Cotton and Woollen Company, Roanoke Navigation Company, Appomattox Company, and several unlisted railroads.[299]

A Brief Sketch of the Expansion of the Securities Sector

The evidence presented here and in the previous chapter shows the early U.S. securities sector to have been dynamic, efficient, expanding, and growth-inducing. The number of brokers grew rapidly over the period under study. When acting as pure brokers, brokers charged very low commissions, usually well under 1 percent. When acting as market makers or dealers, brokers' bid-ask spreads were consistent with the risks that they undertook buying and holding securities with changeable market values. Overall, brokers did a good job of making securities liquid – or, in other words, cheaply and easily salable at a fair market price. A case study (Philadelphia) shows that the market for securities grew broader and deeper each decade. Broad, deep markets attracted investor demand and thereby decreased financing costs for corporations. Indeed, the securities markets probably induced people to invest who otherwise would not have invested at all, or as much. As such, the markets are one of the major causes of the tremendous jump in investment rates that the nineteenth-century U.S. economy experienced.

Nowhere is this more easily seen than in the IPO market. Untried, sometimes unincorporated firms were able to raise significant sums of equity capital without the aid of investment banks or other inter-mediaries. One reason that investors were so eager for shares is that they knew that the shares could be cheaply resold if necessary, perhaps even at a profit. Much evidence suggests that scholars have yet to ap-preciate fully the huge number of early U.S. corporations, almost all of which raised equity capital in unintermediated IPOs and most of which enjoyed at least a rudimentary secondary market for their stock. Clearly, the joint-stock or corporation phenomenon was not limited to the commercial seaboard centers. America's financial revolution may have followed those in Holland and Britain in time, but it now appears possible that the United States experienced its revolution more deeply. Further research in this direction is surely warranted.

[298]Ibid., 1 July 1850.   [299]Ibid., 17 July 1851.

7

The Freest of the Free: Regulation
of the Financial Sector

The early U.S. financial sector was able to integrate and expand quickly in the first few decades of the nation's existence because politicians and judges allowed it to develop largely unfettered. Attempts of state and national governments to regulate securities markets and banks were relatively meager. While securities markets were almost completely unregulated by government and largely self-regulated, regulations fell more heavily on banks, but even here the market was often able to make adjustments that muted the effects of poorly conceived legislation. For instance, the market managed to offset some of the more pernicious characteristics of New York's Safety Fund, a bank liability insurance scheme with highly politicized origins. In addition, bank taxes in many important states were such an important source of revenue that the taxes may have, somewhat paradoxically, induced those states to follow enlightened probanking policies. Massachusetts, for example, led the nation in banking capacity because its reliance on bank tax revenue logically led it to implement liberal banking policies. Undoubtedly because of its English and colonial roots, particularly the fear of a predatory state, the early nineteenth-century United States had one of the freest financial systems in the world, a world considerably freer from financial regulations than today's.[1]

Securities Market Regulations

The new nation inherited many of the legal practices and precedents of the mother country. Securities regulation was little different.[2] That is not to say, however, that early Americans simply produced a carbon copy of England's laws and legal interpretations. Early U.S. regulatory laws were not as stringent as those of England. Additionally, as Horwitz and Banner have shown, U.S. judges interpreted laws so as to encourage enterprise, private property creation, and the growth of free markets.[3] Securities regulation, both case and statute law,

[1] Neal 1990:2.
[2] Except where otherwise noted, this section is based on Banner 1998.
[3] Horwitz 1977; Banner 1998.

was no exception. Despite some politicians' vehement antisecurities rhetoric, the U.S. securities industry was but lightly regulated, much less so than England's. With the possible exception of the Dutch, Americans enjoyed the freest securities market of any importance in the world.

Some Americans expressed dismay over the fact that in the 1780s a few northern speculators purchased many dollars worth of depressed government securities that were later fully funded under Hamilton's financial program. The appreciation of those assets looked to some like exploitation. When the assets appreciated well above par, only to fall back some 20 percent during the Panic of 1792, some Americans summoned the ghosts of the infamous South Sea Bubble and called for securities issuance and trading to be strictly regulated. According to one observer, securities traders were nothing but a:

> Set of sharks, that flouncing in the flood,
> Suppose all kind of fish their proper food:
> A set of hawks, that flying in the air,
> Of harmless birds make up their bill of fare:
> A set of wolves, that prowling 'bout for prey,
> All animals devour that cross their way.

Stockjobbers, some claimed, were able to manipulate stock prices at will in order to profit from innocent investors. "Speculators will aim to keep a fluctuation," the argument went, "as their trade depends on *ups* and *downs*." "The trade of the Alley," another critic claimed, "consists in conspiring to pick the pocket of every body not in the secret. Those who are, can make stocks rise and fall at pleasure, and pocket the difference."

Other Americans did not understand that the securities markets helped to induce economic growth. They saw stock trading as a zero-sum game, a mere shuffling of assets, and hence nonproductive. Thomas Jefferson, for example, thought of securities trading as a form of "gambling" that prevented resources from being invested in "commerce . . . manufactures . . . buildings, etc." He clearly did not understand that the securities represented real investments already made. Luckily, at least some policy makers understood Hamilton's view that securities were merely paper evidences of real investment made more valuable by their liquidity and transparency.

Interestingly, the very success of many early IPOs led to a backlash against them. Investors made too much profit too quickly for comfort. Some early Americans believed that the existence of securities, both corporate and government, would lead to the creation of a moneyed aristocracy that would use its paper wealth to create a predatory state. Such critics noted that many members of Congress and state legislatures owned securities. Others feared that the moneyed aristocracy would be able to bribe or otherwise corrupt even legislators who owned no securities. If under the sway of the moneyed interests, the critics argued, legislative bodies would enact laws further favoring the moneyed rich over the landed and the poor. A huge government bureaucracy composed of worthless pensioners would suck the American yeoman farmer dry economically. His land and political independence gone, the farmers would be forced to become tenants or mere laborers and the Republic would give way to despotism. "Public debt," one organization toasted, "may it be considered as the Charybdis of republicanism and the Scylla of virtue."

Their fears were not unfounded. Such critics, after all, fully understood the principal-agent problem and its implications for governance. Politicians, as mere agents, may act in ways contrary to the interests of the public, the principals. Indeed, many modern nations attempting to establish liberal, market-oriented democracies have allowed their governments to degenerate into predatory states. Luckily, many early U.S. politicians understood that the best way to reduce the risk of politicians' perfidy was not to multiply the number of politicians but rather to check the government's potential rapacity with nongovernmental forces, such as competitive markets. Rather than use fear as an excuse to overregulate the securities industry, therefore, early U.S. politicians allowed the securities sector to develop relatively free from governmental fetters. A free market went hand in hand with political freedom, they correctly reasoned. Policy makers, therefore, generally did not succumb to the rhetoric of the supposed horrors of the South Sea Bubble, even after the Panic of 1792.

The federal government, for example, did little to impede securities markets. One law, passed in 1789 and updated periodically thereafter, prohibited six Treasury Department officials from "directly or indirectly" engaging in commerce or dealing in securities while in office. However, Congress did not extend the act to its own members, and the several states did not follow up with similar enactments. Additionally, the law imposed fines too small to have served as a deterrent, and no one was ever prosecuted under it.

After the Panic of 1792, Congress several times debated a small tax (.05 percent) on public debt transfers. If passed, anyone wishing to sell a federal bond would have been forced to pay a small tax to do so. Opponents successfully argued that the tax was unjust because it would lower the market value of the securities by limiting their liquidity. (See the section in Chapter 5 on the Theory of Portfolio Choice.) They noted that the tax, passed postcontract, would impair the credit of the new government. After some initial support for the tax, deft Federalist political maneuvering crushed it. Of course, in the early national period more onerous taxes, such as taxes on capital gains, were almost completely unthinkable.

The Panic of 1792 induced two states to consider passing minor securities market regulations. New York's legislature actually banned the public auction of securities. Dealers and brokers did not fight the regulation, however, because they had already stopped the practice. In 1817 the state relaxed the regulation, allowing securities to be sold at auction for the benefit of the estate of the deceased or the bankrupt.

In the wake of the panic, New York and Pennsylvania considered legislation forbidding certain time contracts. Pennsylvania tabled the bill, but New York passed it. As of 1792, therefore, New York had on its books a watered-down version of an infamous English securities regulation known as Barnard's Act. In New York, in other words, it was technically illegal to promise to sell government debt or corporate stock that one did not own when the contract was made. The act remained in force in New York until 1858. Massachusetts passed a similar act in 1836 and did not repeal it until 1910. In both states, however, the law was largely a dead letter. Time contracts were simply enforced privately. In a repeated game, dealers and brokers had a strong incentive to fulfill their obligations without recourse to the courts because, if they failed to do so, they would not be allowed to continue to play in the lucrative game. Loss of reputation, in other words, was a strong enough sanction to make most dealers comply with their contracts. Interestingly, the existence of the regulation against time contracts in New York led to the development of the New York Stock Exchange as a self-regulating body. The brokers and dealers were breaking the law, so they could not turn to the state for assistance. They had to police themselves and continue to do so to this day.[4]

States further regulated securities markets through clauses in acts of incorporation that prescribed procedures to be followed during IPOs and secondary stock transfers. Most early incorporations were "special" or, in other words, specific to each corporation. The regulations, therefore, varied widely. The most restrictive of the regulations capped the number of shares to which a particular person, or persons from specified geographical areas, could subscribe. Such regulations sometimes also limited the number of shares that stockholders could vote in corporate elections. Other charters mandated that stockholders could not vote in corporate elections unless they had owned their share(s) longer than some specified period. Some charters mandated minimum holding periods and thereby prevented the transfer of stock for specified periods. Most such restrictions appear to have been attempts to reduce the principal-agent problem in corporate governance

4McCaffrey and Hart 1998.

structure. By expanding the number of stockholders and extending their geographical spread, legislators hoped that corporations would not fall under the control of the unscrupulous.

Variations between charters made it more costly for investors to search for information; nothing could be assumed. Corporate charters, however, were often printed as handbills and widely distributed, so the search costs were not as high as they might first seem. Importantly, if charters were later amended, they were almost always made more liberal; early American legislatures and courts, like their colonial forebears, upheld the sanctity of contracts at almost every turn.

Financial information disclosure requirements were likewise a function of each of the thousands of special charters enacted over the period of this study. Some charters required directors to report periodically to government; individual stockholders, however, had to inquire personally. Directors of most corporations, especially banks, would show investors only balance sheets, but that is about all that even today's investors can view under normal circumstances. Some companies, like the Hamilton Manufacturing Company, allowed any stockholder to view all of the firms' books.[5] Overall, then, the markets were relatively transparent.

State laws against usury did not affect securities trading. State and U.S. courts both followed a seventeenth-century English case that allowed for the payment of a risk premium where "the principal or any considerable part, be put in risque," a realization of the trade-off between risk and return noted by the Theory of Portfolio Choice. People have a right, as one Virginia judge put it, to sell securities "at whatever price is agreed on," as long as the securities, or other forms of property for that matter, were not being used to disguise a loan. (One common way of disguising usury was for the parties to contract to buy and sell an asset at widely different prices. For example, the lender would "buy" a horse, bank share, or other asset from the borrower for $1,000. That is the loan. At the end of the loan period, the borrower bought the asset back for, say, $2,000. That is the repayment of the principal plus an implicit interest charge.)

Some very interesting cases relating to usury show the sophistication of the early financial market. In 1824, for example, a lender agreed to loan $3,000 to Yale College for a year in exchange for the dividends paid on Yale's holdings of $3,000 worth of Eagle Bank stock. The Eagle Bank that year paid 7 percent, 1 percent over Connecticut's usury cap. The court held, however, that the loan was not usurious because the contract was written such that if the Eagle Bank had paid

---

[5] Thomas G. Cary, *Profits on Manufacturers at Lowell: A Letter from the Treasurers of a Corporation to John S. Pendleton of Virginia* (Boston: Charles C. Little & James Brown, 1845).

only 5 percent, or indeed had paid no dividends, the lender would have not received 7 percent. Because interest rate risk was involved, in other words, the contract was legal. Other cases show that it was common for brokers to lend money to investors for the purchase of stock. Courts held that the broker could charge a commission for the purchase, even if his total charges, interest plus commission, would be over the usury cap.

Late in the period under study, Pennsylvania (1841) and Maryland (1842) sought to reduce speculation in securities by voiding futures contracts requiring delivery more than five days after the contract date. The statute did not apply to loans of securities, however, as such an interpretation, as one judge explained, "would invalidate every deposit of stock as a collateral security for a debt, and would very essentially impair the practical value of this kind of property." The statutes had teeth; they voided the contract and imposed stiff fines on both parties. The very teeth of the statute, however, rendered it almost useless. The burden of enforcement rested with the parties who had willingly entered the contract. Again, the state found it difficult to stop a practice that could be enforced extralegally.

Similarly, states did not license brokers until well into the nineteenth century, and then only to raise revenue, not to ensure that brokers met minimum requirements. Only in Maryland, where the license fee was a hefty $1,000, and the fine for brokering $500 *per offense*, were the license laws designed to restrict entry. In 1834 Massachusetts took a slightly different route and taxed the sale of securities at auction.

States also had difficulty making stock transfers costly or time-consuming. Some corporations slowed stock transfers by requiring the board of directors to approve each transfer. Other corporations had the right to buy their own shares rather than allow particular transfers. Some banks had the right to disallow transfers if the seller owed debts to the bank. Courts, however, regularly circumvented restrictive clauses because, as the Delaware Supreme Court noted, "the assignable nature of this kind of property constitutes its chief value," a direct confirmation of the Theory of Portfolio Choice.

Legislatures caught on. Over time, transfer clauses in special charters and general incorporation laws grew more lax. In 1849, for example, New Hampshire voided all sections of its state laws that in any way hindered the transferability of stock. By 1850, most charters mandated only that stockholders inform one of the officers of the corporation of the transfer, and some allowed transferability by mere endorsement. Courts, however, stopped short of turning corporate shares into fully negotiable instruments like bills of exchange. It was an astute conclusion; full negotiability would have decreased the value of securities by rendering their ownership less certain and making fraud easier.

Courts used existing laws and precedents relating to fraud to prosecute securities fraud. They made a distinction between knowingly making false statements and espousing sincere but overly optimistic opinions. *Caveat emptor* was the general rule; only outright lies on the part of the seller could reverse a sale. Directors who sought to deceive the entire market by issuing false financial statements, for example, were held accountable to the entire market and subject to class action suits.

Courts often deferred to brokers' customs when deciding difficult cases. For example, brokers did not disclose their clients' names to other brokers. They, therefore, took nominal title to securities for brief periods, but only in the interest of their clients. The brokers, in other words, were not acting as dealers, although they took temporary title to the securities. The clients, therefore, were liable for any losses incurred (or gains made), in the course of the transaction, not the brokers. Courts supported that practice.

Early American judges, in short, generally sought to accommodate and extend the market for securities. They helped defrauded investors to recover from deceitful corporations, supported brokers' customs, and pushed to make shares easily transferable. Given the relative affluence of most judges, and the widespread ownership of securities, it is probable that judges were acting roughly in their own self-interest as securities holders. They, therefore, sought to shield the market from overzealous regulation while simultaneously seeking to maintain a fair set of game rules. One way that they did so was to allow the securities industry to regulate itself, through organizations like the New York Stock Exchange.

Special Banking Regulations

Bank regulations were stricter than securities regulations.[6] They too, especially until the late 1820s, were usually imbedded in special incorporations subject to the whims of state legislatures. Indeed, legislatures could block the chartering of banks altogether. Unpredictable, widely varying entry requirements were the most important aspect of early bank regulation. Even that regulation, however, was hardly absolute; many banks that could not gain a charter from a particular state legislature simply waited a year until the next legislature convened. Others went into operation as unchartered joint-stock associations.[7] Others gained corporate privileges by paying for them in the form of bribes or

---

[6]Except where otherwise noted, this section is based on Crowder 1942, White 1971, and Wright 1997a.

[7]Sylla 1976.

above-board grants of stock or cash to the state treasury.[8] Overall, however, "state governments made little attempt to regulate banking" de jure and even less de facto.[9]

Early bank charters were mostly concerned with note issue; most failed to define banking even in general terms. In many states, chartered banks had a legal monopoly to issue notes. Many nonbanks and unchartered banks, however, issued notes with relative impunity. Some insurance companies, for instance, issued bearer "bonds" in small denominations designed to pass current as money. Charters often restricted the value of notes the bank could emit at any one time. The values were usually pegged to paid-in capital or specie reserve levels. When too restrictive, such regulations were generally ineffective. Sometimes, when sanctions were not high enough, they were simply ignored. Other times, banks circumvented the restrictions by issuing postnotes, facility notes, or other unregulated bank note substitutes in addition to their legal allotment of standard bank notes. Although banks were not at liberty to increase their capital stock without legislative permission, the stockholders, through the agency of their elected directors, were at complete liberty to retain profits. In addition, generally no restrictions were placed on the size of nonnote liabilities. Banks, therefore, could grow as large as they liked by attracting deposits. Few were forbidden from offering interest on deposits, but few took advantage of the loophole.

Bank charters also typically limited the categories of assets that banks could hold. Banks were generally forbidden to own real estate other than their offices. Banks as a rule could not engage in "commerce" or the buying and selling of "merchandize." Some banks, however, were authorized to build waterworks, railroads, or canals, or to manufacture and sell commodities. Some banks could not own various forms of securities; other banks were required to own certain securities. Charters sometimes limited loans to directors or known usurers. Some charters, usually of banks with names like the "Farmers' and Mechanics' Bank," mandated that a certain percentage of loans be made to individuals with specific occupations. Charters also sometimes limited the collateral that banks could accept, although loopholes generally made such regulations dead letters.

Bank charters often restricted the establishment of branches. A separate, special law was required for each branch. Where branching was not explicitly restricted, it was assumed that banks could not establish branches across state lines. As today, banks charged the highest fees that they could in order to generate significant noninterest revenue streams. Charters and general laws, however, sometimes restricted the

[8]Sylla, Legler, and Wallis 1987.   [9]Krooss and Blyn 1971:32.

amount that banks could charge for fees and for inland exchange premiums.

Bank charters also capped the interest rate that banks could charge for loans, usually at the existing usury ceiling of the chartering state. Unlike unincorporated firms and individuals, which used various ruses to evade the usury ceiling, banks seem to have obeyed the law, although some stretched it by requiring high compensatory balances. Where the law allowed higher interest rates on longer loans, banks naturally urged borrowers to borrow for longer periods. However, when the market price of loans exceeded the legal maximum, applications for loans flooded banks. (People wanted to borrow from banks at 6 percent and relend the funds at 8, 10, or 12 percent.) Banks responded by engaging in nonprice credit rationing. They lent, in other words, only to the safest borrowers.[10]

Some states also taxed banks, sometimes by forcing them to pay a bonus in exchange for a charter and sometimes by an annual levy, usually a small percentage of each bank's capital. Interestingly, the annual, per unit taxes were not as onerous as they at first sound. For some states, the percentage of revenue from such bank taxes was a significant portion of total government revenue. Those governments, therefore, had vested interests in the success of their banking sectors. In such states as Connecticut, Massachusetts, Rhode Island, Pennsylvania, Delaware, North Carolina, and sometimes Maryland, New York, Vermont, and Virginia, the "heavy hand of government" sought to aid banks in order to protect or extend the politically safe revenue that those banks generated. Those states tended to have large numbers of banks, so the tax burden on each bank was light; governments did not want to kill the goose that laid the golden eggs.[11] The point here is not that bank taxes were good things for banks, merely that the existence of taxes does not necessarily mean a large degree of adverse regulation. While banks in those states would have, I suspect, been better off without the taxes, to some degree the taxes redounded to the banking sector's benefit by linking its interests to that of the state, thereby reducing the likelihood of the passage of restrictive legislation or predatory tax levels.

General Banking Regulations in New York: The Revised Statutes, the Safety Fund, and Free Banking

Beginning with the passage of the Revised Statutes in 1827, New York led the nation in general banking laws, regulations that pertained to all banks in the state. A close examination of general banking regulations

---

[10]Wright 1998a.   [11]Wallis, Sylla, and Legler 1994.

in the Empire State is therefore warranted. By the 1820s the size and complexity of the U.S. financial system, coupled with the ill effects of the Panic of 1819, and a still low but increased rate of bank failures, aroused the fears of many Americans.[12] The result was increased government regulation of banking outside of New England, which operated under a system of private regulation known as the Suffolk System.[13] Some of the general government regulations, most notably the Safety Fund, were heavy-handed failures. Others, like the Free Banking acts, though not optimal, freed bank entry from the political process and regularized bank charter requirements.

New York's Revised Statutes were "not only the first attempt to organize the statute law of an English speaking people, but . . . also the first codification of the law of a state."[14] The revisers – banker and lawyer Benjamin F. Butler, politician Erastus Root, and famed jurist James Kent – reduced the fragmentary mass of New York's laws to one whole, systematized set of code. Their efforts remained the groundwork for New York statutory law until the end of the nineteenth century.[15] Where gaps in the law existed, they freely used provisions of the common law, or, as in the case of banking, mixed standard bank charter provisions with recent reform suggestions to develop their own set of restrictions, regulations, and definitions.[16]

The Revised Statutes contained 50 provisions related to banking. Some thought this too much regulation.[17] Some of the statutes resembled the 1826 reform suggestions of John C. Spencer, a powerful New York politician. Spencer, therefore, backed the Butler, Kent, and Root banking provisions.[18] The imposition of full stockholder liability was the leading safeguard.[19] The Revised Statutes also forbade unauthorized reductions of capital, limited total loans, limited loans to directors, and specified a method for calculating profits. Directors were personally responsible for the debts of their banks and were made criminally liable for shortcomings. Insolvencies were considered fraudulent unless proved otherwise.[20] Annual statements to the comptroller

---

[12]Sylla 1985; Wright 1997a.
[13]Whitney 1878; Trivoli 1979; Rolnick, Smith, and Weber 1998; Bodenhorn 2002.
[14]Driscoll 1965.   [15]Butler 1911:7–8.   [16]Driscoll 1965:266.
[17]A Stockholder, *Examination of Some of the Provisions of the "Act to Create a Fund for the Benefit of the Creditors of Certain Monies Corporations, and for other Purposes," Passed April 1829, Particularly to its Effects on the City of New York* (New York, 1829); *Report and Observations on the Banks, and Other Incorporated Institutions in the State of New York* (New York: William Mercein, 1828), iv. Both authors thought men should "trust more to character in their dealings than to penal enactments."
[18]John Cleaveland, *The Banking System of the State of New York* (New York: John S. Voorhies, 1864), xxxviii.
[19]Chaddock 1910; Seavoy 1982.
[20]This was to prevent criminals from escaping by keeping inaccurate or incomplete books, a moral-hazard problem if there ever was one.

were required, the issuance of small notes prohibited, and capital requirements strictly defined and regulated. The statutes also contained
provisions for electing directors. Another section of the statutes reit-
erated the state's prohibition of unchartered commercial banking.

Thanks to the nation's strong belief in the sanctity of contract, the
Revised Statutes' provisions were not applicable to existing corporations, only those to be chartered after 1 January 1828. No banks were
chartered in New York until after the passage of the Safety Fund in
1829, however, so no banks ever operated solely under the provisions
of the Revised Statutes, making an assessment of its merits and problems difficult.[21] Contrary to the assumptions of some historians, those
portions of the Revised Statutes not modified by the provisions of the
Safety Fund Act stayed in effect. In fact, the charters of Safety Fund
banks explicitly referred to the Revised Statutes for definitions, stip-
ulations, and provisions.[22] Albert Gallatin knew this as he organized
his National Bank of New York in 1831. In his plans, he noted that
the bank would be subject "to the 29th, 30th, 31st Sect. aforesd of
Revd Statutes." "It would therefore seem that the affidavit [that the
stock be paid in full before beginning business]," Gallatin lamented,
"must be filed in the County clerk's office (by Rev. Stats) and with
the Comptroller (by charter), and also prove satisfactory to the Bank
Commissioners (by the Safety Fund), before any loans or discounts
can be made."[23]

During the winter of 1828–29, the failures of the Franklin Bank of
New York, the Bank of Columbia, and the Middle District Bank, combined with the cessation of bank entry under the Revised Statutes'
harsh terms, created a money stringency[24] and convinced many that
the time had come for significant bank reform.[25] Some existing banks
seemed unable to reduce the principal-agent problem. The Bank of
Columbia's failure, for example, was laid squarely on "the fraud, ne-
glect or mismanagement of some or all of its officers and agents."[26]

[21]Dewey 1910:255.

[22]See, for example, the third article of the National Bank charter, which read that the
"Said corporation shall possess the general powers of a corporation, as defined in the
eighteenth chapter of the first part of the Revised Statutes." National Bank, "An Act to
Incorporate the President, Directors and Company of the National Bank" (New York,
1829).

[23]Albert Gallatin Papers Miscellaneous papers, forms & plans for the National Bank,
1831, (Philadelphia: Rhistoric Publications, microfilm).

[24]Haggerty Austin & Co. to Simon Newton Dexter, 2 January 1829, no. 753, Letters,
1800–44, Simon Newton Dexter Papers, CUSC.

[25]Abijah Mann to Azariah Flagg, 6 February 1828, in Azariah Cutting Flagg, *Banks and
Banking in the State of New York From the Adoption of the Constitution in 1777 to 1864. Compiled
from Authentic Sources* (Brooklyn: Rome Brothers, 1868), 35–36.

[26]*In the Court for the Trial of Impeachments and Correction of Errors Between the President,
Directors and Company of the Bank of Columbia, Appellants, vs. The Attorney General of the State
of New York, Respondent* (Hudson: S. Curtis Jr., 1829), 3–4.

Unfortunately, New York's "solution," the Safety Fund, actually increased moral hazard. The Safety Fund, it seems clear, was more of a political animal than an attempt to make the banking system safer. Indeed, by 1830 only about 1 percent of the state's revenue came from banks, down from 6 percent in 1820.[27] The state no longer had a strong financial interest in maintaining the health of the banking system, increasing the risk of political shenanigans.

After his election to the governorship, Martin Van Buren began corresponding with an obscure bank reformer, Joshua Forman, about banking issues. Although Van Buren was not even sure where Forman lived,[28] he encouraged the former Federalist to develop his ideas concerning making note issue more secure. Forman claimed he got the idea from "the regulations of the Hong merchants in Canton, where a number of men, each acting separately, have, by a grant of the Government, the exclusive right of trading with foreigners, and are all made liable for the debts of each in case of failure."[29] Forman, in other words, sought to reduce the information asymmetry between banks (as borrowers) and the public (as bank liability holders) by giving banks incentives to monitor each others' activities.

James A. Hamilton, son of Alexander Hamilton, also penned Van Buren a long letter concerning bank reform.[30] After suggesting that a state-owned bank was a plausible alternative, Hamilton backed a bond capital plan first set forth by capitalist Isaac Bronson. Hamilton stressed the necessity of forcing banks to lend according to strict "real bills" rules. He noted that banks did not need any capital at all as long as their discounts matched their receivables.

Van Buren offered the outlines of the Safety Fund scheme in two speeches.[31] The first was given on 23 January 1829. "Having for many years ceased to have an interest in those institutions, and declined any agency in their management," Van Buren explained, "I am deeply conscious of my want of that sort of information which is so important in forming an intelligent and safe opinion upon the subject."[32] "To dispense with banks altogether, is an idea which seems to have no advocate," the Little Magician began, "and to make ourselves wholly dependent upon those established by Federal authority, deserves none." As for a state-owned institution, Van Buren thought such a scheme sure to

[27]Wallis, Sylla, and Legler, 1994.
[28]"Find out the residence of Mr. Forman, and give the enclosed to him." Martin Van Buren to Jesse Hoyt, 15 January 1829, PMVB.
[29]Forman's actual words, as cited in Root 1895.
[30]James A. Hamilton to Martin Van Buren, January 1829, PMVB.
[31]Root 1895:288.
[32]"Annual Message by New York Governor Martin Van Buren Recommending Bank Reform and the Safety Fund, January 23, 1829," in Herman Krooss, ed., *Documentary History of Banking and Currency in the United States* (New York: McGraw-Hill, 1969), 1:636–42.

fail. Unfortunately, Van Buren thought "the reasons for this apprehension" were "so cogent in their nature, so constant in their operation, and of such ready occurrence to intelligent minds," that he need not detail them. He did note that "we cannot close our eyes to the difficulties and pecuniary embarrassments that must result from suddenly stopping the operations of so many and such long established institutions." Van Buren condemned bank charter bonuses, cash or stock payments to the state treasury that some banks used to obtain charter. "Its tendency has been, and must always be," he argued, "to weaken the security of the public in those institutions, for the performance of that in which the public interest mainly consists – the faithful redemption of their paper." "Imposing severe penalties upon acts designed to divert the funds from the appropriation which in justice and policy ought to be made of them, are of value, but necessarily restricted in their operation," the governor argued, implicitly critiquing his former law partner Benjamin F. Butler's Revised Statutes. "The importance of some more efficient safeguard has been felt by former legislatures, and they have endeavored to obtain it through the medium of a personal responsibility of the stockholders," the Albany Regency leader noted. Van Buren promised soon to present a plan proffered by a "disinterested party" that would "make all the banks responsible for any loss the public may sustain by the failure of any one or more of them." Though a "rigorous" solution, Van Buren thought the increased credit of the paper would be more than sufficient compensation.

The future vice-president's second speech, given 26 January, was a much fuller exposition of the proposed act. It appears as though Forman wrote the speech because in a letter dated 24 January the old Federalist scrawled: "The passage you spoke of this morning I have retained."[33] Van Buren noted the idea of insuring bank liabilities had been discussed before. Indeed, as early as 1810 English traveler John Lambert thought the British government ought to secure the deposits of Quebec's poor *habitans*.[34] In 1818 newspaper editor Hezekiah Niles argued that "banks should guarantee the notes of other banks when they proffered them in payment instead of specie or their own notes."[35] The Van Buren–Forman plan merely extended the concept to all bank notes, regardless of how they circulated, and paid for the redemption fund with a special bank tax.

A Senate committee report warmly backed the Van Buren–Forman plan because it thought it necessary to ensure New York's future prosperity. "The lucid and masterly manner in which the Governor has

[33]Joshua Forman to Martin Van Buren, 24 January 1829, PMVB.
[34]John Lambert, *Travels Through Lower Canada and the United States in the Years 1806, 1807, and 1808* (London: Richard Phillips, 1810), 1:245–46.
[35]Quoted in the *Rochester Telegraph*, 14 July 1818.

treated the whole subject, induces the committee to believe, that it
will be out of their power to shed additional light on a matter so ably
examined by the Executive."[36] "The charters of twenty-eight banks,
now in operation in this state, will expire between the present time
and the year 1834; one in 1830; three in 1831; seventeen in 1832; six
in 1833; and one in 1834," the senators continued, citing an 1826
comptroller's report.[37] To force so many banks to close would create
"a degree of distress and embarrassment, such as never has been experienced by the people of this state." Besides the calling in of loans,
nonrenewal would occasion a migration of capital out of the state, the
Senate committee believed. The SBUS would gain too much power if
the legislature allowed the charters of so many state banks to expire.
The senators then backpedaled, arguing that New York's banks, generally speaking, had "sustained their paper at specie value,... regularly
paid the taxes imposed upon them," loaned considerable sums to the
state treasury, and helped build the Erie and Champlain Canals, "the
pride of this State."[38] The losses sustained were like "a mere drop in
the ocean" compared with the benefits that banks brought. Bank failures were also minor compared with the failure of individuals, the
senators concluded.

The Assembly committee on banks and insurance companies produced a similar report.[39] It claimed to have approached the issue with
"single intentions to advance the great interests of the community."
"The system of banking renders almost infinite aids to trade and industry, to the administration of the finances of the government, and
to the whole system of political economy," the assemblymen believed.
"Paper money," the committee argued, "increases the active capital of
a country; which extends labour and industry, and therefore creates
a greater quantity of the products of both, and by producing more
commodities for exportation, accomplished a favourable balance of
trade, and the introduction and increase of gold and silver." This was a
very different, very progrowth, nonagrarian argument that contrasted
sharply with an earlier, widely held belief that banks caused the exportation of specie. The Assembly committee was of course arguing
that banks increased the production of export commodities to such an
extent that the nation's aggregate trade and balance of payments were
placed in the black. Without banks, "we should have beheld nothing
but poverty, inertness and distress," the committee argued. The committee most feared bank note depreciation, so it suggested limiting
bank issues to twice their capitals.

[36] *Report of the Committee on Banks and Insurance Companies, Made to the Senate, January 19,
1829* (Albany: Croswell & Van Benthuysen, 1829), 3.
[37]Ibid., 4.   [38]Ibid., 6.
[39]Bath Farmers' *Advocate and Steuben Advertiser*, 26 February 1829.

The committee rejected Isaac Bronson's suggestion that bank capital should consist of bonds and mortgages because "it would not be practicable to convert these securities into coin with that facility which is necessary to a prompt redemption of the paper issued by the bank."[40] The assemblymen also rejected proposals to create a state-owned and state-controlled bank with branches.[41] "All experience shows that government or financial banks always abuse the trust confided to them," they argued, insinuating that such a bank would overissue notes for political reasons, a clear example of the principal-agent problem. The committee rejected the Revised Statutes because they did not adequately provide security for banks' depositors and noteholders. Furthermore, to do away with all banks "would plunge the whole state in distress and ruin." "The poor and those of small capital, who were rapidly improving their condition, would be absolutely crushed," the assemblymen argued. In fact, the committee believed that the state needed many more banks, wherever "business and commerce will warrant it." The committee was willing to eliminate current taxes on banks in exchange for acceptance of the Safety Fund. It thought the mutual insurance aspect of the plan would prevent banks from running on each other for specie or similarly attempting to disrupt each other's businesses.

Revelations concerning the failure of the Bank of Niagara in 1819 may have influenced some legislators. The Treasury held $14,000 to $15,000 face value worth of Bank of Niagara bills. According to Oliver Forward's February letter to Assemblyman Millard Fillmore (Erie County), after the Niagara's insolvency, Comptroller Archibald McIntyre improperly and without the consent of the legislature took various mortgages and bank-owned real estate as collateral security.[42] Although McIntyre in fact did try to get the legislature's advice on the matter, he apparently did not have title to the land properly conveyed on the Erie County transfer books. The sheriff accordingly sold the lands to satisfy the bank's other debts and the state lost its collateral.

Bank reform became fashionable by the early spring 1829. "The most important & interesting question now before us is the renewal of Bank Charters," William K. Fuller (Madison County) wrote upstate New Yorker Samuel Hatheway in March.[43] Also in March, the American

---

[40]Bronson had put forth a proposal for a bond capital system that made little headway. When later combined with some of Eleazar Lord's ideas and a dose of laissez-faire rhetoric, Bronson's bond capital system would pass as part of the Free Banking Act.

[41]James A. Hamilton, of all people, argued a state-owned bank was a viable alternative. James A. Hamilton to Martin Van Buren, January 1829, PMVB.

[42]Oliver Forward to Millard Fillmore, 3 February 1829, Miscellaneous Documents, NYSL.

[43]W. K. Fuller to Samuel Hatheway, 25 March 1829, no. 2281, Hatheway Family Papers, CUSC.

Institute,[44] a protectionist organization, tried to jump on the bank reform bandwagon to further the cause of domestic manufacturing.[45] "The monied capitals of the banks are drawn from all classes of the community, and are placed chiefly under the control of men interested in and dealing in foreign goods, and by them loaned on notes at sixty or ninety days, to stimulate and encourage the importation and sale of foreign manufactures," the institute asserted, in direct contradiction to the Assembly bank committee's report. "A large majority of the capital of the banks is employed and made subservient, directly or indirectly, to the auctioneers . . . while domestic manufactures are depressed, by having the money of the country drawn into the banks, which would otherwise have been loaned to, or invested in, establishments for their production," the institute complained. The American Institute wanted the Safety Fund to stipulate that banks had to loan a certain amount on the security of real estate.[46] It argued that such loans were more secure and more productive than when lent on "mercantile security." The institute argued it was only seeking domestic manufacturers' "fair proportion of monied accommodations."

Another interest group, New York City's Common Council, also appointed a committee to report on the bank reform issue in late February 1829.[47] The committee's sentiments were similar to Van Buren's and the legislators but added a few new twists. The committee argued that "the funds of these Institutions are now loaned and in active circulation, and are interwoven with the interest and necessities of almost every branch of business or calling, and as the refusal of the Legislature to Re-charter those Institutions would withdraw this large amount from use and circulation at an immense hazard to the solvency of a large class of industrious Citizens, whose want of Capital has obliged them to procure accommodations from these Banks." "The refusal to re-charter these Incorporations," the committee added, "would drive the Citizen to look to the wealthy Capitalist and Broker for his pecuniary accommodations, and to pay to them a rate of interest far exceeding that charged by the Banks." The committee also feared the loss of "a very large Foreign Capital," the sums that Europeans had invested in New York banks. It also noted that to eliminate banks would injure "the funds of Widows and Orphans invested in these Corporations by Testamentary devisees." Recharter of the banks, then, was "highly important to the interest and prosperity of this City." The rest

44 The memorial was signed C. Bolton, President pro tem, and Jonathan Sidell, Secretary.

45 *Memorial of the American Institute, praying for certain regulations in the banking capital of this state, in assembly,* 14 March 1829, doc. no. 160, AAS.

46 "A Stockholder" claimed 75 percent. A Stockholder, *Examination of Some of the Provisions.*

47 23 February 1829, *Minutes of the Common Council of the City of New York, 1784–1831* (New York: City of New York, 1917), 17:672–73.

of the Common Council agreed, and soon drew up instructions for its New York County assemblymen. Though the council did "not deem it in their province to express any opinion as to the terms or Conditions on which these Institutions should be re-chartered," they wanted to make it clear that they believed "*the wants & necessities of the City demand & imperiously require the rechartering of these Institutions.*"[48]

With many strong interest groups fearful of losing most of the state's banks should the overly strict Revised Statutes not be amended, the political situation was ripe for reform. Legislators felt compelled to pass the Safety Fund for fear it was the only option. Indeed, it quickly passed. Its major feature was a scheme of mutual insurance of bank notes and deposits. It also alleviated the harsher aspects of the Revised Statutes. Soon after its passage, applications for banks soared. In 1829 alone, 16 banks renewed their charters under the regulations of the Safety Fund and 11 new banks successfully gained charter.

Safety Fund charters all took the same general form. Some of the provisions had long been a component of at least some of the state's bank charters. Others had only recently come into vogue. All explicitly contained a clause mandating adherence to the provisions of the Safety Fund and those portions of the Revised Statutes not repealed or altered by the new law.

Upstate country bankers generally realized that the fund would give credit to their notes while not unduly taxing their institutions. City bankers, on the other hand, realized that a tax on capital, not note issue, would place most of the burden of the system on themselves while granting no benefits. Martin Van Buren later claimed to have "opened communications with those whom I regarded as the most competent and trustworthy bankers of New York and Albany...and after full discussion we settled upon the plan."[49] His definition of "competent and trustworthy" must not have been very wide because almost all New York City bankers opposed the plan. George Newbold of the Bank of America, for example, wrote to Thomas Olcott in December 1828 to express his dissatisfaction with Forman's plan.[50] "I have not believed nor do I yet think that it is necessary for the Safety of the Public, nor Sound policy as it regards the real & permanent interest of the State that any new provisions of law should regulate the Conduct & operations of banks," Newbold asserted, "beyond an ample sufficient provision that the Capital & the whole Capital incorporated Shall be actually paid in full, possessed before the Bank shall go into operation." He thought all bank failures in New York

[48]2 March 1829, ibid., 17:684.
[49]John C. Fitzpatrick, ed., *The Autobiography of Martin Van Buren* (Washington, D.C.: Government Printing Office, 1920), 221–22.
[50]George Newbold to Thomas Olcott, 17 December 1828, PMVB.

involved "banks which had but little or no original sound Capital." The total volume of bank losses was less than 5 percent of personal losses, he argued, but did not cite a source.[51] "The project in its present form," Newbold continued, "will facilitate the incorporation of New Banks & particularly Country Banks with Small Capitals throughout the State." The Bank of America president thought the .25 percent levy on capital "as being oppressive in addition to the Annual Tax." He thought .125 percent more reasonable provided any sums paid into the Safety Fund were deducted from the general, annual state tax. "The project as it stands is very objectionable because it will enable Banks with Small Capitals to extend the circulation . . . to a great & dangerous degree in as much as the Public no longer relying upon the Bank alone . . . will repose unlimited Confidence in the mutual payment of its bills." Newbold clearly understood that the scheme created a moral-hazard problem. With their notes insured, banks had little incentive to keep their issues in check. Worse still, noteholders and depositors had no incentive to monitor a bank's financial condition because the insurance scheme promised to compensate them in case of bank failure. Freed from close monitoring, bank directors would be free to engage in risky behaviors. The same problem, excessive risk taking by insured banks, has made many economists critics of the Federal Deposit Insurance Corporation (FDIC) and the ill-fated Federal Savings and Loan Insurance Corporation (FSLIC).[52]

To express their dissatisfaction with the Safety Fund, New York City banks virtually stopped discounting, creating an "artificial" scarcity of money.[53] Common investors in New York City showed their opposition to the Safety Fund by not taking up the stock of two new banks[54] – the Merchants' Exchange Bank and the National Bank of New York. Other new banks got on well, however.[55] Despite the already shaky conditions caused by the failure of the Hudson, Middle District, and Franklin Banks, passage of the Safety Fund did not significantly affect the credit of the notes of chartered banks.[56] Although there was some

[51] "A Stockholder" would make a similar suggestion in his pamphlet. The Senate had already made the argument at the end of its report on Van Buren's Safety Fund speeches.
[52] Mishkin 2000; Bodenhorn 2002.
[53] Govan 1959:145.
[54] Edwin Williams, *New York Annual Register for the Year of Our Lord 1830* (New York: J. Leavitt, 1830).
[55] "We have obtain a part of our Bills and Commenced operation moderately have made an arrangement with the N.Y. State Bank at Albany are negotiating with the American Exchange Bank in N.Y. to redeem our Bills there. It is our intention to keep our Bills in a good Credit as any of the Country Banks by the aid of some of our Canal Drafts and other Eastern funds that we shall obtain. Think we shall be enabled to meet all the Bills that are sent to N.Y. promptly. We have found no difficulty in obtaining specie." John Jay Knox to Simon Newton Dexter, Augusta, N.Y. May 27, 1829, no. 753, Letters, 1800–44, Simon Newton Dexter Papers, CUSC.
[56] Norwich *Anti-Masonic Telegraph*, 8 April, 10 June 1829.

stringency in May, by the end of June the banks promised that "all good paper can be done."[57] The cashier of the Dry Dock Bank told Simon Newton Dexter in August 1829 that the business of his bank was "going on prosperously."[58] In September, money was "plenty, very plenty, for the right kind of security" despite the fact that the failure of some "Manufactories is Most Certain, unless Goods Change in Price."[59]

"A Stockholder" presented one of the fullest early critiques of the Safety Fund.[60] He was certain that the new system would "prove destructive to the old and solvent institutions of this city." He argued small, new banks were much more likely to fail than large, old ones. Hence, he insinuated, the Safety Fund was not really an "insurance" scheme as some described it because the premiums (payments into the fund) were not based on likelihood of loss. He also noted that, unlike real insurance schemes, the purchasers of Safety Fund "insurance," stockholders, would never receive any benefit from their "policy" in their capacity as stockholders.[61] If viewed as a tax system the Safety Fund was also "unrighteous" because it levied on capital, not income. City banks rarely divided more than 5 percent, "A Stockholder" contended, whereas country banks often announced 9 percent to 12 percent dividends. Of course, higher returns also meant higher risks. City banks also had to contend with higher real-estate taxes, higher salaries, and higher overall operating costs. The Safety Fund premium on top of the city tax, county tax, state tax, and federal tax, "should it be wanted," was simply too much for city banks to bear. They were mostly banks of discount and deposit, not banks of note issue, "A Stockholder" reminded readers.

"A Stockholder" argued, contrary to contemporary wisdom, that typical stockholders no longer had any real control over the institutions in which they owned stock, or any real idea of their actual condition. Hence, failure was something "in which they have no agency." That was the same argument that Safety Fund advocates had used to urge the protection of noteholders, who they considered "innocent" and hence most worthy of reimbursement. Depositors were less so. Unlike noteholders, who might have to accept the note of a certain bank or receive no payment or change at all, depositors were thought to have some agency in the institutions in which they placed

[57] J. L. Rathbone to Erastus Corning, 26 June 1829, Erastus Corning Papers, 1801–1930, Corning Family Papers, CUSC.
[58] William Stebbins, Cashier, New York Dry Dock Company, to Simon Newton Dexter, New York, 11 August 1829, no. 753, Letters, 1800–44, Simon Newton Dexter Papers, CUSC.
[59] J. L. Rathbone to Erastus Corning, 9 September 1829, Erastus Corning Papers, 1801–1930, Corning Family Papers, CUSC.
[60] A Stockholder, *Examination of Some of the Provisions*.
[61] Though they might in their capacity as a noteholder or depositor.

their funds and some ability to ascertain a bank's financial strength. Others noted that depositors in areas with only one bank had very little choice in the matter. Some argued that most depositors were also stockholders, but it was countered that they should not have to suffer loss in their capacity as depositors as well as stockholders. Safety Fund law reflected this ambivalence; at first depositors were able to make use of the fund[62] but after 1842 they were not.[63] Very few were willing to take "A Stockholder"'s position. In fact, some of the opposition to the Safety Fund came from those who thought full stockholder liability would be sufficient to keep banks from failing because it would give stockholders a strong incentive to monitor directors' activities.[64]

"A Stockholder" also wondered why the Safety Fund applied only to banks. Other types of corporations failed and left creditors in the lurch, he noted. While it was true that banks issued notes, so too did other types of corporations. All emitted "notes of hand, bonds, and bills payable after date," he correctly observed. "The material difference" between bank notes and corporation notes, he argued, "is not perceived." Bank notes were more likely to serve as cash or current money, he admitted, but when serving as such they were a benefit to the people. Hence, the people ought to assume some of the risk. Nonbanks were actually much more likely to fail than banks, he contended, probably correctly.[65]

"A Stockholder" stressed the importance of bank governance structure. "In all matters of trust, the only safe-guard is the vigilance, honesty, and responsibility of those interested in the management," he argued.[66] "Everything depends on the safety of the securities they receive in return for their notes," he further contended. Like Newbold, "A Stockholder" saw moral hazard looming on the horizon. The Safety Fund would create a false sense of security, he predicted, opening the floodgates to all sorts of peculation. He also predicted that the Safety Fund would force specie to leave the state and would reduce the value of New York bank notes in other states. Unfortunately, he did not elaborate on the process involved.

Country accommodation borrowers ultimately paid for the Safety Fund, "A Stockholder" somewhat contradictorily argued. The Safety Fund, he noted, allowed banks to charge 7 percent interest on notes longer than 63 days. Country banks, he reasoned, would take

---

[62]Hedges 1938:22.   [63]Miller 1927:151.   [64]Redlich 1947:94.
[65]He was certainly correct, at least in absolute dollars. The ratio of loss to capital invested would be a more accurate indicator. Bank loss figures are available, but the compilation and analysis of nonbank losses would require a massive study.
[66]Even Joshua Forman believed "the best public security is a sound capital and honest men to manage them." Joshua Forman to Martin Van Buren, 17 December 1828, PMVB.

advantage of the provision and force all accommodation notes to run longer than 63 days to earn the extra interest. In New York City, however, where there were seven banks that would not fall under the provisions of the Safety Fund for many years, if ever, no bank would be able to charge 7 percent on any loan, regardless of its length.[67] That was exaggeration, but the Manhattan lending market certainly was more competitive than most of those upstate.

The bank commissioners created under the Safety Fund were worse than useless, "A Stockholder" believed. Because a bank's condition was a function of the quality of its receivables, general statements were very misleading. The only way to know a bank's condition was to know the intimate details of each discounted note. Not even directors knew the full situation of their bank because each director was acquainted with the quality of only a portion of the paper discounted.[68] Because the commissioners did not have to be bankers, and because they had to visit each bank at least three times a year, there was no way that they would have time to study any one bank's receivables in the necessary detail. "A Stockholder" also wondered if any intelligent, honest man could be induced to hold such a demanding job for a mere $1,500 per year salary. In other words, he saw a principal-agent problem looming; the regulators would not work diligently in the public's interest. The same problem, called "regulatory forbearance," exacerbated the U.S. savings and loan crisis of the 1980s.[69]

Theologian, merchant, insurance company president, and later railroad president Eleazar Lord published a treatise, *Principles of Currency and Banking*, that proved to be a much more subtle and scholarly critique of the Safety Fund.[70] Lord persuasively argued that banking problems were not historical or particular but systemic. As long as banks could increase the volume of currency beyond what was needed for trade or could furnish merchants with fictitious capital with which to trade, there would be bank failures. "Banks ought to be simply offices of discount and deposit," he opined. In other words, Lord believed banks should store money for safekeeping and discount only self-liquidating commercial paper, not mere promissory notes. Lord argued that banks, in order to achieve that ideal, should be required to invest their capitals in permanent government bonds and forbade to loan more than their capital. "It is an advantage of no small consideration, that under this system," Lord argued, "there could be no

[67]In the case of the SBUS branch at New York, the Manhattan Company, and the Dry Dock Company.
[68]This further bolstered "A Stockholders"'s contention stockholders could not be held responsible for failures. It would also have been an argument against punishing directors too harshly for failures.
[69]Mishkin 2000.
[70]Eleazar Lord, *Principles of Currency and Banking* (New York, 1829).

possible objection to the establishment of as many banks as individuals possessing the requisite capital might be disposed to establish." This idea of open competition within general government guidelines and supervision would become the second pillar of the Free Banking Act or Bond Security act of 1838. Lord's exposition was excellent, and if his book had been published in November 1828 instead of November 1829, the Safety Fund concept may have been a mere footnote in the history of banking.

Or maybe not. Many contemporaries and historians believed that Van Buren created the Safety Fund to ensure the control of his party, the Albany Regency, over banking in the state. Robert Chaddock, author of a full-length treatise on the Safety Fund, believed that the system augmented the Regency's power. "After 1829, under the Safety Fund System, the marriage of banks and politics reached its apex," historian L. Ray Gunn likewise argued. Gunn saw the Safety Fund as part of the process whereby political leaders removed important decision making from the control of the increasingly powerful and vociferous democratic masses. Margaret Myers also thought the system politically motivated. Isaac Bronson biographer Grant Morrison thought the plan an Albanian attempt to wrestle banking control of western New York from Wall Street, an intriguing hypothesis. Van Buren biographer Robert Remini, on the other hand, believed the regency leader "for years . . . had been bothered by the general banking conditions in the State and had long wondered if there were not some way he could provide New York with dependable financial institutions, protect the public from wildcat banks and minimize the possibility of a panic." Van Buren's own assertions are the only evidence of such concerns, however, and it is difficult to believe that in the 1820s "wild cat banks," which were largely a phenomenon of the antebellum West, were much on the Red Fox's mind. Fritz Redlich was probably most accurate when he admitted that "it is difficult to decide what actually prompted Van Buren's actions." The Safety Fund was certainly designed to allow for the "orderly expansion of banking," but the question remains whether it was so designed to ensure bank note security, to strengthen a political machine, or both.[71]

Accusations that the Safety Fund was a Regency ploy to acquire control over the state's banks are bolstered by the activities of Regency bankers such as Benjamin Knower. As the impending passage of the Safety Fund promised to open the floodgates for new charters, Knower maneuvered to prepare himself to imbibe heavily of the stock of country institutions. "Sibley says Ben Knower will take a good share of the

[71] Chaddock 1910; Gunn 1988; Myers 1931:83; Morrison 1973:276; Remini 1951:683; Redlich 1947:89; Riesman 1989:30.

Bank Stock – Whew!!" Everard Peck wrote to Thurlow Weed concerning a proposed second bank in Rochester, New York.[72]

As Jacksonians geared up for the war against the SBUS, some New Yorkers began to wonder if Van Buren, a Jacksonian insider, had set up the Safety Fund as an alternative to the national bank. In February 1830 Isaac Bronson warned Nicholas Biddle that he had "good reason for believing the late law of this State [Safety Fund Act] . . . originated in political motives." "If the other States had come into the measure as was recommended," Bronson noted, "the Banks of the country would have become a company of mutual insurers, and probably in the appraisal of the gov't sufficiently safe to be entrusted with the collection and disbursement of the public monies."[73] Of course, Bronson may have been upset his bond capital plan had met rejection.[74] In May 1830 Charles A. Davis, one of the directors of the New York State Bank, wrote Nicholas Biddle about Van Buren's fear of the SBUS.[75] Davis likened Van Buren to an old gun: "It was safer out of reach & harms way for tho it was said to have neither flint or powder in it still it might go off." Davis said he at first thought Van Buren set forth the Safety Fund to become as popular as "Clinton & Canal," an allusion to longtime governor DeWitt Clinton and the profitable system of internal improvements he had helped to construct. Davis now perceived, however, that the Safety Fund could serve as "a substitute . . . and a safe channel for all Govt purposes' sh'd the U.S. Bank be dispens'd with."

The Safety Fund, in other words, may have been designed to help upstate regency-controlled banks to become "pet banks," state banks that would hold large federal deposits after the demise of the SBUS Large New York City Safety Fund banks such as the City Bank perceived it was against their best interest to seek federal deposits during the SBUS crisis and scramble for pet bank status. By limiting the bank's outstanding notes and deposits to two and a half times a bank's capital, the Safety Fund prevented the large city banks from using their large deposits as the basis of discounts as they had when under their original charters, which did not consider deposits as liabilities.[76] To take too many deposits, then, would have cut into the banks' ability to make discounts and hence their profits.[77]

[72]Everard Peck to Thurlow Weed, Rochester, 29 February 1829, Thurlow Weed Papers, University of Rochester, Rochester, N.Y.
[73]Isaac Bronson to Nicholas Biddle, 13 February 1830, in Reginald McGrane, ed., *The Correspondence of Nicholas Biddle dealing with National Affairs, 1807–1844* (New York: Houghton Mifflin, 1919).
[74]Venit 1945.
[75]Charles August Davis to Nicholas Biddle, 21 May 1830, in McGrane, *The Correspondence of Nicholas Biddle*, 102.
[76]The banks were restricted to issuing notes three times debts, "over and above" its deposits.
[77]Cleveland and Huertas 1985:13.

Additionally, Regency Safety Fund banks may have been used against the SBUS In July 1834, for example, Redwood Fisher, son of prominent Pennsylvania lawyer Miers Fisher, told Nicholas Biddle that "the Safety fund Banks of the State, under the influence of the Albany Regency, have considerably curtailed their issues – and refuse to extend them."[78] This, he claimed, threw "all the odium of the present extreme scarcity of money throughout this State upon your Bank." "Gentlemen from many counties of the State have assured me, that the farmers – men of much influence, believe that their suffering is owing to that assigned cause," Fisher continued. "The Regency presses are daily filled with articles calculated to induce this opinion, and it is fast gaining ground," he believed.

Later in 1834 Alexander Hamilton Jr. told New York lawyer John Woodworth that "the regency have resolved, through the Safety Fund Banks, to grant facility to raise, if possible, the price of grain about the commencement of October, in order to satisfy the farming interest that our embarrassments have passed away and that their policy had placed the future prosperity of the country on a permanent footing – this impression is now gaining ground and unless counteracted will give us an uphill labour."[79]

Given the Safety Fund's politicized origins, it is not surprising that views of the Safety Fund's economic performance have been mixed. On the one hand, the noteholders of Safety Fund banks lost only .125 percent to bank failures between 1829 and 1866.[80] That was not bad for a system that regulated as many as 91 banks at one point. New York's Safety Fund banks weathered the Panic of 1837 better than the banks of any other state.[81] By 1840, however, failures had prostrated the system. Although the charter of the last bank incorporated under its provisions expired in 1866, as early as 1853 a bank analyst labeled the Safety Fund "dead."[82] Despite the system's checkered record, it was adopted and did well in several other states, including Vermont.[83]

New York politician and financier Azariah Flagg thought that the Safety Fund's biggest flaw was that it made other banks responsible for the failure of member banks. In other words, he criticized the crux of the entire system. Flagg also believed that the act should have kept bank note plates out of the control of bank directors as the Free Banking Act later would.[84] Such a provision would have limited moral hazard by making it easy to monitor directors' note printing patterns. In 1864

[78]R. Fisher to Nicholas Biddle, 7 July 1834, in McGrane, *The Correspondence of Nicholas Biddle.*
[79]Alexander Hamilton Jr. to John Woodworth, 14 September 1834, in ibid.
[80]Klebaner 1974:48.   [81]Gunn 1988.
[82]Henry Baker, *Banks and Banking in the United States* (Boston: Ticknor, Reed, and Fields, 1853), 11.
[83]Redlich 1947:95.   [84]Flagg, *Banks and Banking in the State of New York.*

John Cleaveland argued that the Safety Fund's prohibition of postnotes (§35) "has been more effectual, during the last twenty-five years, in securing to the citizens of this State a uniform and sound currency, and preventing bank insolvency, than all the restrictions and prohibitions in the statutory regulations of 1827 [the Revised Statutes]." That may have been true, but New England banks did an even better job under a completely private, if somewhat coercive, system, the Suffolk System.

Financial historian Margaret Myers believed that the Safety Fund "exercised for some years a large and on the whole beneficial influence upon banking and the money market."[85] Compared with the Bond Security or Free Banking Act that would follow, the Safety Fund created a more elastic currency. Both systems proved to give about equal protection to bank creditors. The Safety Fund's initial costs were higher, but Safety Fund banks could keep more notes in circulation than free or bond security banks. The cost differential, then, depended on the performance of the bond banks' securities. L. Carrol Root suggested that the two systems complemented each other. Safety Fund banks provided much needed currency elasticity while the free banks provided much needed entry.[86]

One benefit of the Safety Fund that scholars like Root often overlook, however, is that it too eased entry into banking. Legislators, relieved of the political responsibility for poorly performing banks by the insurance fund, became more willing to charter banks. The number of new banks chartered in New York jumped in the early 1830s. By demonstrating the benefits of easier entry, the Safety Fund may very well have laid the basis for its successor, the Free Banking Act.[87]

Overall, however, the Safety Fund must be counted as a failure. It attempted to regulate too much, created a major moral-hazard problem, allowed smaller banks to free-ride on larger banks, did not rid the banking system of political influence, and generally was inferior to New England's private Suffolk System. Worse yet, it was probably created to help Van Buren's Albany Regency as much as to reform banking. No one saw the Safety Fund's problems more clearly than New Yorkers, who passed legislation creating a parallel banking system, the so-called free-banking system, in 1838.

Free banking's biggest advantage was that it more clearly divorced bank entry from politics. Legislative approval was not necessary to obtain a free-banking charter. Potential bankers merely had to meet certain requirements in order to begin operation – supply $100,000 of capital, back 12.5 percent of its notes with specie, and submit two financial statements to the comptroller each year. Additionally, free banks were required to hold their capital in the form of government

85Myers 1931.   86Root 1895.   87Wright 1997a.

bonds and mortgages. The banks would earn interest on the bonds and mortgages, which could be sold for specie if necessary to redeem note issues.[88]

Between 1837 and 1863, 18 states in addition to New York enacted free-banking laws. The details varied from state to state, as did the outcomes. In some western states the passage of free banking led to the creation of infamous "wild cat" banks that issued huge sums of bank notes on the security of nearly worthless bonds. Such banks tended to have very mobile offices deep in frontier forests, hence their nickname. After a rough start, however, the act succeeded in eastern states like New York. Importantly, the free-banking concept formed the basis of the National Banking Act, a major federal banking law passed during the Civil War.

Adam Smith would have taken issue with some of the regulation of the early U.S. financial system, including much of the Revised Statutes and the Safety Fund. Overall, though, he would have been cheered by the financial system's relative de facto freeness. He was, after all, a realist who was not so "absurd as to expect that an Oceana or Utopia should ever be established."[89] Given the nature of legislatures, government regulation of some sort was well nigh inevitable. Despite the many political machinations surrounding important legislation, such as the Safety Fund, the early United States generally managed to avoid onerous regulation of the financial system. A Lockean conception of government and a solid understanding of moral hazard, both largely products of its English political system and colonial experience, prevented early America from succumbing to a predatory state. Relatively unfettered by government strictures, the financial system was poised to aid economic development by meeting the borrowing needs of the commercial, manufacturing, and agricultural sectors.

[88]Seavoy 1982; Gunn 1988.   [89]Smith 1776: book 4, chapter 2.

8

Finance-Directed Economic Development

Thomas Willing, Michael Hillegas, Alexander Bryan Johnson, Eleazar Lord, and scores of other early U.S. financial pioneers understood that none of the major means of economic growth hitherto explored by economic historians could have flourished without modern capital markets. The great triad of the early U.S. economy – trade, agriculture, and manufacturing – all relied on the financial sector. Indeed, one is hard pressed to find a single major economic activity or innovation that did not receive crucial support from banks, other types of financial intermediaries, or securities markets. The *root cause* of early U.S. economic growth (1780–1850), therefore, is the development of the financial sector, not transportation and communication improvements, not foreign trade, and not manufacturing firms.

Banks supplied short-term liquidity credit to merchants and traders, corporate transportation companies, and manufacturing concerns of all types. Banks, especially local, country banks, lent directly to farmers.[1] The agricultural sector gained most, however, from banks' loans to merchants and transportation companies. The merchants paid farmers with cash; by decreasing transportation costs, the internal-improvement companies increased the demand for farmers' products, "expanding the market" in Smithian terms.

Securities markets were also of prime importance. The sale of corporate equities and bonds or the sale of state bonds financed internal improvements. Increasingly, manufacturing firms assumed corporate form in order to tap long-term investment funds. Merchants rarely incorporated into trading companies, but they used the securities markets much as banks did, to keep relatively safe, liquid, interest-bearing assets on their balance sheets.

The early U.S. financial sector was not perfect, or optimal, but it was far superior to that of the colonial period, and to those of most other nations. The combination of banks and securities markets created an unquantifiable synergy where banks supported capital markets, which, in turn, supported banks.[2] First, banks supported the securities

---

[1]Wright 1997a.   [2]Sylla 1998.

markets by lending to brokers and dealers. Those securities special-
ists, in turn, made the secondary market for bank (and other corporate) shares liquid, thereby lowering banks' long-term borrowing
costs. Second, major financial instruments were all forms of "money"
and hence were almost completely fungible. With minimal cost and
effort, bills of exchange, bank liabilities, or specie could also be used
to purchase securities, and securities could be used to purchase bills
of exchange, bank liabilities, or specie.[3]

Together, the two major parts of the financial sector, banks and securities markets, managed to reduce problems of information asymmetry
and other lending-related costs and risks enough to allow significant
amounts of passive investment to occur. From there, it needed only to
support trade, agriculture, and manufacturing in order to spark per
capita increases in GDP.

Financing Trade

Short-Term Bank Financing

The importance of short-term bank financing of trade has been thoroughly described elsewhere recently, so I do not dwell upon it here.[4]
Generally speaking, merchants (and other borrowers) obtained short-
term loans from banks on the basis of two forms of collateral, a bill
of exchange or draft or a promissory note. The former often arose in
the course of "real" trade and was essentially a postdated check drawn
on a nonbank payer. The latter was a simple IOU. Bankers obviously
preferred lending on real bills because goods in shipment and the
general credit of all of the parties who made, endorsed, or accepted
the bills served as collateral for them. Only the general credit of the
maker and any cosigners backed an IOU.

Banks literally discounted – that is, paid the discounted present
value of – the bills or notes receivable. The equation that they used,
the present value formula, was identical to the one used today, $PV = FV/(1+i)^n$ where PV = present value, FV = future value or principal, i = interest rate, and n = the number of years to maturity.
Thus, if a merchant discounted a bill or note of \$1,000 payable in
exactly 1 year, at 6 percent interest, he would receive from the bank
\$943.40 today [\$943.40 = \$1000/(1.06)]. The merchant would do
so if he believed that \$943.40 today was preferable to \$1,000 in one
year, which he might believe if he had a debt to pay or an opportunity that promised to return him more than \$1,000 within a year.

[3]Philip Livingston to Alexander Hamilton, 27 March 1792, *PAH*, 26:663.
[4]Bodenhorn 2000, 2002; Wright 2001.

By essentially paying the interest at the beginning of the loan, the merchant saved a few dollars compared with the cost of a simple loan ($56.60 instead of $60, the difference stemming from compounding). By discounting the receivable rather than making a simple loan, the banks fully collateralized both principal and interest. The merchant owed $1,000, the exact amount of the receivable. (With a simple loan, the merchant would owe $1,000 plus the $60 interest, leaving the interest payment uncollateralized.)

By discounting their notes and bills (accounts receivable), banks allowed merchants to anticipate future income, thereby allowing them to conduct a safer, or larger, business. In other words, banks supplied merchants' liquidity needs. Unlike his colonial predecessor, an early national merchant with access to bank discounts did not have to be terribly concerned with the amount of specie that he had on hand. He could turn his bank notes, his receivables, and his securities into specie virtually at will. If specie was in short supply, he could use the bank to obtain some other form of money acceptable to his creditor, such as a draft drawn on New York or simply a bank credit.

The liquidity banks afforded also allowed businessmen to diversify their concerns because project completion did not have to be coordinated with expected cash outlays. For example, if a merchant wanted to undertake a trading expedition with an expected duration of nine months, he need not be concerned if he had to pay for the transported goods in six months because he could borrow on collateral of the goods in transit, or even just his own good name, while he patiently awaited for his goods to reach market.

"The bank, by the operation of discounting," some Americans understood as early as 1785, created "the important and substantial advantages of both prompt payment and credit."[5] Banks, in other words, assumed the risks and rewards of lending, allowing merchants and retailers to specialize on trade. Increasingly, traders could insist on payment in ready funds like specie, bank notes, or bank check, and eschew credit terms. That was especially true in the urban retail trade, and in all wholesale dealings. Wholesale merchants and retailers made heavy use of their bank accounts to make disbursements and to safekeep receipts. Thomas Willing, for example, funneled most of his income through his bank account, depositing and disbursing over $160,000 in 1790 alone.[6] Similarly, banks helped small or new traders to obtain goods that they could not purchase on credit. In 1815, for example, Jacob Leonard sought a loan from the Bank of Columbia so that he could purchase "a stock of goods" in his "line" from "some houses where

[5] *Pennsylvania Gazette*, 16 February 1785.
[6] Thomas Willing Bank Book no. 4, 1790–91, HSP.

I shall be a stranger" and some that had already "declined business" on credit terms.[7] Bankers, after all, were better at making credit decisions than other potential lenders.[8]

Most merchants truly depended on short-term credit to remain competitive. To buy most advantageously they needed cash, not cash when their customers decided to buy, but cash when the market was low. Indeed, merchants devoid of access to bank credit complained bitterly about it.[9] Therefore banks, at the margin, could make or break mercantile houses. Banks, in other words, served the very useful economic function of separating the efficient from the inefficient firms, forcing the latter to become more efficient or to exit.[10]

Securities as Means of Payment

Early U.S. merchants had little need for long-term capital, so they rarely formed corporations. The securities markets were important to merchants mainly as a convenient vehicle for investment. Merchants were very much like banks in that they needed to maintain a degree of liquidity in order to meet punctually bills as they fell due. Rather than tie up large amounts of their assets as specie, they turned to banks to provide short-term liquidity loans. Banks could not always be relied upon, however. Sometimes banks overextended and had to stop discounting until their balance sheets improved. At other times, there was too much demand for bank loans. Because usury laws capped the interest rate, banks could not meet the higher demand with interest rate increases. They, instead, engaged in nonprice rationing and made very selective lending decisions.[11] Merchants, therefore, kept securities as a form of "secondary reserve" that could be hypothecated to secure loans. If merchants could not raise cash at bank, even through hypothecation, they raised it by outright selling their securities, for a minor brokerage fee, in one of the nation's several liquid capital markets. If they did get the loan, they collected the coupon and dividend payments from their securities. The current yields on such investments were usually high enough to compensate for the interest on the loan.[12]

Then, as today, government securities also served as "safe havens" in troubled times. Shortly after the sacking of Washington during the War of 1812, John Jacob Astor argued "what times are these I think after all 6 p Ct. are our best property."[13] During minor panics and money shortages, prices of U.S. bonds often increased (and yields decreased),

[7]Jacob Leonard to Dr. John Ott, Georgetown, 17 August 1815, LCP.
[8]Bodenhorn 2000.   [9]Wright 1997a.   [10]Bodenhorn 2000.
[11]Wright 1998a.   [12]Krooss and Gilbert 1972:115.
[13]John Jacob Astor to D. A. Smith, 31 August 1814, John Jacob Astor Papers, BLHU.

indicating a sort of "flight to quality" similar to that experienced in world financial markets to this day.[14]

Securities were also useful as a means of domestic and international remittance, in lieu of specie, drafts, or bills of exchange.[15] "The fact is," Charles Haines told readers in 1824, "the stocks of the monied institutions in a city like New York, are perpetually circulating – passing from one to another, and serving as commercial facilities, and commercial means to companies and to individuals."[16] Indeed, after the sacking of Washington in 1814, large nominal differences in domestic prices developed. The further one was from Boston, the banks of which did not suspend specie payments, the higher the nominal price one had to pay. Southerners making payments in Baltimore and New York, therefore, were greatly disadvantaged and could suffer "considerable loss." Southerners who purchased securities before the suspension, however, found that the securities were "a good remittance."[17]

When it was to their advantage, merchants also used securities as a means of international remittance. When spot exchange rates were very high, or in other words when it was costly for U.S. merchants to make payments overseas using bills of exchange, merchants had three options. They could ship commodities, specie, or securities. Often, securities offered the most attractive alternative.

Early in the 1790s the fact that the coupon payments on U.S. bonds were payable only in the United States somewhat dampened foreign demand because the policy put European investors to extra expense. As early as 1790 British investors tried to induce Congress "to appoint a reputable banking house at London, to pay interest in London of American bonds, in the same manner as the bank of England pays interest of government debt."[18] An easy means of transferring the securities in London was also suggested. The U.S. government was also to "pay all expences, remitting to Europe, premium to banker, &c. for his trouble." "In this way," it was argued, "their friends in Britain could be of assistance in laying out their loose money in that property, and thereby raise the credit and same of the American States, when it was seen through Britain and Europe, how high the American stock sold." The advocates of this plan noted that the Irish and British governments made similar arrangements in Amsterdam, in order to induce Dutch investment. The United States, however, made no such provisions. In 1794 English traveler Henry Wansey noted that foreigners desirous

---

[14]Sylla, Wilson, and Wright 2002.   [15]Myers 1931:64.

[16]Charles Glidden Haines, *Arguments Against the Justice and Policy of Taxing the Capital Stock of Banks and Insurance Companies, in the State of New York* (New York: G. F. Hopkins, 1824), 14.

[17]Henry Remsen to John P. Van Ness, 16 June 1815, Henry Remsen Papers, NYPL.

[18]*Pennsylvania Gazette*, 3 November 1790.

of investing in the "American funds" could make arrangements with "any American house" to receive and remit the income for "a small commission."[19]

In 1795 the market stepped in to provide a better solution.[20] A group of London bankers argued that "the Resources of the United States of America being, in proportion to the Debt, probably superior to those of any European Government; and they having made ample Provision for the Payment of the Interest of their Stocks, only two Arrangements more seem necessary to make them a very eligible Property to People in this Country; viz. 1st. To make them transferable in London; and, 2d. To provide Means for paying the interest or Dividends, in London, punctually on a certain Day without Expence." With the help of U.S. trustees, the bankers devised a private system for payments and transfers of U.S. securities in London. The U.S. trustees received the payments in America and remitted the whole sum to a London bank, "without expense." The London bank, which also kept the local transfer books, made payments to the current owners. Holders still had the option of registering their shares on the books of a U.S. loan office, or they could trade the securities in London via assignment.[21]

As early as 1794 some English creditors argued that "Stocks" were the "best remittance" in many circumstances. By the end of 1794 "a great deal of money [had been] made by remittance in them and at least one broker predicted that "American Stocks are sure to sell well in London."[22] By 1797 European demand for U.S. securities was strong enough that a Philadelphian could publicly argue that "if good bills should become scarce, the public funds, bank stocks, and insurance stocks of the United States, offer very safe means of placing money now in Europe, being at present at moderate prices here; and if transmitted to England they can be sold or not according to the state of money matters there."[23] In late 1799 U.S. merchants sent federal securities, including transferable script in a new

---

[19]Henry Wansey, *Journal of an Excursion to the United States of North America in the Summer of 1794* (1796), 233.

[20]*Dunlap's American Daily Advertiser*, 6 August 1795.

[21]"Every purchaser of American stock receives a certificate, declaring that the United States are indebted to him or his assigns, the amount therein specified, and the assignment of these certificates constitutes the mode of transfer in these funds. The holders may at any time have them registered in their names in the treasury book at Washington, or at the loan office of any particular State, and receive new certificates in their own name, for which purpose a power of attorney must be made out by a notary public." Bernard Cohen, *Compendium of Finance: Containing an Account of the Origin, Progress, and Present State of the Public Debts, Revenue, Expenditure, National Banks and Currencies of France . . . and Shewing the Nature of the Different Public Securities, with the Manner of Making Investments Therein* (London: W. Philips, 1822), 277.

[22]George Nelson to Samuel Bellamy, 28 July 1794; to George Bell, 24 December 1794, George Nelson Letter Book, UNCSC.

[23]*Merchants' Daily Advertiser*, 29 April 1797.

U.S. loan, to England "in reams...in remittances for goods."[24] Similarly, after the Panic of 1819, securities, including shares of the SBUS,[25] became a good means of remittance to London.[26] In 1830, according to John Jacob Astor, exchange rates strongly affected domestic demand for securities. "Exchange on Europe is fallen," he told Albert Gallatin in 1830, "which make our Stocks less valuable here for that market."[27]

Securities could also be used to finance international trade proactively. During the War of 1812, John Jacob Astor sent Six Percents and other U.S. securities to Europe where his agents sold or hypothecated for them for loans, the proceeds of which they used to buy bills of exchange on Canton.[28] From New York, Astor directed his London bankers, Baring Brothers and Company, to sell his U.S. Sixes in Amsterdam at 96 percent of par or higher.[29]

Over the first half of the nineteenth century, major international private bankers emerged as important conduits in the sale of American securities abroad. In addition to the Barings, the Browns, George Peabody, William Corcoran, and, to a limited extent, Nathan Rothschild purchased and resold American public securities, especially government debt instruments.[30]

The sums that moved overseas were substantial. By 1798 it was well known "that Europe[ans] hold [a] full 2/3 of the U States funded & Bank Stock & that Chiefly in England."[31] In 1827 almost $20 million of the U.S. national debt, which then stood about $69 million, was in the hands of foreigners, about $13.6 million in Britain, $3.2 million in Holland, and just over $3 million in other European nations.[32] SBUS stock was also strong in international markets; at times as much as 30 percent was held in Britain. Similarly, in the late 1830s foreigners owned over half of Louisiana's banking capital.[33]

The securities market helped to buffer the world macroeconomy from the destabilizing effects of large, unexpected specie flows. For example, in 1818 "the immense quantities of specie...exported to India...occasioned a great scarcity of money...which [w]as...

[24]*Philadelphia Aurora*, 30 December 1799.   [25]*Richmond Enquirer*, 13 April 1821.

[26]*The Paradox Solved, or, a Financial Secret Worth Knowing: With the Means of Dissipating Dearth and Desolation, by the Due Encouragement of National Industry, in a Letter to the President of the United States, by the Author of Statisticus* (Baltimore: Joseph Robinson, 1820).

[27]John Jacob Astor to Albert Gallatin, 30 January 1830, Albert Gallatin Papers (Philadelphia: Rhistoric Publications, microfilm).

[28]John Jacob Astor to Baring Brothers & Co., 19 June 1813, vol. 16, copy of letter, J. J. Astor, 1813–15, John Jacob Astor Papers, BLHU.

[29]John Jacob Astor to Baring Brothers & Co., 29 April 1814, ibid.

[30]Hidy 1949:150–52, 194–202, 260–69, 476–77; Perkins 1975:58; Cohen 1971; Hidy 1978:375, 379; Ferguson 1998:389–96.

[31]George Nelson to Alex Shirras, 5 August 1798, George Nelson Letter Book, UNCSC.

[32]*Philadelphia Public Sale Report*, 15, 29 December 1827.   [33]Wilkins 1989:61–63.

pressingly experienced at Baltimore, Philadelphia, New-York, &c."
"The consequence" of the specie outflow was "that money borrowers,
to meet their payments, have been obliged to bring stock and exchange
into the market, and thereby occasion its depression in price."[34]
Sometimes, securities flowed back to the United States. In early 1797,
for example, some British investors remitted BUS shares instead of
specie.[35]

Merchants, in other words, used securities as specie substitutes in
both internal and external trade. Securities, particularly government
bonds, but also some corporate equities, were a form of money in
the wholesale trade, roughly similar to the Federal Reserve System's
monetary aggregate M3 or, at the very least, L.[36]

Additionally, of course, foreigners' purchases of U.S. securities increased America's capital stock, effectively making more funds available to finance growth-enhancing projects. Every dollar of U.S. securities owned by a European was an extra dollar available in the U.S. to
develop new technology, to increase the division of labor, or to improve
infrastructure. True, foreign owners earned dividend and coupon payments in dollars, but of course, on average, securities issuers were earn-
ing more than what they were paying to investors or they would not
have issued the securities in the first place.

Some foreign investors with good information about the U.S. were
even willing to keep the bulk of their assets in U.S. securities. Take, for
example, the case of George Nelson, an Englishman who ran a retail
shop and securities dealership in Charleston in the late 1780s and early
1790s. As he prepared to return to England in late 1792, he made a
strong case for leaving his wealth in the United States. As he explained
to a fellow Englishman, "you think I had better bring my property
home with me but as the greatest part of it is in the American funds
& pays abt. 7 pr. Ct. & I think very safe that I think it will be best to let
it remain & have the Interest remitted half yearly in London." Nelson
eventually did return to England and became a dealer specializing in
U.S. securities.[37]

Closely tied to trade, of course, were issues concerning internal
improvements – bridges, roads, canals, railroads, and other physical
infrastructure. A healthy competition between the merchants of the
major commercial centers helped to spur merchants to support infrastructure projects designed to make it easier for farmers, millers,
and manufacturers to bring their foodstuffs and wares to market.
Merchant Thomas Cope of Philadelphia, for example, spent much of

[34] *Boston Columbian Centinel,* 14 November 1818.
[35] *Federal Gazette & Baltimore Daily Advertiser,* 24 March 1797.   [36] Mishkin 2000.
[37] George Nelson to Mr. Lambert, 3 November 1792; to Josiah Adams, 28 April 1794; to
Mr. Nelson, 5 March 1794, George Nelson Letter Book, UNCSC.

1809 "endeavouring to thwart a scheme of the Baltimoreans of robbing us of much of our interior trade, by forming a turnpike road from the Conewago falls on the river Susquehanna to Yorktown, from whence a turnpike is already in forwardness to Baltimore."[38] Baltimoreans, for their part, lamented the dearth of banks in Baltimore, citing the abundance of short-term credit in Philadelphia as the reason why Philadelphia merchants "are enabled to extend their commerce to all parts of the globe" while Baltimore merchants spent much of the day seeking "short credit . . . upon an usurer's interest."[39]

Financing Farming through Internal Improvements

Commercial banks sometimes made direct loans to farmers. Other financial intermediaries, especially insurance companies, savings banks, and lombards, frequently did so. The most significant aid that the financial market provided the agricultural sector, however, was less direct. Banks and capital markets financed the creation of the nation's transportation infrastructure, the roads, canals, railroads, and ports that made the shipment of agricultural products cheaper. The financial sector, in other words, greatly extended the market for farm produce, America's primary output in the late eighteenth and early nineteenth centuries. Farmers without access to markets tended to live close to subsistence levels. Once an internal improvement came to the area, however, most farmers responded by increasing production, usually to pay for consumption of manufactured goods. Almost all significant early U.S. internal improvements relied on the nation's capital market and banking system.

Early Americans learned from England's example that internal improvements, including canals, roads, bridges, and waterworks, could be efficiently undertaken by private companies, "without one penny expence to government," one of the great insights of Adam Smith. In December 1791, for example, an American writer extolled the virtues of the New River Company of London, which supplied Londoners with fresh water. Notwithstanding the "immense expence" of the undertaking, and the "low charge for water," the stock of that company sold "for more than 50 per cent. above par, and [was] esteemed the safest of all public securities."[40]

Cash-strapped states, therefore, were more than happy to allow private companies to build waterworks, bridges, roads, canals, and, later,

[38]Eliza Cope Harrison, ed., *Philadelphia Merchant: The Diary of Thomas P. Cope, 1800–1851* (South Bend, Ind.: Gateway Editions, 1978), 235.
[39]*Federal Gazette & Baltimore Daily Advertiser*, 6 February 1804.
[40]*Pennsylvania Gazette*, 7 December 1791.

railroads. Banks aided those private internal improvement companies in two ways, by purchasing their equities and by granting them short-term liquidity loans.[41]

The Manhattan Bank, itself a private water utility, made one of its first loans to the Cayuga Bridge Company.[42] About the same time, the BUS supplied short-term loans to the Philadelphia waterworks committee.[43] When the Potomac Company defaulted on loans to the Bank of Columbia in July 1814, it felt obliged to provide a full explanation.[44] "The extreme depressed state of Commerce equal almost to a total stagnation," the company spokesperson explained, had decreased "the revenue of the Company for the last twelve months" to less than 20 percent of its expected level. The spokesman included a revenue report designed to dispel any "apprehension of misapplication of funds" and to show "that the delinquency arises from causes not with in the control of the Company." Engineer Benjamin H. Latrobe also obtained liquidity loans from the Bank of Columbia to help to build the water system of Washington, D.C. In order to obtain the loan, Latrobe had to sketch briefly the terms of the water company's charter, his reasons for needing the loan, and a repayment schedule and obtain three cosigners.[45]

Internal improvement companies also used banks to pay dividends to stockholders, store receipts, make collections, and provide other financial services. The Philadelphia and Lancaster Turnpike, for example, had accounts with the BNA and the BUS.[46]

Banks also made long-term equity investments in internal-improvement companies. In 1804, for example, the Bank of Philadelphia subscribed to 10 shares of the "Turnpike from the Nescopack falls on the river Susquehanna to the Lehigh."[47] The next year, it purchased $1,000 worth of shares in the Berks and Dauphin Counties Turnpike Company.[48] At various times, it also owned shares in the Columbia Bridge Company,[49] the Susquehanna and York turnpike, the Centre turnpike, the Lancaster, Middletown and Elizabethtown turnpike, the Susquehanna and Lehigh turnpike, and the Downingtown, Euphrata, and Harrisburgh turnpike.[50] Similarly, the Bank of Pennsylvania's

[41]Minutes of the Proceedings of the Board of Directors of the Offices of Discount and Deposit at Reading, 3 July 1816, Bank of Pennsylvania Records, HSP.
[42]28 November 1799, Journal no. 1, Chase-Manhattan Bank Archives, New York.
[43]Harrison, *Philadelphia Merchant*, 41.
[44]Elie Williams to the President & Directors of the Bank of Columbia, 21 July 1814, LCP.
[45]B. H. Latrobe to the General Mason, President &c. of the Bank of Columbia, 26 December 1811, LCP.
[46]*Pennsylvania Gazette*, 22 August 1792.
[47]Directors' Minutes, Bank of Philadelphia, 9, 11 May 1804, Philadelphia National Bank Records, HSP.
[48]Ibid., 22, 24 May 1805.   [49]Ibid., 16 December 1813.   [50]Ibid., 9 April 1821.

branch at Reading purchased 8 shares of the stock of the Reading
Water Company in 1821.[51]

By 1809 banks and securities markets had allowed New Yorkers to
create an impressive system of internal improvements.[52] The Empire
State in that year bragged of 67 turnpike companies, maintaining
3,071 miles of road, with an authorized capitalization of $5,141,750.
By that year, New York was also home to 21 bridge companies with
an additional $450,000 par capital value. By 1820, however, at least
according to Mathew Carey, "the exertions of Philadelphia...far
exceeded those of any city in the Union, for the promotion of
internal improvement."[53] Philadelphians had furnished the capital
for the Permanent Bridge Company ($300,000), the Upper Ferry
($124,000), the Susquehanna and Schuylkill Canal ($950,000), the
Schuylkill Navigation Company ($1,500,000), the Lehigh Coal Com-
pany ($500,000), the Chesapeake and Delaware Canal Company
($900,000), and sundry turnpikes ($2,910,000), for a total investment in Delaware Valley infrastructure of over $7,100,000. Those
were all important improvements. The Permanent Bridge, for example, enabled the farmers of "nearly Twenty Townships on the west
side of Schuylkill" to bring their produce to Philadelphia without "the
Expence & Difficulty of" fording or ferrying across the Schuylkill River,
an obstacle to trade that was "at all Times injurious to the Prosperity
& Welfare of the People."[54]

New York leapt ahead again with the completion of the Grand Canal
and its feeders. The Empire State financed the canal through the sale
of state bonds, many of which ultimately found their way to Europe.
Indeed, as early as 1791 European bankers believed that individual
American states "might make loans here advantageously."[55] Although
the State of New York owned the canal system, private banks aided in
its creation by affording "loans and other facilities during the progress
of the work."[56] Had not the domestic securities markets developed,
New York would not have been able to sell its bonds. It is not clear
that it could have paid for the canal out of current taxes. Indeed,
in 1829 the *American Jurist* argued that the "large sums" raised for
"carrying on private business, as well as improvements of great public utility" could not have been begun and completed "successfully
without corporations."[57]

[51] Minutes of the Proceedings of the Board of Directors of the Offices of Discount and Deposit at Reading, 15 February 1821, Bank of Pennsylvania Records, HSP.
[52] *Baltimore Evening Post*, 19 October 1809.   [53] Carey Manuscripts, LCP.
[54] Schuylkill Permanent Bridge Papers, Captain Richard Peters Papers, HSP.
[55] William Short to Alexander Hamilton, 22 February 1791, *PAH*, 8:59.
[56] *Report of the Committee on Banks and Insurance Companies, Made to the Senate, January 19, 1829* (Albany: Croswell & Van Benthuysen, 1829), 6.
[57] "Manufacturing Corporations," *American Jurist* 2 (1829): 94.

When combined, the trade networks of merchants and the physical infrastructure of bridges, roads, and canals allowed for profitable manufacturing. Raw and intermediate goods could be shipped longer distances more cheaply.[58] By 1809, for instance, pits as far away as Burlington, New Jersey, supplied "the glass works at Albany" with sand. Finished and intermediate goods also traveled those networks and internal improvements to their final markets. As early as 1801, the city of Reading was "noted for its hatters," who made "large quantities of wool hats of good fabric" for sale to "Philada. Hatters" for dispersion "in every direction." "They manufacture them so cheap & their work is in such credit that no person in Philada. attempts the same business," one contemporary explained.[59] The division of labor and specialization that characterized Philadelphia's regional economy in the first half of the nineteenth century, in other words, ultimately depended upon the financial sector.[60]

The aid of the financial sector was also necessary to help to create the final product. Until recently, most scholars argued that "there were credit as well as labor scarcities in the new republic." "Indeed," many scholars argue that "the country had a primitive banking system at the time." Banks "acted more to facilitate trade through short-term loans than to promote industrial undertakings." The significance of securities markets did not even register with most scholars. Ergo, the financial system could not have been involved "in bankrolling large-scale enterprises."[61] Manufacturers, the story goes, had to raise capital from private investors and retained earnings. That hoary story must be eschewed; it was never plausible and is now known to be just plain wrong in many circumstances.[62]

Financing Manufacturing

"A Tradesman,... having a number of Apprentices employed," Philadelphia lawyer and businessman Miers Fisher noted circa 1790, "may have a considerable quantity of his manufacture upon his hands for which he cannot find an immediate Market." The lack of short-term credit was disastrous, Fisher argued. "His stock worked up, – without money to purchase more, – demands upon him for Rent, market-money, Fuel &c., his workmen must stand idle; unless, by, sacrificing his goods at a public sale, for less than half their value, he procures a sufficiency to supply his necessities."[63] Though perhaps less eloquent,

---

[58]Rothenberg 1992.   [59]Harrison, *Philadelphia Merchant*, 81, 241.
[60]Lindstrom 1978.   [61]Licht 1995:84–86.
[62]Lamoreaux 1994; Bodenhorn 2000; Wright 2001.
[63]"A Plan for the Support of the Poor, and for the Relief of the Necessitous," Miers Fisher Papers, HSP.

the bank loan application letter of soap boiler John Wirt made the same points even more poignantly:

> I ask the favour of inlargeing my accommodation as I have been making soap & candles in the small way & find it will answer well in my town & I have built a house for a factory of 62 feet by 23 feet & have the part witch is occupied for soap making done & commenced work in it & will make from 3 to 4000 weight soap per week if I can get Capitall to Lay in Stock. . . . I wish my accommodation in all to be for 4000$ witch will pay all my notes & give me about 1500$ to go on with witch in able me to do something for my self as well as a greater convineance for the town in General as there has been large sums of money sent to Baltimore & other place for the article of Soap & Candles But without Capital I cant do anything as my opponent in Washington Mr. Docker has offered the Butchers in our Market the Cash in advance to Get their tallow from me. I have as Good workmen & a steady man imployed by the Year. . . . It [is] my intention if you Grant me this favor to go to Frederick & Hagerstown Winchester & the other Neighbor town[s] in a few day[s] to procure Tallow to Go on with as this is the Season to Get it.[64]

Philadelphia shipbuilders also complained that they were "often put off for a long Time before they can procure Payment for their Bills to their great Damage" because they could not easily seize the "Body Tackle Furniture" of ships.[65]

Those were not isolated instances. The BNA lent widely to artisans and manufacturers. As early as 1786, less than five years after the birth of the bank, Philadelphians argued that "houses and ships were built, and improvements in manufactures of all kinds were carried on, by money borrowed occasionally at the bank." "Commerce and arts flourished in Philadelphia, while they declined in every other city in America," it was argued, "from the want of that credit which the bank produced in our city." Occupations that benefited from bank loans included ship and house carpenters, blacksmiths and anchor smiths, nailers, painters, sail and mast makers, riggers, brickmakers, and masons.[66] Recent scholarly research has verified those claims.[67]

Philadelphia was not unique. For example, the Bank of Utica, from two offices in upstate New York, readily lent to artisans and manufacturers.[68] In 1818 the Bank of Columbia made short-term loans to the Building Company of Georgetown, near Washington,

[64]John Wirt to the President, Directors of the Bank of Columbia, 5 October 1815, LCP.
[65]Philadelphia Ship Builders Petition, box 4a, folder 5, HSP.
[66]*Pennsylvania Gazette*, 29 March 1786.   [67]Wright 1998a, 1999a.
[68]Wright 1997a.

D.C.[69] Similarly, in 1829 Joseph Ellicott noted that "the two Banks in Canandaigua, the one in Geneva and the one in Rochester had discounted liberally for Merchants, Millers &c. in the seven western counties" of New York.[70] When manufacturers could not get bank loans directly, they often joined forces with merchants in order to obtain access to short-term funds.[71]

That artisans received bank loans should not be surprising. Artisans were, after all, businesspeople who had to contend with many of the same problems, essentially problems of asset and liability management, that merchants and farmers did. Take, for example, the situation of Philadelphia brickmaker Nicholas Esling. He made and delivered almost $60 worth of bricks for John D. Coxe in June and July 1802, but Coxe offered only a promissory note, due in November, in payment. In the meantime, Esling had numerous small cash payments to make to pay workers and to buy materials. So, he discounted Coxe's note at the BNA, paid his bills in cash or with checks, and then repaid the loan when Coxe paid the note.[72] Artisans used banks extensively even when they did not need loans. Philadelphia brewer Reuben Haines, for example, received no discounts from the BNA in 1792, yet his account was extremely active, with total credits over $52,000. Haines used the bank to pay his suppliers by check and to safekeep and collect his receivables. Numerous other artisans did likewise. Other artisans, such as cooper Matthias Pinyard, received intermittent discounts. Still others, such as tanner Jonathan Meredith, received numerous discounts. Discounts, 48 different ones totaling just over $70,000, made up 35 percent of Meredith's credits (deposits) in 1795, for example.[73]

Ground rents were an important source of long-term financing for artisans in the Middle Atlantic states. Ground rents were misnamed; they were not leases or rents but a type of special, perpetual mortgage. They were used extensively in Pennsylvania, Delaware, and Maryland from the late seventeenth century until the Civil War. One of the few recent scholars to study ground rents concluded that the institution encouraged entry into the real-estate market of small-scale entrepreneurs, notably building tradesmen.[74] Indeed, almost three-quarters of the purchasers of land by ground rent in Philadelphia between 1770 and 1820 were artisans. With their lots paid for out of current earnings, those artisans could use their savings to erect

[69]Joseph Nourse to the Bank of Columbia, Georgetown, 12 March 1818, LCP.
[70]Robert W. Bingham, ed., *Reports of Joseph Ellicott As Chief of Survey (1797–1800) and as Agent (1800–1821) of the Holland Land Company's Purchase in Western New York* (Buffalo: Buffalo Historical Society, 1937–41).
[71]Livesay and Porter 1971.
[72]Society Miscellaneous, box 1a: Miscellaneous Bills, HSP.
[73]See Individual Ledgers, 1792, Bank of North America Records, HSP.
[74]Rilling 2001.

buildings and purchase tools.[75] Ground rents also helped to establish inland towns. "The easie rents of Lots at first in York Reading and Carlisle," Edward Shippen wrote James Hamilton in 1769, "were the only means of their being so well Settled as they are."[76] Shippen could easily have added Pottstown, Philadelphia, and most other substantial towns in the lower Middle Atlantic states to that list. Sources suggest that ground rents played important roles in the growth of Lancaster and other county seats in Pennsylvania; Wilmington, Delaware; and Baltimore, Maryland.[77] Ground rents were so salubrious that Alexander Hamilton established a ground rent–like system for the artisans of the SEUM in Patterson, New Jersey.[78]

Artisans outside of those states needed to find personal or institutional lenders for long-term capital. Their long-term capital needs, however, were not large.[79] If their businesses needed funds in order to grow, artisans could turn to insurance companies,[80] savings banks,[81] or merchants.[82] In antebellum New England, growing artisanal and manufacturing concerns could also attempt to create or capture a bank.[83] Finally, larger firms could obtain a corporate charter and raise equity in the capital markets while continuing to tap the institutional loan market.[84]

The much-maligned SEUM was one of the first manufacturing concerns to form a joint-stock corporation. The first joint-stock manufacturing company in America was "The United Company of Philadelphia for Promoting American Manufactures." A large putting-out and shop system started in 1775, the unincorporated company issued shares of £10 each to fund the activities of some 500 individuals who spun thread at home and in a factory-like setting. The Revolution squelched that firm. Soon after the war, the New York Manufacturing Society, a joint-stock corporation, issued shares to fund its 130 spinners and 14 weavers.[85]

The SEUM, yet another brainchild of Alexander Hamilton, had a propitious beginning. Investors filled the initial SEUM subscription of $100,000 in July and August 1791. Investors subscribed an additional $625,000 and elected directors in late 1791. Although a complete list of the stockholders is not extant, many of the most important are known. William Constable, Nicholas Low, Herman LeRoy, George Scriba, James Watson, and the firms of Sutton and Hardy

[75]Wright 1998b.
[76]Edward Shippen to James Hamilton, 9 March 1769, Edward Shippen Letter Books, American Philosophical Society, Philadelphia.
[77]Wood 1970.   [78]*PAH*, 12:12–13.   [79]Bodenhorn 2000.
[80]James 1942:85; Fowler 1888:61.
[81]Keyes 1876; Manning 1917; Horne 1947; Olmstead 1976.
[82]Livesay and Porter 1971.   [83]Lamoreaux 1994.   [84]Rothenberg 1992:122.
[85]Clark 1929:183–92.

and Ten Brook and Chapman were merchant importers. Constable, Andrew Craigie, Abijah Hammond, Richard Harrison, LeRoy, Philip Livingston, Low, Matthew McConnel of Philadelphia, Alexander Macomb, and Cornelius Ray were or soon became directors in the BONY, the BUS at Philadelphia, or the BUS's New York branch. Brockholst and Philip Livingston, W. P. Smith, and Robert Troup were lawyers, and Harrison was federal district attorney for New York. John Pintard was a stockbroker, insurance man, and Tammany officer.[86]

Hamilton's role in the SEUM was as large and as constant as possible given his other duties. He went so far as to hire skilled immigrants from England and advanced them his personal funds so that they could begin to work on models and full-sized prototypes of machines. Hamilton knew that the SEUM's recruiting violated English laws preventing the emigration of skilled artisans and machine parts. According to the closest and most recent student of this issue, Hamilton "wholeheartedly supported technology piracy."[87] Hamilton also collected information and made recommendations about which types of manufacturing to begin. At the same time, he arranged for surveys of prospective manufacturing sights and participated in the careful decision-making process that selected Patterson. The site chosen was one of the best in the country.[88] "Fine sites for cotton and woollen factories exist in every State which I have visited," British traveler Henry Fearon noted in 1818, "the Falls of Pasaic, near New York, cannot, for such purposes, be exceeded. Mr. Casey, lately of Liverpool, is endeavouring to form a cotton twist establishment at this place." That prime location would later save the SEUM.

The SEUM soon attracted a devoted following. In August 1792, for example, SEUM stockholder Moore Furman expressed surprise at "short sighted Speculators that they dont catch at the Manufacturing Scrip at par." "Well," he concluded, "I'll keep it and reap the profits my self then."[89] By October of that year, the SEUM had "near 200 hands employed" at Patterson, New Jersey, printing and staining calico.[90] Unfortunately, soon thereafter the SEUM foundered under the direction of a French architect who was more interested in style than in functionality or speed. By 1796 the SEUM was moribund. It went "dormant" for a time, but its stockholders did not dissolve it. It later revived and thrived as a sort of venture capital firm and landlord. It played a major, though quiet, role in the development of Patterson.[91]

[86]Davis 1917:393.   [87]Ben-Atar 1995:390.
[88]Henry Fearon, *Sketches of America: A Narrative of a Journey of Five Thousand Miles Through the Eastern and Western States of America* (London: Longman, Hurst, Rees, Orme and Brown, 1818), 304.
[89]Moore Furman to William Edgar, 30 August 1792, William Edgar Papers, NYPL.
[90]*Brunswick Gazette*, 23 October 1792.   [91]Davis 1917.

Although the direct impact of the SEUM was small, its indirect effect was to give publicity to manufactures, and to encourage productive use of capital so that land speculators and fops did not dissipate the nation's new liquid wealth.

The number of incorporated joint-stock manufacturing concerns grew steadily over the decades. Many of antebellum America's big manufacturing firms, such as the Amoskeag mills and the Tredegar Iron Works, were joint-stock companies that raised equity capital in the nation's securities markets. In 1843, for example, the equities of 26 manufacturing firms were listed in the major Boston commercial newspaper, the *Boston Shipping List*. By 1853 that number had increased to 40.[92] According to contemporary observers, the prices of those equities were rationally determined. Consider, for example, the following:

The present price of the stocks in the Lowell companies varies, from the par value of one thousand dollars, up to twenty-seven per cent. advance, or twelve hundred and seventy dollars for a share, at which rate that of one company, the "Merrimack," is held. You see, then, that purchasers know how to discriminate. They have, in truth, all the information that they could desire for doing so. The accounts of the companies cannot be concealed from stockholders, to whom a full annual exhibit is always made. Still less can they be concealed from directors; and when men are made directors, they do not give up the right to buy and sell shares, nor can they control two or three hundred stockholders, so far as to prevent them from putting their shares into the market or to compel them to do so. The market price, then, is the true indication of the value of the share. Fifty men, at least, stand ready to buy or sell, as any advantage is to be gained either way. Their calculations are founded upon an exact knowledge of what is the amount reserved; what is the stock of goods unsold, and what the latest report of prices from Canton or New York; what is the stock of cotton on hand for each mill, and what the latest price, with the tendency up or down, at Liverpool or New Orleans.[93]

Notice the author's stress on information dissemination, first in the reduction of information asymmetry between principals (stockholders) and agents (the firm's officers) and second in the market's ability to correctly value the stock given changes in relevant macroeconomic variables and insider trading. The same author also noted that the manufacturing firms, like the nation's financial firms, were widely held.

[92]Sylla, Wilson, and Wright 2002.
[93]Thomas G. Cary, *Profits on Manufacturers at Lowell: A Letter from the Treasurers of a Corporation to John S. Pendleton of Virginia* (Boston: Charles C. Little & James Brown, 1845), 12.

For instance, 390 different persons owned shares in the Merrimack Company. Of that number, 46 were merchants, 68 were female, 52 were retirees, 80 were holders in trust, 23 were lawyers, 18 were doctors, 3 were literary institutions, 15 were farmers, 40 were clerks or students, and 45 were mechanics and machinists, many *"in the actual employment of the Company."*[94] Such employees owned $60,000 worth of shares.

Conclusions

The early U.S. financial system aided the commercial, agricultural, and industrial sectors of the economy, though in slightly different ways. It aided commerce through short-term liquidity discounts. Merchants who received such discounts could conduct business more safely or more profitably. The financial system also provided merchants with an alternative means of remittance in both domestic and international payments. When foreigners purchased U.S. securities, or accepted them as remittances, they increased America's capital stock, essentially funding the wealth-producing ideas of U.S. entrepreneurs.[95]

The financial system aided the nation's many farmers directly by making them loans that they used to improve the efficiency of their farms. The system also helped farmers, and other small businesses, indirectly, by providing short- and long-term financing for internal-improvement corporations, including turnpike companies, canals, and railroads, that increased the extent of the market and decreased transportation costs and information travel times.

Manufacturers, too, benefited from the financial system. Manufacturers, like merchants and farmers, obtained short-term liquidity loans from banks.[96] In addition, manufacturers raised equity capital in the nation's strong IPO markets. Not all manufacturing firms tapped those markets, but the largest ones, like New England's textile mills, did, and to good effect.

Common sense tells us, therefore, that the financial system was crucial to early U.S. economic growth. In this instance, common sense is fully backed by recent economic theory. Ross Levine, Robert King, Sara Zervos, and others have empirically tested the finance-led growth hypothesis and confirmed it in each instance. Such studies have found that financial and economic development occur simultaneously. They also show a high correlation between the initial extent of financial development and subsequent economic growth rates extending decades into the future. Greater financial depth, in other words, stimulates economic growth in both the short and long run. Rousseau and Sylla

[94]Ibid., 13.   [95]Wilkins 1989.   [96]Bodenhorn 2000.

argue that the process was essentially autocatalytic or, in other words, a positive feedback cycle.[97]

Additionally, Bodenhorn argues, convincingly I might add, that evidence from the early nineteenth-century United States suggests a similar causal relationship between financial development and economic growth. Using advanced statistical techniques that control for the effects of nonfinancial factors, Bodenhorn shows that increases in bank credit had a statistically significant effect on the rate of income growth.[98]

Again, however, econometric analysis is not necessary to understand the importance of finance to economic growth. Adam Smith, more than 200 years ago, recognized the crucial role of finance in economic growth. It is to his argument that we now turn.

[97]Rousseau and Sylla 1999.   [98]Bodenhorn 2000, 2002.

9

Conclusion

Adam Smith made very clear that the direct causes of the wealth of nations are free trade, infrastructure improvements, labor specialization, and economies of scale and scope. Those things, alone or in concert, increase efficiency and real per capita aggregate output. None of those things simply comes about, however. Each must be funded, mostly through borrowing. Borrowing and lending is far from a simple process. Problems of information asymmetry, namely adverse selection, moral hazard, and the principal-agent problem, collude to limit effective lending. The riskiest borrowers seek loans most eagerly. Once a loan is made, the borrower must be monitored to reduce fraud or risky behavior. Owners too must monitor their agents and employees lest defalcations occur. Reducing information asymmetry is not cheap, so large, specialized firms or transparent markets best undertake it. Only when the financial system is sufficiently advanced to reduce information asymmetry can significant numbers of major, wealth-creating projects be profitably undertaken.

Can those findings, however, really be considered a rediscovery of the beliefs of Adam Smith, the founder of modern economics? After all, Smith was extremely careful to differentiate the substance from the fluff, the wheat from the chaff, the real from the merely nominal. He rightly considered interest on money "always a derivative revenue."[1] He also rightly noted that, "though the wages of the workman are commonly paid to him in money, his real revenue, like that of all other men, consists, not in money, but in the money's worth; not in the metal pieces, but in what can be got for them."[2] Smith is most remembered, and revered, for his vivid descriptions of the division of labor in action in pin factories, his stunning critique of government interference in the market, and, of course, his metaphor of the "invisible hand." One might think, therefore, that Smith ignored, or abhorred finance as mere superfluity. Such, however, was not the case.

Smith devoted the second book of his *Wealth of Nations* to "the nature, accumulation and employment of stock." In the introduction to

[1] Smith 1776: book 1, chapter 5.   [2] Ibid., book 2, chapter 1.

that second book, he clearly states that "labour can be more and more subdivided in proportion only as stock is previously more and more accumulated." Of course by "stock," Smith had physical assets in mind. Later in the second book, however, Smith makes a strong case for bank money, a financial asset, as a substitute for specie, a physical asset. He likened the invention of bank money to the invention of "some improvement in mechanics," a metaphor also used by early Americans.[3] Smith therefore endorsed the cautious extension of banking, noting "that the trade of the city of Glasgow doubled in about fifteen years after the first erection of the banks there; and that the trade of Scotland has more than quadrupled since the first erection of the two public banks at Edinburgh." He doubted that banks caused all of the increase, but he argued convincingly that banks contributed "a good deal" to the increase. "It is not by augmenting the capital of the country," Smith argued in his usual, cautious way, "but by rendering a greater part of that capital active and productive than would otherwise be so, that the most judicious operations of banking can increase the industry of the country." In other words, "the judicious operations of banking, by substituting paper in the room of a great part of this gold and silver, enables the country to convert a great part of this dead stock into active and productive stock; into stock which produces something to the country."[4] Smith's views on paper money of course apply to wider monetary aggregates, such as the securities that blossomed in the early United States. If the replacement of specie with bank liabilities could convert dead into productive stock, so too could the replacement of specie or other inert physical assets with equities and bonds. Although Smith believed a national debt to be "pernicious," he realized that its existence was in some ways beneficial. Investors in the national debt, for example, often lend to the government on "extremely advantageous" terms, including the easy transferability of the debt instruments to "any other creditor." In other words, "the merchant or monied man makes money by lending money to government, and instead of diminishing, increases his trading capital."[5] The indirect benefit of a national debt, its salubrious effects on investment, was considerable.

After all, Smith reminds us, "some part of the capital of every master artificer or manufacturer must be fixed in the instruments of his trade." "This part, however, is very small in some" businesses, such as tailoring. "In other works," however, "a much greater fixed capital is required."

[3] "A bank upon these principles is like mechanic powers in producing force, compared with strength of hands in advancing improvements and prosperity of a country." *Pennsylvania Gazette*, 19 July 1786. See also *PAH*, especially Hamilton's 1781 claim that banks were "the happiest engines that ever were invented for advancing trade." [4] Smith 1776: book 2, chapter 1.   [5] Ibid., book 5, chapter 3.

Industrial concerns, such as ironworks and coal works, require "instruments of trade which cannot be erected without a very great expense."[6] If some way cannot be found to finance such great, expensive endeavors, they are not built, and their advantages remain unrealized. Because few can afford to build great factories out of their own stock, they must borrow it from others, if they can.[7]

Smith understood that adverse selection and moral hazard could disrupt credit markets and pointed to banks as a major means of reducing those problems. He noted, for example, that merchants preferred "the home trade" over the foreign and carrying trades because in the latter pursuits it was too easy to be "deceived." "In the home trade," on the other hand, the merchant "can know better the character and situation of the persons whom he trusts." He also recognized the adverse-selection problem, arguing that interest rates "so high as eight or ten per cent" attract only "prodigals and projectors, who alone would be willing to give this high interest." "Sober people," he continued, "who will give for the use of money no more than a part of what they are likely to make by the use of it, would not venture into the competition."[8] Smith also noted that banks in Scotland reduced moral hazard by closely monitoring their customers' accounts. "The banking companies of Scotland . . . were . . . very careful to require frequent and regular repayments from all their customers." The practice enabled the bankers "to make some tolerable judgment concerning the thriving or declining circumstances of their debtors, without being obliged to look out for any other evidence besides what their own books afforded them; men being for the most part either regular or irregular in their repayments, according as their circumstances are either thriving or declining."[9]

Smith also understood the principal-agent problem. "The directors of such companies," he wrote in *Wealth*, "being the managers of other people's money than their own, it cannot well be expected, that they should watch over it with the same anxious vigilance with which the partners in a private copartnery frequently watch over their own." The solution to the principal-agent problem, Smith argued, was to form joint-stock corporations, especially in banking, insurance, transportation concerns, and waterworks.[10] Those, of course, were the very types of companies that Americans were mostly likely to incorporate.

Importantly, there is much evidence that early Americans had read and understood Smith perfectly. By 1785 American banking advocates regularly cited, quoted, and excerpted Smith and other probank

[6]Ibid., book 2, chapter 1.   [7]Ibid., book 2, chapter 4.   [8]Ibid.
[9]Ibid., book 2, chapter 1.   [10]Henderson 1986:111–15.

theorists, such as Sir James Steuart.[11] By 1786 the intermediation role of banks was fully understood. "Common Sense," probably Thomas Paine himself, explained that he had "kept cash at the bank" for almost a year without receiving "a single farthing interest." He kept "between eight and nine hundred pounds" in the bank because he thought it "safer under the care of the Bank, until I have occasion to call for it, than in my own custody." In the meantime, he noted, "this money the country has had the use of."[12] By 1804 many Americans understood that additional banks could help the economy by further reducing information asymmetry. More banks "would increase the number of directors, and give a greater scope of information as to who ought and ought not to be accommodated from the banks."[13] By the 1810s the United States had its own bank theorists, such as Alexander Bryan Johnson.[14] Finally, contemporaries well understood that nations with physical endowments similar to the northern United States, most notably Canada, were not destined to economic greatness if they lacked a sufficiently complex financial system. British observers stated the case very clearly. George Hebert, for instance, lamented the sorry state of Canada in 1833, noting the prevalence of bartering and the dearth of bank liabilities as major causes of the north country's backwardness.[15] James Buchanan, the British consul in New York in the 1820s, also noted Canada's relative "torpidity, and indolence." Buchanan argued that the major difference between the two nations was their respective financial sectors. U.S. banks and securities markets drew "forth the energies of the people," unlocking productive capabilities that "in the history of nations affords no parallel."[16]

---

[11] See, for example, *Pennsylvania Gazette*, 7 September 1785; "A Citizen of New York," *Remarks on That Part of the Speech of His Excellency the Governor, to the Legislature of the State of New-York, Relative to the Banking System* (New York, 1812), 4, 8.
[12] *Pennsylvania Gazette*, 21 June 1786.
[13] *Federal Gazette & Baltimore Daily Advertiser*, 6 February 1804.
[14] Alexander Bryan Johnson, *An Inquiry into the Nature of Value and of Capital and into the Operation of Government Loans, Banking Institutions, and Private Credit* (New York, 1813); Todd 1977.
[15] George Hebert, *Present State of the Canadas; Containing Practical and Statistical Information* (London: 1833), 152–53.
[16] As quoted in Hubbard 1995:71–72.

References

Adams, Donald R. 1978a. "The Beginning of Investment Banking in the United States." *Pennsylvania History* 45:99–116.

1978b. *Finance and Enterprise in Early America: A Study of Stephen Girard's Bank, 1812–1831*. Philadelphia: University of Pennsylvania Press.

Baldwin, Simeon. 1903. "American Business Corporations before 1789." *Annual Report of the American Historical Association* 1:253–74.

Banner, Stuart. 1998. *Anglo-American Securities Regulation: Cultural and Political Roots, 1690–1860*. Cambridge: Cambridge University Press.

Barnes, Andrew W., ed. 1911. *History of the Philadelphia Stock Exchange, Banks and Banking Interests*. Philadelphia: Cornelius Baker.

Baskin, Jonathan, and Paul Miranti. 1997. *A History of Corporate Finance*. Cambridge: Cambridge University Press.

Ben-Atar, Doron. 1995. "Alexander Hamilton's Alternative: Technology Piracy and the Report on Manufactures." *William and Mary Quarterly* 52:389–415.

Bessembinder, Hendrik, and Herbert M. Kaufman. 1997. "A Comparison of Trade Execution Costs for NYSE and NASDAQ-listed Stocks." *Journal of Financial and Quantitative Analysis* 32:287–311.

Bodenhorn, Howard. 1999. "Short-Term Loans and Long-Term Relationships: Banks and Borrowers in the Nineteenth Century." Lafayette College, Easton, Pa. Unpublished manuscript.

2000. *A History of Banking in Antebellum America: Financial Markets and Economic Development in an Era of Nation-Building*. Cambridge: Cambridge University Press.

2002. *State Banking in Early America: A New Economic History*. New York: Oxford University Press.

Bogue, Allan, and Margaret Bogue. 1957. "'Profits' and the Frontier Land Speculator." *Journal of Economic History* 17:1–24.

Brewer, John. 1989. *The Sinews of Power: War, Money, and the English State, 1688–1783*. Boston: Unwin Hyman.

Bruchey, Stuart. 1965. *The Roots of American Economic Growth, 1607–1861: An Essay in Social Causation*. New York: Harper & Row.

Buel, Richard. 1998. *In Irons: Britain's Naval Supremacy and the American Revolutionary Economy*. New Haven: Yale University Press.

Butler, William Allen. 1911. *A Retrospect of Forty Years, 1825–1865*. New York: Charles Scribner's Sons.

Carosso, Vincent P. 1970. *Investment Banking in America: A History*. Cambridge, Mass.: Harvard University Press.

Chadbourne, Walter W. 1936. *A History of Banking in Maine, 1799–1830.* Orono, Maine: University Press.

Chaddock, Robert E. 1910. *The Safety Fund System in New York State, 1829–1866.* Washington, D.C.: Government Printing Office.

Chandler, Alfred, Jr. 1977. *The Visible Hand: The Managerial Revolution in American Business.* Cambridge, Mass.: Harvard University Press.

1990. *Scale and Scope: The Dynamics of Industrial Capitalism.* Cambridge, Mass.: Belknap Press.

Clark, Victor. 1929. *History of Manufactures in the United States.* Vol. 1, *1607–1860.* New York: McGraw-Hill.

Cleveland, Harold, and Thomas Huertas, et al. 1985. *Citibank, 1812–1970.* Cambridge, Mass: Harvard University Press.

Cohen, Henry. 1971. *Business and Politics in America from the Age of Jackson to the Civil War: The Career Biography of W. W. Corcoran.* Westport, Conn.: Greenwood.

Cowen, David J. 2000a. "The First Bank of the United States and the Securities Market Crash of 1792." *Journal of Economic History* 60:1041–60.

2000b. *The Origins and Economic Impact of the First Bank of the United States, 1791–1797.* New York: Garland.

Crothers, A. Glenn. 1997. "'The Projecting Spirit': Social, Economic and Cultural Change in Post-Revolutionary Northern Virginia, 1780–1805." Ph.D. diss., University of Florida.

1999. "Banks and Economic Development in Post-Revolutionary Northern Virginia, 1790–1812." *Business History Review* 73:1–39.

Crowder, Edward. 1942. "State Regulation of Banking in New York." Ph.D. diss., New York University.

D'Arcy, Stephen, and Neil Doherty. 1990. "Adverse Selection, Private Information, and Lowballing in Insurance Markets." *Journal of Business* 63:145–64.

Davis, Joseph S. 1917. *Essays in the Earlier History of American Corporations.* New York: Russell & Russell.

deVries, Jan, and Ad Van Der Woude. 1997. *The First Modern Economy: Success, Failure, and Perseverance of the Dutch Economy, 1500–1815.* Cambridge: Cambridge University Press.

Dewey, Davis R. 1910. *State Banking before the Civil War.* Washington, D.C.: Government Printing Office.

Dickson, P. G. M. 1967. *The Financial Revolution in England: A Study in the Development of Public Credit, 1688–1756.* New York: St. Martin's Press.

Doerflinger, Thomas. 1986. *A Vigorous Spirit of Enterprise: Merchants and Economic Development in Revolutionary Philadelphia.* Chapel Hill: University of North Carolina Press.

Driscoll, William. 1965. "Benjamin F. Butler: Lawyer and Regency Politician." Ph.D. diss., Fordham University.

Duke, Basil W. 1895. *History of the Bank of Kentucky, 1792–1895.* Louisville: John P. Morton.

Egnal, Marc, and Joseph Ernst. 1972. "An Economic Interpretation of the American Revolution." *William and Mary Quarterly* 29:3–32.

Evans, George, Jr. 1948. *Business Incorporations in the United States, 1800–1943.* New York: National Bureau of Economic Research.

Fenstermaker, J. Van. 1965. *The Development of American Commercial Banking: 1782–1837*. Kent, Ohio: Kent State University.

Ferguson, E. James. 1961. *Power of the Purse: A History of American Public Finance, 1776–1790*. Chapel Hill: University of North Carolina Press.

Ferguson, E. James, John Catanzariti, Elizabeth Nuxoll, Mary Gallagher, et al., eds. 1973–99. *The Papers of Robert Morris, 1781–1784.* 9 vols. Pittsburgh: University of Pittsburgh Press.

Ferguson, Niall. 1998. *The World's Banker: The History of the House of Rothschild.* London: Weidenfeld & Nicolson.

Flaumenhaft, Harvey. 1992. *The Effective Republic: Administration and Constitution in the Thought of Alexander Hamilton.* Durham, N.C.: Duke University Press, 1992.

Fowler, J. A. 1888. *History of Insurance in Philadelphia for Two Centuries (1683–1882).* Philadelphia: Review Publishing and Printing Company.

Garbade, Kenneth D., and William L. Silber. 1978. "Technology, Communication and the Performance of Financial Markets: 1840–1975." *Journal of Finance* 33:819–32.

Garg, Sonali. 2000. "Innovations in Communications Technology and the Structure of Securities Markets: A Case Study of the Telegraph and the Rise of the NYSE to Preeminence, 1830–1860." Ph.D. diss., Ohio State University.

Govan, Thomas. 1959. *Nicholas Biddle: Nationalist and Public Banker, 1786–1844.* Chicago: University of Chicago Press.

Gunn, L. Ray. 1988. *The Decline of Authority: Public Economic Policy and Political Development in New York, 1800–1860.* Ithaca: Cornell University Press.

Gwyn, Julian. 1973. "Private Credit in Colonial New York: The Warren Portfolio, 1731–1795." *New York History* 54:269–93.

Harrison, Paul. 1994. "The More Things Change the More They Stay the Same: Analysis of the Past 200 Years of Stock Market Evolution." Ph.D. diss., Duke University.

Hedges, Joseph E. 1938. *Commercial Banking and the Stock Market before 1863.* Baltimore: Johns Hopkins Press.

Henderson, James P. 1986. "Agency or Alienation? Smith, Mill, and Marx on the Joint-Stock Company." *History of Political Economy* 18:111–32.

Henretta, James. 1998. "The 'Market' in the Early Republic." *Journal of the Early Republic* 18:289–304.

Hidy, Muriel. 1978. *George Peabody: Merchant and Financier, 1829–1854.* New York: Arno Press.

Hidy, Ralph. 1949. *The House of Baring in American Trade and Finance: English Merchant Bankers at Work, 1763–1861.* Cambridge, Mass.: Harvard University Press.

Horle, Craig, Joseph Foster, et al., eds. 1991. *Lawmaking and Legislators in Pennsylvania: A Biographical Dictionary.* Philadelphia: University of Pennsylvania Press.

Horne, Oliver. 1947. *A History of Savings Banks.* London: Oxford University Press.

Horwitz, Morton. 1977. *Transformation of American Law, 1780–1860.* Cambridge, Mass.: Harvard University Press.

Hubbard, J. T. W. 1995. *For Each, the Strength of All: A History of Banking in the State of New York.* New York: New York University Press.

Hunt, Carleton. 1936. *The Development of the Business Corporation in England, 1800–1867.* Cambridge, Mass.: Harvard University Press.

James, Marquis. 1942. *Biography of a Business, 1792–1942: Insurance Company of North America.* New York: Bobbs-Merrill.

John, Richard R. 1995. *Spreading the News: The American Postal System from Franklin to Morse.* Cambridge, Mass.: Harvard University Press.

Jones, Alice Hanson. 1980. *Wealth of a Nation to Be: The American Colonies on the Eve of the Revolution.* New York: Columbia University Press.

Kaminski, John Paul. 1972. "Paper Politics: The Northern State Loan-Offices during the Confederation, 1783–1790." Ph.D. diss., University of Wisconsin.

Karmel, James. 1999. "Banking on the People: Banks, Politics and Market Evolution in Early National Pennsylvania." Ph.D. diss., State University of New York at Buffalo.

Keyes, Emerson. 1876. *A History of Savings Banks in the United States.* New York: B. Rhodes.

Kilbourne, Richard H., Jr. 1995. *Debt, Investment, Slaves: Credit Relations in East Feliciana Parish, Louisiana, 1825–1885.* Tuscaloosa: University of Alabama Press.

King, Robert, and Ross Levine. 1993. "Finance and Growth: Schumpeter Might Be Right." *Quarterly Journal of Economics* 108:717–38.

Klebaner, Benjamin. 1974. *Commercial Banking in the United States: A History.* New York: Dryden Press.

Kohn, Meir. 1999. "Finance, Business, and Government before the Industrial Revolution." Dartmouth College Working Papers 99-01-99-07. Hanover, N.H.

Krooss, Herman E., and Martin R. Blyn. 1971. *A History of Financial Intermediaries.* New York: Random House.

Krooss, Herman, and Charles Gilbert. 1972. *American Business History.* Englewood Cliffs, N.J.: Prentice-Hall.

Kulikoff, Allan. 1992. *Agrarian Origins of American Capitalism.* Charlottesville: University Press of Virginia.

Lamoreaux, Naomi. 1994. *Insider Lending: Banks, Personal Connections, and Economic Development in Industrial New England.* Cambridge: Cambridge University Press.

Landes, David. 1998. *The Wealth and Poverty of Nations: Why Some Are So Rich and Some Are So Poor.* New York: W. W. Norton.

Larson, Henrietta. 1931. "S&M Allen – Lottery, Exchange, and Stock Brokerage." *Journal of Economic and Business History* 4:424–45.

Larson, John. 2001. *Internal Improvements: National Public Works and the Promise of Popular Government in the Early United States.* Chapel Hill: University of North Carolina Press.

Lebergott, Stanley. 1985. "The Demand for Land: The United States, 1820–1860." *Journal of Economic History* 45:181–212.

Lee, C. H. 1990. "Corporate Behaviour in Theory and History: I. The Evolution of Theory." *Business History* 32:17–31.

Levine, Ross, Norman Loayza, and Thorsten Beck. 2000. "Financial Intermediation and Growth: Causality and Causes." *Journal of Monetary Economics* 46:31–77.

Levine, Ross, and Sara Zervos. 1998. "Stock Markets, Banks, and Economic Growth." *American Economic Review* 88:537–58.

Licht, Walter. 1995. *Industrializing America: The Nineteenth Century*. Baltimore: Johns Hopkins University Press.

Lindstrom, Diane. 1978. *Economic Development in the Philadelphia Region, 1810–1850*. New York: Columbia University Press.

Livesay, Harold, and Glenn Porter. 1971. "The Financial Role of Merchants in the Development of U.S. Manufacturing, 1815–1860." *Explorations in Economic History* 9:63–87.

Lockard, Paul A. 2000. "Banks, Insider Lending, and Industries of the Connecticut River Valley of Massachusetts, 1813–1860." Ph.D. diss., University of Massachusetts.

Maier, Pauline. 1993. "The Revolutionary Origins of the American Corporation." *William and Mary Quarterly* 50:51–84.

Majewski, John. 2000. *A House Dividing: Economic Development in Pennsylvania and Virginia before the Civil War*. Cambridge: Cambridge University Press.

Mann, Bruce. 1987. *Neighbors and Strangers: Law and Community in Early Connecticut*. Chapel Hill: University of North Carolina Press.

Manning, James. 1917. *Century of American Savings Banks*. New York: B. F. Buck.

Martin, Joseph G., and Clarence Barron. 1975. *The Boston Stock Exchange*. New York: Arno Press.

Matson, Cathy. 1985. "Fair Trade, Free Trade: Economic Ideas and Opportunities in Eighteenth-Century New York City Commerce." Ph.D. diss., Columbia University.

Mayer, Lewis. 1883. *Ground Rents in Maryland*. Baltimore: Cushings and Bailey.

McCaffrey, David, and David Hart. 1998. *Wall Street Polices Itself: How Securities Firms Manage the Legal Hazards of Competitive Pressures*. New York: Oxford University Press.

McCurdy, Linda. 1974. "The Potts Family Iron Industry in the Schuylkill Valley." Ph.D. diss., Pennsylvania State University.

McCusker, John J. 2000. " 'The Freshest Advices': The Emergence of Robert Morris's Philadelphia as the Early Center of Trade and Commerce in Post-Revolutionary United States and the Development of an Indigenous American Commercial and Financial Press." Paper presented at Re-Examining the Economic and Political History of the Confederation through the Papers of Robert Morris, a conference in celebration of the completion of *The Papers of Robert Morris, 1781–1784*, New York, 7 April.

McCusker, John J., and Cora Gravesteijn. 1991. *The Beginnings of Commercial and Financial Journalism: The Commodity Price Currents, Exchange Rate Currents, and Money Currents of Early Modern Europe*. Amsterdam: NEHA.

McCusker, John J., and Russell Menard. 1985. *The Economy of British America, 1607–1789*. Chapel Hill: University of North Carolina Press.

McDonald, Forrest. 1958. *We the People: The Economic Origins of the Constitution*. Chicago: University of Chicago Press.

———. 1979. *Alexander Hamilton: A Biography*. New York: W. W. Norton.

Merrill, Michael, and Sean Wilentz, eds. 1993. *The Key of Liberty: The Life and Democratic Writings of William Manning, "A Laborer," 1747–1814*. Cambridge: Cambridge University Press.

Michener, Ron. 1988. "Backing Theories and the Currencies of Eighteenth-Century America: A Comment." *Journal of Economic History* 68:682–92.

——— 2000. "Colonial Currency in New York." University of Virginia, Charlottesville. Unpublished manuscript.

Michie, Ranald. 1981. *Money, Mania, and Markets: Investment, Company Formation, and Stock Exchange in Nineteenth-Century Scotland*. Edinburgh: John Donald.

——— 1999. *The London Stock Exchange: A History*. New York: Oxford University Press.

Miller, Harry E. 1927. *Banking Theories in the United State before 1860*. Cambridge, Mass.: Harvard University Press.

Mishkin, Frederic S. 2000. *The Economics of Money, Banking, and Financial Markets*. New York: Addison Wesley.

Morrison, Grant. 1973. "Isaac Bronson and the Search for System in American Capitalism, 1789–1838." Ph.D. diss., City University of New York.

Munsell, Joel. 1850. *Annals of Albany*. 10 vols. Albany: J. Munsell.

Myers, Margaret G. 1931. *The New York Money Market*. Vol. 1, *Origins and Development*. New York: Columbia University Press.

Neal, Larry. 1990. *The Rise of Financial Capitalism: International Capital Markets in the Age of Reason*. Cambridge: Cambridge University Press.

North, Douglass. 1961. *Economic Growth of the United States, 1790–1860*. New York: W. W. Norton.

Officer, Lawrence. 1996. *Between the Dollar-Sterling Gold Points: Exchange Rates, Parity, and Market Behavior*. Cambridge: Cambridge University Press.

Olmstead, Alan. 1976. *New York City Mutual Savings Banks, 1819–1861*. Chapel Hill: University of North Carolina Press.

Pammer, Michael. 2000. "Economic Growth and Lower Class Investments in Nineteenth Century Austria." *Historical Social Research* 25:25–48.

Papenfuse, Edward C. 1975. *In Pursuit of Profit: The Annapolis Merchants in the Era of the American Revolution, 1763–1805*. Baltimore: Johns Hopkins University Press.

Patterson, John A. 1971. *Ten and One-Half Years of Commercial Banking in a New England Country Town: Concord, Massachusetts, 1832–1842*. Sturbridge, Mass.: Old Sturbridge Village.

Perkins, Edwin. 1975. *Financing Anglo-American Trade: The House of Brown, 1800–1880*. Cambridge, Mass.: Harvard University Press.

——— 1994. *American Public Finance and Financial Services, 1700–1815*. Columbus: Ohio State University Press.

Pred, Allan R. 1973. *Urban Growth and Circulation of Information*. Cambridge, Mass.: Harvard University Press.

Priest, Claire. 1999. "Colonial Courts and Secured Credit: Early American Commercial Litigation and Shay's Rebellion." *Yale Law Journal* 108:2413–50.

Rappaport, George. 1996. *Stability and Change in Revolutionary Pennsylvania: Banking, Politics, and Social Structure*. University Park: Pennsylvania State University Press.

Rawson, David A. 1998. "'Guardians of Their Own Liberty': A Contextual History of Print Culture in Virginia Society, 1750 to 1820." Ph.D. diss., College of William and Mary.

Redlich, Fritz. 1947. *Molding of American Banking: Men and Ideas.* New York: Johnson Reprint.

Remer, Rosalind. 1990. "Old Lights and New Money: A Note on Religion, Economics, and the Social Order in 1740 Boston." *William and Mary Quarterly* 47:566–73.

1996. *Printers and Men of Capital: Philadelphia Book Publishers in the New Republic.* Philadelphia: University of Pennsylvania Press.

Remini, Robert. 1951. "The Early Political Career of Martin Van Buren, 1782–1828." Ph.D. diss., Columbia University.

Riesman, Janet. 1989. "Republican Revisions: Political Economy in New York after the Panic of 1819." In William Pencak and Conrad E. Wright, eds., *New York and the Rise of American Capitalism: Economic Development and the Social and Political History of an American State, 1780–1870,* 1–44. New York: New-York Historical Society.

Rilling, Donna J. 2001. *Making Houses, Crafting Capitalism: Builders in Philadelphia, 1790–1850.* Philadelphia: University of Pennsylvania Press.

Rolnick, Arthur, Bruce Smith, and Warren Weber. 1998. "Lessons from a Laissez-Faire Payments System: The Suffolk Banking System (1825–58)." *Federal Reserve Bank of St. Louis Review* 80:105–20.

Root, L. Carrol. 1895. "New York Bank Currency: Safety Fund vs. Bond Security." *Sound Currency* 2:285–308.

Rosen, Deborah. 1997. *Courts and Commerce: Gender, Law, and the Market Economy in Colonial New York.* Columbus: Ohio State University Press.

Rostow, Walt W. 1960. *The Stages of Economic Growth: A Non-Communist Manifesto.* Cambridge: Cambridge University Press.

Rothenberg, Winifred B. 1992. *From Market-Places to a Market Economy: The Transformation of Rural Massachusetts, 1750–1850.* Chicago: University of Chicago Press.

Rousseau, Peter, and Richard E. Sylla. 1999. "Emerging Financial Markets and Early U.S. Growth." Paper presented at the Economic History Association Conference, Baltimore, 9 October.

Ruwell, Mary E. 1993. *Eighteenth-Century Capitalism: The Formation of American Marine Insurance Companies.* New York: Garland.

Schwartz, Anna. 1947. "The Beginning of Competitive Banking in Philadelphia." *Journal of Political Economy* 55:417–31.

Schweitzer, Mary M. 1987. *Custom and Contract: Household, Government, and the Economy in Colonial Pennsylvania.* New York: Columbia University Press.

Seavoy, Ronald. 1982. *The Origins of the American Business Corporation, 1784–1855: Broadening the Concept of Public Service during Industrialization.* Westport, Conn.: Greenwood.

Sellers, Charles. 1991. *The Market Revolution: Jacksonian America, 1815–1846.* New York: Oxford University Press.

Smith, Adam. 1776. *An Inquiry into the Nature and Causes of the Wealth of Nations.* London: W. Strahan and T. Cadell.

Snowden, Kenneth A. 1987. "Mortgage Rates and American Capital Market Development in the Late Nineteenth Century." *Journal of Economic History* 47:671–91.

Sturm, James L. 1969. "Investing in the United States, 1798–1893: Upper Wealth-Holders in a Market Economy." Ph.D. diss., University of Wisconsin.

Sylla, Richard E. 1976. "Forgotten Men of Money: Private Bankers in Early U.S. History." *Journal of Economic History* 46:173–88.

———. 1985. "Early American Banking: The Significance of the Corporate Form." *Business and Economic History* 14:105–23.

———. 1998. "U.S. Securities Markets and the Banking System, 1790–1840." *Federal Reserve Bank of St. Louis Review* 80:83–104.

———. 1999a. "Emerging Markets in History: The United States, Japan, and Argentina." In Ryuzo Sato, Rama V. Ramachandran, and Kazuo Mino, eds., *Global Competition and Integration*, 427–46. Boston: Kluwer Academic Publishers.

———. 1999b. "Shaping the U.S. Financial System, 1690–1913: The Dominant Role of Public Finance." In Richard Sylla, Richard Tilly, and Gabriel Tortella, eds. *The State, the Financial System and Economic Modernization*, 249–70. Cambridge: Cambridge University Press.

Sylla, Richard, John B. Legler, and John J. Wallis. 1987. "Banks and State Public Finance in the New Republic: The United States, 1790–1860." *Journal of Economic History* 47:391–403.

Sylla, Richard E., Jack Wilson, and Robert E. Wright. 1997. "America's First Securities Markets, 1790–1830: Emergence, Development and Integration." Paper presented at the Cliometrics Conference, Toronto, 17 May.

———. 2002. "Database of Early U.S. Securities Prices." ICPSR, Ann Arbor, Mich.

Syrett, Harold, and Jacob E. Cooke, eds. 1961–87. *The Papers of Alexander Hamilton*. 27 vols. New York: Columbia University Press.

Taylor, George. 1958. *The Transportation Revolution, 1815–1860*. New York: Rinehart.

Thorp, Daniel B. 1991. "Doing Business in the Backcountry: Retail Trade in Rowan County, North Carolina." *William and Mary Quarterly* 48:387–408.

Todd, Charles. 1977. *Alexander Bryan Johnson: Philosophical Banker.* Syracuse: Syracuse University Press.

Trivoli, George. 1979. *The Suffolk Bank: A Study of Free-Enterprise Clearing System.* Leesburg, Va.: Adam Smith Institute.

Van Winter, Pieter J. 1977. *American Finance and Dutch Investment, 1780–1805, with an Epilogue to 1840*. Trans. James C. Riley. New York: Arno Press.

Venit, Abraham. 1945. "Isaac Bronson: His Banking Theories and Financial Controversies." *Journal of Economic History* 5:201–14.

Wainwright, Nicholas B. 1953. *History of the Philadelphia National Bank: A Century and a Half of Philadelphia Banking, 1803–1953*. Philadelphia: William M. Fell.

Wallis, John, Richard E. Sylla, and John B. Legler. 1994. "The Interaction of Taxation and Regulation in Nineteenth-Century U.S. Banking." In Claudia Goldin and Gary Libecap, eds., *The Regulated Economy: A Historical Approach to Political Economy*, 121–44. Chicago: University of Chicago Press.

Werner, Walter, and Steven T. Smith. 1991. *Wall Street*. New York: Columbia University Press.

Wettereau, James O. 1985. *Statistical Records of the First Bank of the United States*. New York: Garland.

White, Roger S. 1971. "State Regulation of Commercial Banks, 1781–1843." Ph.D. diss., University of Illinois.

Wilkins, Mira. 1989. *The History of Foreign Investment in the United States to 1914*. Cambridge, Mass.: Harvard University Press.

Whitney, David R. 1878. *The Suffolk Bank*. Cambridge, Mass.: Riverside Press.

Wood, Jerome H. 1970. "The Town Proprietors of Lancaster, 1730–1790." *Pennsylvania Magazine of History and Biography* 94:346–68.

Wright, Robert E. 1996. "Thomas Willing (1731–1821): Philadelphia Financier and Forgotten Founding Father." *Pennsylvania History* 63:525–60.

——— 1997a. "Banking and Politics in New York, 1784–1829." Ph.D. diss., State University of New York at Buffalo.

——— 1997b. "The First Phase of the Empire State's 'Triple Transition': Banks' Influence on the Market, Democracy, and Federalism in New York, 1776–1838." *Social Science History* 21:521–58.

——— 1998a. "Artisans, Banks, Credit, and the Election of 1800." *Pennsylvania Magazine of History and Biography* 122:211–39.

——— 1998b. "Ground Rents against Populist Historiography: Mid-Atlantic Land Tenure, 1750–1820." *Journal of Interdisciplinary History* 29:23–42.

——— 1999a. "Bank Ownership and Lending Patterns in New York and Pennsylvania, 1781–1831." *Business History Review* 73:40–60.

——— 1999b. "Israel Jacobs (1726–1796) of Providence Township: Farmer, Weaver, Quaker Congressman." *Bulletin of the Historical Society of Montgomery County* 31:300–11.

——— 2000. "Capital Market Integration and Investment: Ownership of Corporate Equities in Antebellum Maine." *New England Journal of History* 57:1–22.

——— 2001. *Origins of Commercial Banking in America, 1750–1800*. Lanham, Md.: Rowman & Littlefield.

——— ed. 2002. *History of Corporate Finance: Development of Anglo-American Securities Markets, Laws, and Financial Practices and Theories*. 6 vols. London: Pickering & Chatto.

Index